NEEDS ASSESSMENT

Concept and Application

NEEDS ASSESSMENT

Concept and Application

Roger Kaufman
The Florida State University

Fenwick W. English
American Association of School Administrators

EDUCATIONAL TECHNOLOGY PUBLICATIONS
ENGLEWOOD CLIFFS, NEW JERSEY 07632

Library of Congress Cataloging in Publication Data

Kaufman, Roger A
  Needs assessment.

  Includes bibliographies and index.
  1. Curriculum planning. I. English, Fenwick W.,
joint author. II. Title.
LB1555.K365   375'.001   78-13628
ISBN 0-87778-130-3

Printed in the United States of America.

Library of Congress Catalog Card Number:
78-13628.

International Standard Book Number:
0-87778-130-3.

First Printing: January, 1979.

ACKNOWLEDGEMENTS

This work represents the authors' independent thinking and work, done on our own time, and thus does not and should not be construed as the position of either of our respective professional affiliations. We do thank them, however, for intellectual stimulation, personal encouragement, and a base for professional experience.

Additionally, we would like to mention just a few of the people who have influenced us, and have, either personally or professionally, directly or indirectly, contributed to (but who are not responsible for the errors of) this effort:

Bob Stakenas, Bob Morgan, Bob Branson, Bob Gagne, Bruce Stone, Michael Knight, Mary Jane Ward, Mickey Andrews, Dave Feldman, Ted Blau, George Albee, Al Mayrhoffer, Leon Lessinger, Harold Greenwald, Jim Rudolph, Ron Wood, Dick Handley, Andrew Carron, Joe Mills, Ken Eaddy, C.M. Lawrence, and Janice, Jac, and Naomi Kaufman.

Ruth Dewey, Stan Schoenfeld, Fran MacEachron, Victor Schacter, John Gonder, Eunice Lloyd, Marge Lieneck, Pete Perkins, Mike Turillo, Dan Donovan, Terry Saario, Rod Roth, Bill Viall, Jack Rand, Paul Salmon, Louis Zeyen, Jerry Melton, and Lolita English. And our thanks to the many graduate students at Florida State University and United States International University who served to teach us much about this topic.

Finally, we would also like to thank the following people for helping this book become a reality: Carol Marlin for editorial suggestions, Becky Smith for typing above and beyond the call of duty, and Francie Stoutamire for looking after a number of details which helped things appear on time.

PREFACE

In education (and in training, too) we have tried almost endless approaches and innovations. We have altered content, we have re-shaped the teaching-learning relationship, and we have automated various aspects of instruction. On the national level we have increased educational expenditures to the poor and financed countless projects to increase creativity and to improve performance. Still we are faced with the prospect that, in sum, we appear not to have made the necessary impact to substantially improve the schools. Our efforts don't seem to make much of a positive difference.

We believe that the reason is not a lack of energy or dedication, but some less-than-productive thinking. We in education and training are not usually able to specify and demonstrate our impact because our desired outcomes are not usually specified. And when they are specified, they are frequently not relevant. It is difficult to know whether one has achieved a targeted objective when there are no clear targets, or when the targets are, in reality, only the implementation of whatever "how-to-do-its" were tried at the time. Most often the targets are not related to a useful and valued set of outcomes.

Picking the correct and appropriate problems and finding the best solutions are the keys to educational success. Needs assessment is a critical tool for doing just that. Needs assessment is a basic tool for productive, rational, and logical thinking about problems and solutions. It is a tool to be used to functionally separate means and ends. It is a way in which any educator, trainer, learner, or parent can make sense of intended innovations, ranging from program budgeting to locus of control, by learning how to ask (and answer) the right questions. Unlike a fad which does not change anything permanently, needs assessment is the first step in functional, useful, planned change. What is needs assessment, and how does one do it? These two questions are the subject of the book.

The first part of this work explains the conceptual framework of needs assessment. It has been written from the experiences of several years in the design and implementation of needs assessments in many states at levels ranging from state departments of education to a single classroom. The work is based upon concept, thought, application, and mistakes. It is not perfect nor complete, but represents our best thinking and observations until now. Critics will find much to fault, for it is neither an action kit which pretends to be all things for all people, nor is it a report of empirically-based research. It is frankly pragmatic. The first section of this book is partially based upon research and writings which have gone before and which come together here with new information and experiences added to the mixture. Tomorrow will bring fresh insights and new perspectives.

The second part of the book deals with more of the how-to-do-its from operational experiences in education and training.

A professor and an administrator have jointly produced this work in an attempt to bring together theory and application, so that someone who wants to measurably improve education may take the first rational and logical steps toward defining problems and eliminating non-problems. Educational planning and success depend singularly on knowing *what* has to be accomplished before methods and means are implemented for doing the job.

Kaufman is primarily responsible for chapters one through five, eight, nine, and thirteen; English for chapters six, seven, and ten through twelve; although we have both contributed to all chapters.

Roger Kaufman
Fenwick W. English

TABLE OF CONTENTS

NEEDS ASSESSMENT

Concept and Application

Section One

THE CONCEPTUAL FRAMEWORK OF NEEDS ASSESSMENT

INTRODUCTION TO SECTION ONE

This book deals with the first critical step in identifying and resolving problems: needs assessment.

While the major emphasis and examples will be from the context of educational planning and accomplishment, the concepts, models, and procedures are applicable to government, business, industry, and the military. To include examples from all fields would provide a very cumbersome volume, so we have chosen to exemplify education and ask other readers to generalize as they move through the material. This first section has seven chapters and provides the conceptual and definitional background for understanding that there are several kinds of needs assessments and that there is one most basic variety which obtains its criteria for planned change from the world external to the intervening agency. It places needs assessment in the larger context of systematic planning and accomplishment, defines terms such as "input," "process," "product," "output," and "outcome," and then relates these in turn to two central educational themes, management and curriculum.

This is the base for successful identification and verification of problems, and determining that a problem symptom is representative of the requirements for change.

With this information and understandings, the way is prepared for considerations in Section Two of how to apply needs assessment tools and concepts.

Chapter 1

WHY NEEDS ASSESSMENT?

Intervention or meddling? Tinkering or change? Useful or benign? Positive or disruptive? Whenever we presume to change something, we run the risk of not accomplishing that which we set out to accomplish. Or worse, sometimes the situation deteriorates. Almost no one, when being candid, will think that our educational system is working the way it should. When we presume to educate a child, we are attempting to change the course of events, usually by changing or manipulating the means to certain ends.

Education is a means, a set of processes and how-to-do-its which are intended to help learners to survive and contribute in the world in which they currently live and to which they will be going when they legally exit from our schools (Kaufman, 1972). But for all the means we utilize, for all of the resources expended, for all the effort put into planning, development, implementation, and use, many feel that our educational agencies are failing or not "doing their job." Frustration, anger, and cries for change are frequently expressed. Some want to tear it all down, some want to dramatically change and modify, and some want things to stay just as they are.

Controversy. Our society seems fueled by the desire for change. Newspapers and the media tend to write about that which is "newsworthy" and in a style which is simple to understand. This leads to reporting which is frequently different from the facts at hand (just read the headlines and story about something with which are you intimately knowledgeable). Controversy surrounds much of education today, the way it engulfed business and industry in earlier years.

7

Change. Change to what? Change from what? Why change? If we change, what do we use to change? These are critical questions which can make the difference between useful and less-than-constructive change.

Needs assessments are tools for constructive and positive change—not change solely driven by controversy, "quick-fixes," and situational crises, but rational, logical, functional change which meets the needs of citizens, educators, and learners. They represent formal, systematic attempts to determine and close the more important gaps between "what is" and "what should be." As we will see in Chapters 3 and 4, there are several varieties of needs assessments. We will be recommending one which is the base for all of the other methods and strategies, one which will require the determination of needs from outside of the organization involved and charged with bringing about change.

For now, we define needs assessment as a formal process which determines the gaps between current outputs or outcomes and required or desired outcomes or outputs; places these gaps in priority order; and selects the most important for resolution. "Need" is defined as a gap between current outcomes or outputs and desired (or required) outcomes or outputs.

A needs assessment, then, is an identifying, harvesting, justifying, and selecting of gaps (or needs) to be closed. The nature and importance of the gaps are critical, for if we choose trivial or incorrect needs to resolve, then we will not achieve the results we set out to accomplish. We suggest that it is the inappropriate or incorrect selection of needs which is at the root of much educational failure; and, further, we strongly suggest that the use of appropriate needs assessment tools, techniques, and strategies can greatly improve educational success.

Needs assessment, then, is central to selecting the correct problems for resolution and will provide the necessary information for determining appropriate interventions. If we are to change, it makes sense to correctly identify what should be changed; armed with this information, we are better able to know what interventions to select to bring about the required change.

This strongly indicates that in order to pick the correct means—how-to-do-its useful in bringing about desired results—we must know the required ends, outputs, or outcomes which are valued and important. If we first know the ends to be achieved, then selection of the appropriate means can be more successful.

The Confusion of Means and Ends

Our past educational solutions didn't seem to work well, but not because they were not useful or even powerful tools by themselves. They were usually applied with high hopes but without proper diagnosis. Our tools are *means;* they represent potential *ways* to bring about *valued results.* Too often the solutions themselves were the sole reason for implementation, i.e., they existed, so they were applied. They became ends in and of themselves rather than ways to achieve desired results. This appears to be especially true in technological societies, where we seem to have an endless source of means—techniques, procedures, how-to-do-its, methods, strategies, and tools. Unfortunately, we don't often select these tools on the basis of the *ends* we are to achieve. To paraphrase Albert Einstein, we have a proliferation of means and a confusion of ends.

Can almost all of our educational innovations be wrong? Useless? Just fads? Should we go back to the old model of assigning Mark Hopkins to one end of a log and a single learner to the other? Should we have "readin', writin', and 'rithmetic" and let it go at that? What should we do?

If we are to ask, "What teaching method should we use, massed or distributed practice?," the answer would probably be, "Who is the learner? What does the learner know? What is the content? What previous experiences has she had?" You have to define the problem and specify the required outcomes (ends) before you can make sensible judgments about the process (the means) to solve the problems.

"Ends" are outcomes, outputs, results, products—that which happens when we are finished with the application of any technique, intervention, or strategy.

"Means" are the vehicles and procedures, the solutions, and how-to-do-its which we use to achieve the desired ends.

Means and ends are different, and they are related. When we confuse them, useful concepts and tools tend to fail for the wrong reasons. Our hopes and aspirations for helping learners help themselves don't materialize.

What has happened in education is that we have lived with a general mind-set about judging means that leaves out much or all discussion and consideration of the ends.

The demarcation between means and ends sounds simple; but when it is applied in the operation world, it may become quite complicated. To illustrate, in the checklist below, which are means and which are ends?

MEANS OR ENDS?

Item	Means	Ends
1. Poor planning		
2. Inadequate teacher evaluation		
3. Busing		
4. Inadequate tax base		
5. Excessive class loads		
6. Split School Board		
7. Parental interference		
8. Dehumanized schools		
9. Poor pupil discipline		
10. Vandalism/violence in schools		
11. Low test scores		

For example, is "poor planning" (item #1) a means or an end? What happens if the school system doesn't plan well? How do we know we have "poor planning?" What things will "better" planning ameliorate? Do any of these things that are "better" help students learn?" If not, then perhaps we have a solution to the wrong problem. If planning and learning are related, there should be some relationship between improving the schools' planning capability and improving learning. What is meant by improved learning? Can we be specific? What learning? When? How much? Why?

In successful planning and accomplishment, the relation between means and ends must be specific and clear. If we select a means before identifying and justifying the appropriate end, we risk good ideas and tools failing for the wrong reasons. Powerful tools and approaches, such as differentiated staffing, system planning, team teaching, programmed instruction, instructional television, computer-assisted learning, computer-managed instruction, and the whole host of technological applications (the "things" or hardware of learning and instructional intervention, as distinguished from "soft" educational technology which is a systematic planning and doing process; Stakenas and Kaufman, 1977a,b,c) often do not meet their promise simply because they were selected and implemented without solid evidence of what they should accomplish.

When a result is poorly defined, just about any route will take you there. On the other hand, if you do not know where you are going, it is very difficult to know when you have arrived (Mager, 1975). When you do not know where you are going and select a method for getting there, you are open to failure at best, and failure plus severe criticism at worst.

It does not have to be this way. We can select successful interventions if we first define and justify the ends which we are to achieve, and then select the alternative means to get there. Failure to determine "what" should be accomplished before selecting "how" to get there will surely waste precious resources, time, and worst of all, will brutalize learners who could be learning things which will be useful to their survival, contribution, and well-being in society.

Continuation of current methods and means for delivering education just because we are familiar with them and feel comfortable with them is not productive; nor is change for change's sake. Needs assessment represents a formal set of tools and techniques *and* a way of viewing the world; of intervention and positive, productive change for putting means and ends into useful perspective. This book is dedicated to presenting both the rationale and tools for achieving the first steps toward bringing about this educational success.

Figure 1.1. The relationship between means and ends.

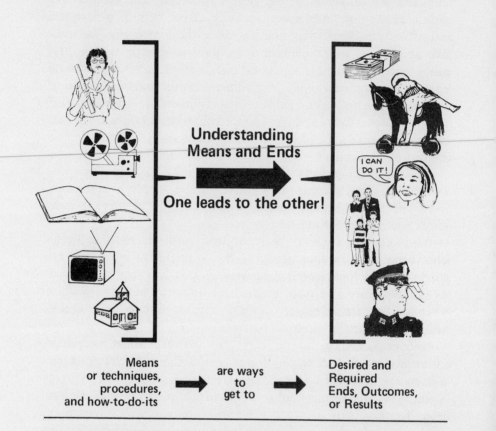

Understanding
Means and Ends

One leads to the other!

| Means or techniques, procedures, and how-to-do-its | are ways to get to | Desired and Required Ends, Outcomes, or Results |

Consistency. Most people feel comfortable with that which currently exists. We get used to ways of doing things, and our environment and surroundings provide stability and solidity in a world of change. We value reliability, sameness, consistency. In our day-to-day work, we tend to continue those things with which we are familiar. In teaching, we tend to use those techniques which were used with us, and we tend to include the content and materials which are known and familiar. In and of itself, this is not bad. It is only inappropriate when change would bring about more valuable results.

Achievement. Another culturally valued element is achievement. We like results; we like things which are promised to be delivered. We prize the worker whose work is always on time and is done as promised. We like people who are on time to pick us up, and who bring back items which we ask them to get. We look favorably upon those who achieve good grades in schools and colleges, and we like those who graduate from our institutions of learning. Those who score well on tests and who make lots of money are generally prized by others. Achievement is getting done something which one sets out to accomplish. In schools, we define "validity" as the characteristic of accomplishing that which one sets out to accomplish.

Usefulness. We also like that which is useful and important. We do not like waste; and thus we like to see money well spent and results of efforts which "make a difference." We decry money which was spent without results, and we deplore "achievers" who are not achievers, such as the person who gets a college degree but who is not practical and cannot solve reasonable problems. We do not like to see high school graduates who cannot read, write, and speak simple declarative sentences. Not only do we tend to prize achievers, but we additionally prize achievement which is useful and functional.

Reliablity, Validity, and Utility. In education, we can measure the reliability of a test or procedure. Reliability is an index of the consistency of something; the repeatability, the dependability of it. A test is reliable if it measures the same thing consistently. We can depend upon it to be consistent. As we may depend upon a reliable test to deliver the same thing time after time, we can depend upon a set of tools of teaching, such as the lecture method, to reliably produce the same thing time after time. We tend to opt for reliable means when other things are equal.

But what about the outputs of tests and teaching techniques which are reliable? Do they deliver that which they said they would deliver? Are they "valid?" Does a test in reading actually test the extent to which a child can read? Does the reliable teaching technique deliver learner skills, knowledges, and attitudes which it was intended to achieve; or put another way, did these reliable methods and means meet their objectives?

And even if they were both reliable and valid (consistent in meeting the objectives), were the objectives *worth* achieving? Were the objectives important? Did the objectives have "utility" in that they were worth accomplishing?

This is perhaps an analogy in educational design and development with some of the more familiar concepts of statistics and measurement: reliability and validity. Perhaps stretching the analogy with testing, in education we achieve reliability of process when we do things consistently. Our methods tend to be "reliable." With the new thrusts of accountability (Lessinger, 1970) and measurable behavioral objectives (Mager, 1975; Kibler, Barker, and Miles, 1970; and Kibler and Bassett, 1977), we have increasing concern not only with "how" to teach, but also with "what" to teach as well (Kaufman, 1978). A well-formed and formatted behavioral objective will supply the basis for measuring and determining the validity of results—did we achieve that which we set out to achieve?

But is this enough? Can we be content only with validity in education and training? Is it enough only to ask "Did we achieve that which we set out to achieve?" Or should we ask the additional question of "Was it worth achieving in the first place?" This latter question is one of "utility," or worth and value of the objectives attempted to be achieved.

This issue will be dealt with in more detail in Chapter 4, but we think it important to consider here—in order to achieve educational success, we must not only have measurable objectives which are tight, precise, and measurable, but we should have ones which are worthy and important. Reliability and validity, perhaps, are not sufficient; necessary, but not sufficient.

An appropriately designed and executed needs assessment can help us to achieve reliability, validity, and utility. We can be effective as well as consistent and efficient. We can achieve, consistently, results which are also worthy and important.

Means and Ends—Further Implications for Successful Planning

Process and product, means and ends—our world is made up of both of these elements. Both are important—critical—to success. But elaborate/sophisticated means are useless unless they achieve necessary and worthwhile ends.

Figure 1.2

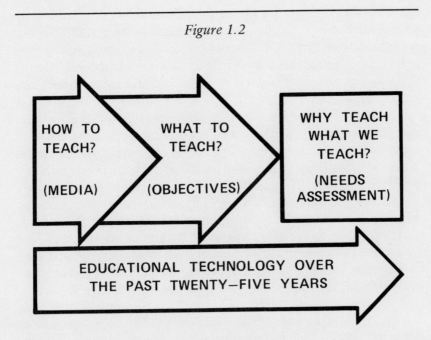

There has been a migration of concern by technologists from "how" to teach, to "what" to teach, and to "why" teach what we teach. This is a movement of thought and concern from "how" to "what" to "why." We are thus becoming more inclusive and "holistic" in our professional interests and concerns.

Again, this point cannot be overemphasized—there is an important difference, yet interrelationship, between means and ends. It is the difference between *how* we do something and *what* that something accomplishes.

This point will not be comfortable for everyone. Most of the people reading this book have been successful. They have lived in a world which emphasizes process, which tends to reward the how-to-do-its, ignores or assumes the utility of the results. For years education has derived its very existence from advertising and dealing with the processes—staffing, teachers, class hours, a whole host of things which are input or process variables—not results.

Our legislators mandate process variables in the laws they pass—measurable objectives, stringent fiscal accountability, salary scales, years of service, teacher-pupil ratios, facilities, equipment, aides, staff ratios. We respond (react?) to legislation and legislatures which mandate in terms of means and assume they are getting useful ends.

The traditions of the law, of the legislative, executive, and political processes, reinforce and reward the preoccupation with means. Our laws are written emphasizing means and almost always assuming that they will yield useful ends. But these ends are poorly if ever specified, and when they are made explicit, they are almost always "en-route" ends—results which are really necessary to achieve *on the way* from our current situation to the survival and contribution of the learners. These "en-route" ends are important, but they must be seen in their most useful perspective, as way-stations and enablers for getting students from "what is" to "what should be" in terms of survival and contribution in society.

We have potential "learners" in the schools—breathing, feeling, caring, growthful, and hurtable children who should be able to perform, able to have the tools necessary to survive and contribute in the world to which they are going and which they can have a part in improving.

The current system, however, tends to reward dealing with means, not with ends desired and accomplished.

It isn't anyone's fault, really. There is no one to blame—the responsibility has been diffused. It is the way the system is, but we are encouraging you and others to make it different, to make it responsive to learners, now and in the future.

This new responsiveness is not angry at the old, is not blameful of the old, is not scapegoating—it is interested in improving upon achievements of the old and in fashioning a humane and responsive new. It wants to shift from focus upon process to a focus upon learner results—useful and validated learner results.

A process of systematic planning and doing, starting with an assessment of needs, can achieve useful ends. All can benefit from this change.

If we are to be successful, we can only reasonably select the means *after* we know the legitimate, valid, and useful ends. Otherwise, we risk having solutions to unknown problems.

If there is one single important concept in this book for the understanding of educational planning (a means) and educational success (an end), it is the critical difference but interrelationship between means and ends.

Hypothetical Case Involving
the Difference Between Means and Ends

Superintendent Cronin had just attended a national professional meeting where he had one week's training in differentiated staffing. He was "sold." It made sense to him. The whole notion of allocating jobs to people on the basis of what they did best with and for children was exciting, and exactly why he went into education 23 years ago. He read extensively in the area and had a consultant in to talk to him and his administrative staff. They were "infected"—the idea was stimulating to them. They proposed the idea to the teachers in the intermediate school (they seemed most open to change); and after much discussion and reading, they decided to try a three-year experiment with it to raise the sagging scores in this lower-middle class neighborhood. A proposal was written to the school board; and after two public hearings and an accusation that it was a left-wing plot, the board approved the budget. The teachers went off for workshops at a northeastern university, and the consultant was retained to "see them through" the period of trial and adjustment. Mr. Cronin also brought in a teacher who had worked with differentiated staffing. Together, they were to work with the intermediate schools during the trial period—he primarily with the administrators, and she with the teachers.

The first year was spent in preparation, pre-testing learners, and building curriculum models and materials—the whole school was abuzz with work and anticipation.

The second year brought the beginning of operation, and there were a number of kinks in procedures that had to be worked out. One teacher claimed he could not teach under these conditions, asked for a transfer, and received it. At first, everyone seemed confused, but soon things worked out, and the whole system was "humming." An evaluator was hired to test the children and analyze the data.

The data after the first year of operation seemed disappointingly similar to the scores from previous years, but it was noted that the period was one of adjustment and that scores would get better. The teachers loved it—it had to be good. The program continued.

The second year of operation was smoother—the new roles were more comfortable and more people knew what they were doing and why. Visitors were coming by almost daily to see the wonder of the program. The consultant and the principal wrote an article for a teachers' magazine.

The data for the second year were collected, analyzed, and reported—and faces dropped. It was just about the same as the control group's—differentiated staffing had not wrought the miracle that it had promised. There was a flurry of activity; rationales were drawn, including a sociological one which noted that the average income of the catchment area had decreased by $170 in the last year and the number of divorces had increased. Also considered was the fact that the changes which were *really* important might not show up for ten or twenty years—what testing could really show the glint in a child's eye or a better self-concept?

The program was dropped as being too costly; and the teachers, administrators, and some parents were disappointed. "Innovation is out of the question with this board," they grumbled, "Creativity wasn't wanted here," they thought. Superintendent Cronin was wounded—he had staked his reputation on this, and he felt that he had been let down by the teachers—if they had really tried harder, he thought, the program would have been successful. He up-dated his vita papers and hit the job-hunting circuit.

Possible analysis. Differentiated staffing is a powerful tool—it attempts to allocate different functions to those resources which are best capable of performing them. Those who design learning packages best do that, and those who communicate best with learners do that in the classroom. It makes sense. However, differentiated staffing is a solution, a means, a process, a type of intervention—it is *not* an end, but it was treated as such by this school. Differentiated staffing will not assure that the *content* of what is taught is relevant, useful, or necessary; it can only deliver that which has been put into it. This school never realized that in order to pick a useful tool (such as differentiated staffing), it was necessary to know the valid and useful ends, record the discrepancies between current results and required results, and then select the best methods and means to do the job. Perhaps differentiated staffing was ideal and they just didn't have the right content. Or perhaps another method would have been more responsive to the gaps in results for these learners—provided that valid goals and objectives of learning had been derived. It seems likely that a solution (differentiated staffing) was chosen before the problem (discrepancies in outcomes to be reduced or eliminated) was selected, documented, and justified. In our hypothetical example, a good idea failed for the wrong reasons.

Accountability. Lessinger (1970) defines this as showing that you have done what you said you would do. We agree, and we feel that this concept is here to stay in education. Agreed, it gets used punitively in some places, but that doesn't negate the concept.

More and more we are called upon to demonstrate that what we have been doing (or will be doing) makes a difference for children. We are always accountable for money spent and where the children are when they are in school, but we tend to balk when it comes to accountability for results—for ends. We will not rehearse the excuses made; they have appeared in the books and articles that all of us have read, and they get repeated each time something appears to threaten the status quo.

We feel that it is important, and humanistic, for us to be accountable for the results we achieve. If we don't make a difference for children, then we should be doing something else. If we aren't accomplishing positive things for children, we should change. If we are doing destructive things for children, we *must* change. We can only know these things if we are accountable for results.

There have been more than a few attempts to deflect the accountability thrust by focusing on means, not ends. For example, many feel that educators should only be accountable for the techniques they use (such as knowing the appropriate reading materials or selecting the proper math workbooks), not for the final results. We feel that it is important for us as professional educators to be responsible for *both* the means *and* the ends. If we cannot predict and achieve results, sooner or later the "buyers" of education (parents, children, community members) will get smart and take their money and business elsewhere. If we don't change learners' skills, knowledges, and attitudes, or if we don't change them appropriately, then why should we be hired?

Accountability, under these concepts, becomes a type of

"truth-in-labeling" pledge for education—we will tell what we intend to do, why we intend to do it, what results we expect, and document the results we achieved. If we insist on becoming only accountable for the process, sooner or later someone will start keeping score on the results achieved, and then the judgments will be presented anyway. We have to deliver results, not just processes.

It seems fair to assume that we want to help learners—why else did we get into education? Most of us are in education, certainly, not for the money alone, but for the "psychic income" from helping learners help themselves. We don't like hassles, and we don't like to be attacked by those who least understand the complexities and problems of education. But we want children to learn and perform. We want the system to work.

It seems reasonable that accountability for results will be with us, and it also seems reasonable that most of us want good results. Why fight something which will help us and help children? Why not use accountability to justify getting the resources necessary for appropriate and proper results? If we are to be accountable for results, if we are to justify the outcomes, then our boards and administrators and publics have to supply us with justified resources, or *they* become accountable for the results. Accountability can be a shared one—*all* of the educational partners (the learners, the educators, and the community) agree upon the results and do their part to achieve them. Thus, we can shift *from* a procedure which "burns" educators when something goes wrong, places them in a position to plead for resources, turns them down for lack of money (another process being treated like a product), and then blames them for poor results anyway!

If we shift from an emphasis upon process (means) to one of product (ends), we are in a much better position to: (1) help learners help themselves to measurable success; (2) plan better on the basis of what ends we are to achieve rather then upon what "nifty" means (how-to-do-its) come along; (3) accomplish more results and feel better about what we do for a living; and (4) improve the image of ourselves and our profession to the rest of the world.

With an accountability for means, we may all lose. With an accountability for ends, we may all win.

Hypothetical Case Involving Accountability

The school board was angry! The reading scores were down again, and the math scores were dismal! That settled it—no more money for frills and fads. It was going to be just good old programs: solid, proven, reliable. And by hook or by crook, there would be "accountability" around here! No more teacher aides, and no more trips to conferences to learn about silly notions which didn't work. This is a big city, and we had to get back to basics. Make the kids work, make the teachers work, and make the administrators make it happen!

They tried to get a merit pay system going, but a threat for a strike got that quieted down. They thought about taking away tenure and granting it for a long record of accountability. That was nixed by the county council. But the board continued to threaten, and the educators were deeply concerned. Collective bargaining came into being; and the teachers negotiated for more pay, shorter hours, and agreed to be accountable for "knowing the right procedure and materials to use with children." They felt that they could not be accountable for what children learned— after all, many came from broken homes, parents uninterested and unconcerned, and many were just "bad." The school board acquiesced, wrote a contract thinking that accountability would be obtained, and settled back for another year, assuring themselves that this year the city's test scores would be back up, at least toward the middle of the distribution for the state.

They were not. In fact, the decline in standardized test scores continued. The board was angrier than ever and threatened to call in a private company to conduct education under contract and to get the state legislature to approve vouchers for children to spend in any school they desired. The teachers argued and brought facts to bear; but a long, angry, frustrating, and threatening siege seemed ahead for both sides again.

Possible analysis. Both sides are wrong! They have viewed accountability as accounting for process, not for results; and they both hoped to improve education, learners, and teachers on process alone. Knowing the correct thing to do is critical, but getting the job done—meeting the needs and achieving the required results—is the proof for learners, teachers, and school board members. How does one publish the results of what teachers know about how to teach? Does this make any sense to the parent of a child who is unable to read in the fifth grade?

The parents and school board members were sure that the teachers were lazy, slothful, and incompetent, and the teachers thought the same of the board. Children *might* have been learning, but who would know it from the tests? Perhaps the tests weren't even appropriate to what children ought to know and be able to do in the world external to the schools! The results were based upon criteria which were only *assumed* to be valid and useful, and everybody thought that changing the process was all that was required.

Accountability, instead of being productive and enhancing, was punitive and not relevant to learners and other humans in our system.

It doesn't have to be so! Education can be responsible for results, even accountable for humanism—the improved self-concept and improvement of every living person that is touched by the schools. And this may be demonstrated in measurable terms.

Planning to Achieve Useful Results

If we are to be accountable for results, and if we are to define results in terms of outputs and outcomes, instead of processes, then what can we do to assure success? Who wants to be accountable for results if there is no way to achieve the required results?

Planning, *sensible* planning, is the key.

Planning is something you do when you don't want to risk the results of your efforts. If you don't care what happens, don't bother to plan. Planning does not mean inflexibility, being "locked-in," or the blind following of something previously specified. It is (or at least can and should be) responsive, responsible, thoughtful, and flexible—it is a tool, nothing more and nothing less.

In some places, it is fashionable to shun planning—to write it off as dehumanizing, unresponsive, blind. This is a reasonable response only to "poor" planning.

In earlier efforts and writings, a concept of planning and doing was developed which attempted to help educators (and other serious behavior change specialists) achieve measurably greater success. This work was built upon many programs, projects, and experiences. It was called a System Approach (Kaufman, 1968, 1970, 1972) because it attempted to put means and ends into useful perspective and because it intended to design, from "scratch," a system—a set of ways and means to identify, verify, and resolve problems. Not just solving (or resolving) problems was considered useful, but the additional and earlier identification and verification of problems before attempting to resolve them.

This "system model" broke with past tradition by clearly identifying and justifying (through appropriate documentation) problems prior to the selection of solutions. Most planning models, such as those incorporated into Planning-Programming-Budgeting Systems (PPBS) in the fifties and sixties, usually made the assumption that the problem was already identified and justified, and that planning was merely the vehicle to put into practice a selected and "best" solution.

Planning, as frequently used in education, therefore, did not face the formal responsibility of separating means and ends; and additionally did not separate useful ends from conventional ends. Poverty programs, teacher training projects, and innovative concepts were all separately identified as ends in themselves, worthy of funding and dissemination on their own. What problems they solved effectively often remained unknown or conjectural.

Planning is the critical activity by which (1) means and ends are distinguished; and (2) guidelines are drawn for administrator, educator, and the public which identify the problem and how one solution is selected and others discarded to solve a validated and useful problem. Contrary to "conventional wisdom" or "common sense" notions in education, the ability to differentiate means and ends does *not* come naturally. It requires disciplined and trained staff and a certain amount of risk-taking potential. In education, asking "what should our business be?" carries with it the possibility that the answer may be "not the business in which we currently find ourselves." Possible threats to job security, existing power relationships, political orientation, and vested interests make assessment difficult. The tendency will be to begin with the status quo as the base for determining what the business should be—meaning that schools will continue with the current set of practices they are now using.

The *system approach,* and with it the first critical tool of *needs assessment,* flies in the face of such conventional wisdom. First, the approach identifies future desired and required outcomes. Then one works back to the present to determine to what degree current outcomes may be short or discrepant. This difference is a "gap," or "need."

"Conventional wisdom" usually begins with a test: administer it and define gaps by the test outcomes. Planning on the basis of a system model says a test is valid only to the degree that it assesses what our business should be; otherwise, it has no inherent validity or utility for determining whether or not a given level of learner performance may be either satisfactory or unsatisfactory.

It is clear that planning can separate means and ends only if it provides the basis for differentiating the "what" from the "how." Essentially, the difference is the ability to discriminate what the problem is and should be, before any "hows" may be considered. Planning must expose the assumptions underlying the "how" and make them part of examining the problem. First and foremost in the planning process is the activity of "problem definition" and justification.

Problems are needs selected for closure—if there is no gap, there is no problem. The problem identification, properly done, starts with an appropriate assessment of needs. A Needs Assessment is the determination of documentable and important gaps between current outcomes and desired outcomes, and the placing of those gaps in priority order for closure.

Planning, Problems, and Needs

Education is a means, a set of interventions which are inputs and processes intending to achieve valued and valuable outputs and outcomes. The basic outcome it should achieve (minimal, not maximum) is that by the time the learner legally exits from the educational agency, she or he should be able to survive and hopefully contribute to society. An economic utility model has been offered which measures indicators of this in terms of consumption and production (Kaufman, 1972).

It is the prime responsibility of schools and the educators who run them to plan for learner success which will at least minimally achieve individual survival and contribution. The basic problem for the schools is to close the gap between current outcomes and required outcomes for its learners. This can be determined by identifying learners' entry skills, knowledges, and attitudes (SKAs), and matching them against the minimal SKAs for their ultimate survival and hopeful contribution in the future society to which they will be going. These future SKAs would have "utility" in that they would allow learners to be fully functioning. They would also represent minimal, not maximum, capability.

The gaps between the entry SKAs and the exit SKAs are "needs" (gaps in results). Any gaps between the exit SKAs and SKAs required in the external world to survive and contribute are also "needs," but ones of much higher priority and criticality for achieving educational success.

Other "needs" may be determined in the chain which extends from the entry levels SKAs of learners through their ultimate ability to survive and contribute outside of school. This sequence is shown in Figure 1.3. It might be noted that a needs assessment, a harvesting of gaps between current results and desired results, may be conducted relative to any two points along this chain; but the most crucial and critical is the one which is conducted between the two extremes—input and outcome.

The basic internal problem confronting schools relates to the degree and kind of learning going on in them. Everything else becomes a secondary problem to the extent that the learning and methods impede or assist the ability of schools to deliver relevant SKAs. In other words, we have no curriculum problems if students are learning that which is stated must and should be learned.

Needs assessment begins with the clients, i.e., the learners, the communities, and the educators. The conceptual difference between this approach and "conventional wisdom" is the difference between a problem focus and a process focus. A process focus begins with teachers, curricula, facilities, or socioeconomic level. A process (or "solution") focus is the debate over class size, "open" classrooms, or various types of school construction formats, leaving out what learners are to learn. These are not problems derived after the conduct of a needs assessment. While much administrative activity may be properly concerned with

---

Figure 1.3

| Entry Skills, Knowledges and Attitudes $\rightarrow$ | In-School Skills, Knowledges and Attitudes $\rightarrow$ | School Exit Skills, Knowledges and Attitudes $\rightarrow$ | Survival and Contribution Skills, Knowledges and Attitudes |

The entry level of learners in terms of their skills, knowledges, and attitudes (SKAs) should serve as the basis for determining the means (teaching techniques, strategies, tools, methods, environments, materials) to move the learners toward further development of the SKAs until such time as they are able to survive and contribute in the world external to the schools. Thus, there may be a progression of needs (gaps in results) at any two points along this scale of progression of individual growth and competency development. The most basic gap to guide educational planners and implementers should be the one between Entry SKAs and Survival/Contribution SKAs.

---

changing means within the schools, one does not usefully begin there to define educational problems. The ability of the schools to identify desired and required student learning is one of stating the outcomes of the educational process in terms that are understandable and assessable and useful.

Some Philosophical Perspectives

As soon as the spectre of identifying the outcomes for education (or training as well) is broached, there is a frequent temptation to enter into a philosophical dialogue over whether knowledge as something to be learned really exists outside of the learner. Other arguments abound, such as if we could agree that a given sphere of information or skill were important, would it be of the same importance tomorrow? Twenty-five years from now? Since it can be demonstrated that no particular set of factors or skills is absolutely essential or completely predictable over a period of time, this may be used as a basis for attempting to discredit such efforts. (Frequently, fright in some individuals might cause them to "philosophize"—to shift the discussion from current and future realities to vague and emotional discourse. This is an understandable but not productive strategy. Philosophy, like theory, is not loose or slippery, and such behavior may be viewed as a "call for help" from someone not feeling secure with the prospects of change.)

The response to such "philosophical" debates is to point out that the schools now teach something and that something is learned in them. In spite of a lack of agreement, teachers do not work with students in a vacuum. Even teachers who profess a disbelief or lack of adherence to a curriculum (or plan, or structure) in the classroom do structure activities to the level of existing student experience, whatever that is. The point is that no matter what method is stated, a plan, a method, a strategy, a philosophy, and a curriculum exists, even if only by default. Students are taught *something;* they always interact with a teacher(s) within a context of previously learned experience.

School is a structured, non-haphazard environment, or it would not exist. The whole purpose of constructing a school in any society is to increase the probability that what is deemed essential for social survival is taught and learned. As Friedman points out (quoting Max Gammon), in "a bureaucratic system . . . increase in expenditure will be matched by fall in production . . . Such systems will act rather like 'black holes' in the economic universe, simultaneously sucking in resources, and shrinking in terms of 'emitted' production."

If every teacher is the *real* plan and the *real* curriculum, then the quality of that curriculum and hence student learning is teacher-controlled. Under such circumstances *teachers* can be realistically held accountable for all learning. To the extent that the system itself makes demands, or attempts to configure the school with teachers perceived and used as means to that end is the extent to which the *sysem* is accountable for those outcomes. The level of institutional accountability for learning is the degree to which it is responsible for better than unsystematic learning if there were no schools, or if teachers alone determine the curriculum.

Philosophical inquiry is important when it helps uncover the various assumptions which undergird practice. The system approach is a pragmatic one. It is grounded on the following premises:

1. The outcome of education should be those skills, knowledges, and attitudes which are deemed by any social order as necessary to its and each individual's survival and growth.
2. School is a place created by the social order to enhance the probability that what is judged by the social order as critical is indeed learned for the preservation and enhancement of that order.
3. What is deemed essential by any given social order is subject to change over a period of time; no one set of skills, knowledges, and attitudes is ever totally permanent.
4. What is important in schools is that which is decided upon by a given society. Validity and utility are socially defined. Schools not only reflect society, but also to a certain extent they change society, though often very slowly.
5. What currently exists to be learned in schools has occurred chiefly by default and not by any systematic effort to define and justify *a priori* the outcomes of the educational process.

The critics of answering the question, "What should the learner learn?" raise the fear of indoctrination, the fear that schools would become dehumanized by a return to rote memory practices, the fear that a defined curriculum would largely be a reflection of the trivial, and that such schools would be racially and socially discriminatory. Of course, what they are describing is schools as they *now* exist without such defined products. It is the contention of the authors that schools have incorporated current practices because there are no reasonable and responsible standards by which these non-functional ways may be expunged. If schools are supposed to be humane places, then they must be defined and planned to be that way, and practices which are not humane should be abandoned. We do not believe this will ever take place until the expected and desired outcomes of the schools are collectively, cooperatively, and substantially defined in terms which are reliable, are valid, and have demonstrated utility.

Any philosophy of education must ask and attempt to answer the question of social utility set within the expectations of the American people. School must serve all the people. It must train, educate, and enlighten all the population. It must be both present and future oriented; and it must provide American society with a repository of general skills, knowledges, and attitudes to preserve a functional way of life during the process of responsive and responsible change. The lag between the current social order and the schools can be reduced by defining measurable expectations for the schools. This bridge lies not so much through incorporating new technologies as in acquiring a change strategy within the schools aimed at adopting mutually defined, measurable, valid, and useful educational outcomes. The clear differentiation at any point in time between means and ends is the absolute requirement of those concerned with improving school effectiveness. Needs assessment offers a realistic and proven method for making such differentiation.

What About Values?

Planning and planners often get accused of ignoring values. We could not even if we wanted to, for they are a part of working with people.

Values are orientations toward existing and possible goals and objectives in life; they are predispositions to act in a given manner in a specified situation. Education and training occur in a context of values.

When one is planning interventions where people are involved or impacted, the values and valuing behavior of those persons are of paramount importance.

When needs are being identified, when determinations of "what is" and "what should be" are being delineated, the values of people are part of their behavior. Thus, by asking people what outcomes they expect and desire from the schools, or what should be the outputs of the schools, values are the screen through which perceptions and actions are strained. Values of people, individually and collectively, are an integral and undeniable fact of needs assessment and planning.

The study of values and valuing is certainly well-known, if not precisely predictable. The works of Lasswell (1948, 1960), Rucker (1969), and more recently Hoban (1977) have made it abundantly clear that any functional and practical design of successful interventions cannot take human values for granted or as constants. We cannot legislate values, nor may we assume them to be the same for all people.

As the fields of educational planning and educational technology (both technological applications and "soft technology") move forward, we see that more emphasis is being placed (and will continue to be placed) upon the social aspects of change, and that change will be increasingly concerned with improving the human condition and for accommodating and promoting relevant and responsive as well as responsible individual differences and values. Differences between people are axiomatic, and since facts do not cease to exist simply because one chooses to ignore them, their continuation and encouragement are basic.

Movement will go toward increased "humanization" of the curriculum and planning in terms of making learning and learning opportunities responsive to individual differences in interests, capabilities, backgrounds, and desired directions. Values and valuing behavior will be part of planning and needs assessment, and more work will be accomplished in order to assure that these differences are responded to in intervention design and development (Kaufman, 1978).

Humanism is not for sissies, it is responsible and responsive education. Education is by human beings for human beings, and as such it cannot attempt to be homogenizing, for it will surely fail, for that would be counter to the most basic and fundamental truths known about humans and behavior change.

Of particular interest to needs assessors and planners will be the value patterns identified by Lasswell (affection, enlightenment, rectitude, respect, skill, power and wealth, and well-being) and the modification made by Rucker (love, respect, skill, understanding, influence, goods and services, well-being, and responsibility). With these conceptual models, one may understand that people—all people—have values, the differences between people being mainly in the emphasis upon some of the values. Arranging the value patterns of different "significant others" involved in educational planning will allow educators, learners, and citizens to include that which is important to all.

What Is Needs Assessment?

All of this seems to lead up to the subject of this book—Needs Assessment. It is a tool for determining valid and useful problems which are philosophically as well as practically sound. It keeps us from running down more blind educational alleys, from using time, dollars, and people in attempted solutions which do not work. It is a tool for problem identification and justification. This tool has been a long time in evolving, and more will be done in future years, even future generations.

Needs Assessment is a *humanizing process* to help make sure that we are using our time and the learners' time in the most effective and efficient manner possible. Do we owe our children and ourselves any less?

KEY CONCEPTS

1. Education is a means to an end.
2. Learning and learners can be exciting, vital, and useful.
3. Many of our failures in education are not due to poor methods and procedures; they are due to selecting methods without carefully considering and determining the results, or outcomes, of education.
4. Educators, by and large, are committed to learning and learners, and they feel frustrated with the system and with themselves in being unable to achieve the results they would like to achieve.
5. There is a critical, vital, and useful difference between "means" and "ends," between the procedures and techniques which can be used and the results that these means can achieve.
6. Most people, including educators, confuse means and ends, and tend to select the means without documenting and justifying the ends.
7. Appropriate planning differentiates means and ends, and

supplies the tools and proper rationales for relating means and ends.

8. Defining the gaps between current ends and desired/required ends is a useful starting place for humane, responsive, and responsible planning.

9. A formal process for harvesting outcome gaps, placing the gaps in agreed-upon priority order, and selecting the needs (gaps) or highest priority for action is called "needs assessment."

10. With a needs assessment and a meaningful planning process, we can become reasonably accountable for ends as well as for means. Accountability can be an enhancing force in professionalism and in education.

11. There can be nothing more caring and humanistic than a process which formally takes into consideration each learner and attempts to find the best ways and means to help her or him to grow, to learn, to earn, and to achieve those legal things in life which makes each happy.

12. Outcomes may be valued by those who are involved in education, or they may be valued only by educators. Validity speaks only to accomplishment of objectives, utility adds the additional dimension of the worthiness of the accomplishment.

13. Values are predispositions to behave in a predictable manner in given situations. The critically important consideration of individual differences necessary to achieve success lies in accounting for, and being responsive to, differences in individual values.

REFERENCES AND BIBLIOGRAPHY

Alchian, A.A. The meaning of utility measurement. *The American Economic Review,* 1953, 26-50.

Carron, A. Needs assessment in government: Rearranging the deck chairs on the ship of state. *Educational Technology,* November 1977, *17*(11), 27-28.

English, F.W., and Kaufman, R.A. *Needs assessment: Focus for curriculum development.* Washington, D.C.: Association for Supervision and Curriculum Development, 1975.

Friedman, M. Gammon's "black holes." *Newsweek,* Nov. 7, 1977.

Gagne, R.M. Discovering educational goals. A paper presented at AERA Annual Meeting, New York, April 4-8, 1977.

Hoban, C.F. Educational technology and human values. *AV Communication Review,* Fall 1977, *25*(3).

Illich, I. *Deschooling society.* New York: Harper and Row, 1970.

Kaufman, R. *Educational system planning.* Englewood Cliffs, N.J.: Prentice-Hall, 1972.

Kaufman, R. *Identifying and solving problems: A system approach.* La Jolla, Calif.: University Associates Publishers, 1976.

Kaufman, R. *Needs assessment.* San Diego: University Consortium for Instructional Development and Technology, 1976.

Kaufman, R. Organizational improvement: A review of models and an attempted synthesis. *Group and Organization Studies,* December 1976.

Kaufman, R. Needs assessment: Internal and external. Paper presented at the 1977 meeting of the Association for Educational Communications and Technology (AECT), Miami Beach, April 1977.

Kaufman, R. A possible taxonomy of needs assessments. *Educational Technology,* November 1977, *17*(11), 60-64.

Kaufman, R. From how to what to why. *Educational Communication and Technology Journal,* Summer 1978.

Kaufman, R.A. A system approach to education: Derivation and definition. *AV Communication Review,* Winter 1968.

Kaufman, R.A. System approaches to education—discussion and attempted integration. In Piele *et al.,* Part III of *Social and technological changes: Implications for education.* Eugene, Oregon: University of Oregon, 1970.

Kaufman, R.A. A possible integrative model for the systematic and measurable improvement of education. *American Psychologist,* March 1971, *26*(3).

Kaufman, R.A., and English, F.W. *Needs assessment: A guide to improving school district management.* Arlington, Va.: American Association of School Administrators, 1976.

Kaufman, R.A., Feldman, D., Snyder, E., and Coffey, W.C.

Human dimensions of school improvement. Philadelphia: Research for Better Schools, 1975.

Kibler, R.J., Barker, L.L., and Miles, D.T. *Behavioral objectives and instruction.* Boston: Allyn and Bacon, 1970.

Kibler, R.J., and Bassett, R.E. Writing performance objectives. In L. Briggs (Ed.), *Instructional design: Principles and applications.* Englewood Cliffs, N.J.: Educational Technology Publications, 1977.

Knight, Michael R., Breivogel, W., and Pyatte, J. *Needs assessment materials: An annotated bibliography.* Gainesville, Fla.: Florida Educational Research and Development Council, 1976.

Lasswell, H.D. *The communication of ideas.* New York: Harper and Row, 1948.

Lasswell, H.D. *Psychotherapy and politics.* New York: Viking Press, 1960.

Lessinger, L.M. *Every kid a winner.* Chicago: Science Research Associates, 1970.

Mager, R.F. *Preparing instructional objectives.* Second Edition. Belmont, Calif.: Fearon Publishers, 1975.

New Jersey Department of Education. MODELOG. Trenton, N.J.: Author, Division of Research, Planning, and Evaluation, 1975.

Reusch, J. *Knowledge in action.* New York: Aronson Publishers, 1975.

Rogers, C. Toward a modern approach to values: The valuing process in the mature person. *The Journal of Abnormal and Social Psychology,* 1964, *LXVIII* (2).

Rucker, W.R., Arnspiger, V.C., and Brodbeck, A.J. *Human values in education.* Dubuque, Iowa: William C. Brown Co., 1969.

Schultze, C.L. The public use of private interest. *Harper's,* May 1977.

Stakenas, R.G., Kaufman, R.A. *et al. Florida school finance study; costs and effectiveness of technological applications in education: A literature review.* Florida State University, Tallahassee, January 1977.

Stakenas, R.G., Kaufman, R.A. *et al. Florida school finance study: K-12—educational technology in Florida: Scenarios for five alternative futures.* Florida State University, Tallahassee, July 1977.

Stakenas, R.G., Kaufman, R.A. *et al. Florida school finance study: Educational technology and cost reduction in higher education: Five alternative futures.* Florida State University, Tallahassee, August 1977.

Stigler, G.J. The development of utility theory, II. *The Journal of Political Economy,* October 1950, 373-396.

Witkin, B.R. *An analysis of needs assessment techniques for educational planning at state, intermediate, and district levels.* Hayward, Calif.: Alameda County School Department, 1975.

Chapter 2

PLANNING-GATEWAY TO TOMORROW

Planning is a substitute for good luck. If you could count on good luck, you would not have to sustain the pain and bother of planning. But most of us are not consistently lucky, and we do not want to depend upon fate. We want to make sure that our tomorrows turn out as well as possible.

In order to plan for the future, we have to take stock of today. We must determine what it is we want the future to be like and how we will know when our future turns out to be successful. This determination of the gaps between the "today" and the desired "tomorrow" is the essential nature and function of a needs assessment. We plot the discrepancies between our today and our tomorrow, but we plot them on the basis of the *outcomes*, not on the basis of processes. Needs are gaps between "what is" and "what should be" in terms of results, not processes or conditions. If the first step in planning is to determine the gaps between current results and desired results, what is the balance of the process? We suggest that it is a systematic process which moves sensibly and sensitively from the current set of results to a desired set of results. This process, which has been called a "system approach," will be summarized here and will serve as a basic referent for this book.*

The suggested process for planning and doing is a six-step

*Those desiring a detailed discussion of a system approach are invited to review *Educational System Planning*, Prentice-Hall, Englewood Cliffs, N.J., 1972, by Roger Kaufman.

system approach which is ordered and sequenced so that one goes from one step to the other when each preceding step is completed. There is an ongoing evaluation which determines when a function or step has been accomplished.

It is termed a "system approach" because it intends to identify, define, justify, design, implement, evaluate, and revise a system from the beginning. It assumes very little about how things are currently accomplished.

If there are needs of high priority, then the process continues in order to bring about predictable results. If there are no needs (no gaps in results), then the process stops there and then—there is no sense in designing a system to replace a system which is already operating well enough so that there are no needs!

Planning and Doing—A System Approach

There is no one "correct" model for planning. There are a number which are available and that work. Some work better than others in given conditions; some are more conceptual than practical; and some are more practical than conceptual. Which one should you use? There is a model which might help you choose between alternative methods and means for planning (and doing, for that matter), and which seems to be a generic process for both identifying and resolving problems.

This "system approach" model is unique in that it starts with an *external referent* for identifying and resolving problems (see Chapters 3 and 4), and proceeds from there to identify requirements for resolution, to select solution alternative(s) from identified alternatives, to implement them, to determine their effectiveness and efficiency, and to revise as required. Each of the six steps is summarized as follows:

1.0. IDENTIFY PROBLEM BASED UPON NEEDS. Here, gaps between current outcomes and desired outcomes are determined, placed in priority order, and the most important selected for action. This is the critical step to assure that the problem-solving process is valid, useful, and important. The basic tool for accomplishing this task is needs assessment. This first step differentiates this system approach process model from others which exist. It makes few assumptions about solutions or even about institutions which are currently in place and operating (such as training organizations, federal or state agencies, schools, or school districts) and only attempts to identify gaps in societal outcomes to which alternative methods (such as education or training) might be responsive.

In making this successful beginning to the problem identification and resolution process, the careful distinction between means and ends must be maintained. Here we are considering gaps between outcomes, such as ability to survive and contribute in the external world (Kaufman, 1972), as compared to current survival. The referent used here is gaps in results (needs) not gaps in processes (or how-to-do-its), such as lack of money, trained teacher, teaching/learning materials or the like. The outcomes desired are called the mission objectives.

2.0. DETERMINE SOLUTION REQUIREMENTS AND IDENTIFY SOLUTION ALTERNATIVES. Given that the gaps between current results and desired results have been now identified, documented, verified, and justified, and those of highest priority selected for action, this function determines the detailed requirements for successfully moving from the current outcomes to the desired outcomes. A tool frequently utilized here is behavioral objectives (cf. Mager, 1975, or Popham, 1966) where outcome statements are made in measurable terms. A behavioral objective is defined as one which:

- states what skills, knowledges, and/or attitudes will be displayed after any intervention (regardless of which one is eventually chosen) has been implemented and completed;
- states who or what will display these behaviors or characteristics;
- states under what conditions the skills, knowledge, and/or attitudes will be displayed;
- states the criteria by which the behaviors may be measured to determine success or failure to meet the objective; and
- leaves no room for confusion about what is to be accomplished, who or what will accomplish the behaviors, where and how the behaviors will be observed, and the criteria to be used to judge success or failure.

In this second step or function, the array of detailed specifications which determines all of the requirements for success are generated, through several levels of analysis (termed mission, function, and task analysis). Each function and subfunction analyzed and listed will have detailed performance requirements which give the complete requirements as specified in the definition of a measurable objective listed above. In addition, for each identified function (see, for instance, the example in Figure 2.1 of a possible mission profile and some derived functions) there will be performance requirements (here used interchangeably with the term objectives).

Further, each time a function and associated performance requirements are identified, possible methods and means (how-to-do-its, such as media, programmed instruction, television, communication satellites, computer-assisted learning) are identified which could accomplish those performance requirements (or *clusters* of performance requirements which go together), and the advantages and disadvantages of each possible methods-means are listed. The reason for listing these possible methods-means and their relative advantages and disadvantages is so that:

1. possible constraints (a performance requirement for which there is not a single possible methods-means) may be identified and eliminated or a decision made that further work is not feasible or possible; and
2. possibilities will be listed for later selection of the methods means in the next system approach step.

This second function is where the detailed analysis can occur, where detailed performance requirements are identified and analyzed, and where feasibility of the system plan may be determined by assuring that at least one methods-means is potentially available for each performance requirement or group of related performance requirements. Thus, this second system approach step is one where both planning and feasibility of problem resolution are determined.

3.0. SELECT SOLUTION STRATEGY(IES) FROM AMONG ALTERNATIVES. Here the methods-means (identified in 2.0) are selected on the basis of which have the greatest possibility, both individually and in interaction with each other, to meet the mission objective and thus reduce or eliminate the identified need. This is a short step to describe here, but in reality it calls for great sophistication to assure that the selections:

- are the most likely to meet the performance requirements;
- are the most efficient as well as effective; and
- will work by themselves as well as with the other selected methods-means.

Such tools as systems analysis, cost-effectiveness analysis, and Program Planning and Budgeting Systems (PPBS) are possible tools for accomplishing this function.

4.0. IMPLEMENT SELECTED METHODS AND MEANS. Here is where most other approaches really start. The needs have been identified and justified, the detailed performance requirements listed, and alternative methods-means selected. The time for design, implementation, and installation is at hand.

Here, if methods-means have been selected which are not already available, they must be either built or bought. They must then be tried out, revised, and made ready for use in the field. Other resources must be scheduled and obtained. Training of personnel to implement selected tools and techniques, if required, must be accomplished as part of this function. This is the "design and doing" portion of the system approach model. (An excellent source book on instructional system design is provided by Briggs *et al.*, 1977, and another extensive model by Branson, *et al.*, 1975, as well as by Mager and Pipe, 1976.)

Whereas the other steps are analytic and build the basic framework for achieving learning success, this is the central part of educational system design and development. It is where the doing gets done.

5.0. DETERMINE PERFORMANCE EFFECTIVENESS. Now that everything has been designed, developed, and used in the operational setting, it is time to see what worked and what did not work. The effectiveness and efficiency of the methods-means are here determined (called by some "summative evaluation").

Based upon the needs identified in the first function and the detailed performance specifications generated in the second function, the actual results are compared to the objectives. Where there are gaps, these are noted for action. Where success is obtained, the maintenance of the methods-means is installed.

6.0. REVISE AS REQUIRED. This, actually, is an ongoing step which is accomplished with all previous functions. At each step

Figure 2.1

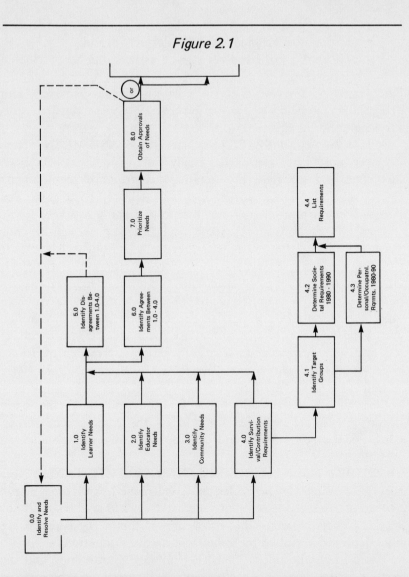

An example of a mission profile (functions 1.0 through 19.0) to show the possible functions and relationships required to identify and resolve needs. Additionally, there is a "break-out" of a function (4.0) to show that each function may be broken-down into constituent, component functions. Note that the functions only identify possible outputs, and do not specify any specific methods-means for accomplishing that function.

Figure 2.1 (Continued)

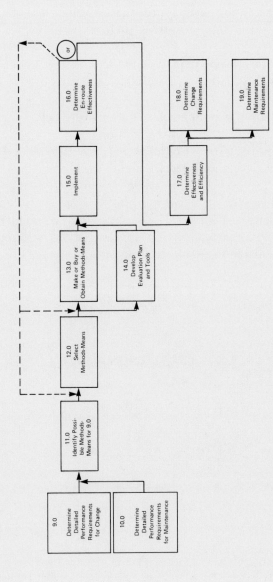

along the way, there is a constant determination of the extent to which each and every performance requirement has been achieved; and when it has not been, appropriate revisions and changes are to be accomplished. This en-route evaluation is also called "formative evaluation."

Thus, there are six steps or functions in this system approach process model, as shown in Figure 2.2.

Some Tools and Techniques Associated with Each Function of the System Approach Model

When we read the literature of educational planning and instructional design and development, we hear of many tools and techniques. Following is a possible way to view many of these in terms of their use in accomplishing a system approach to any planned change. Figure 2.3 is the same as Figure 2.2, but associated with each function is a suggested relationship with currently available tools and techniques.

Figure 2.2

General Problem-Solving Process

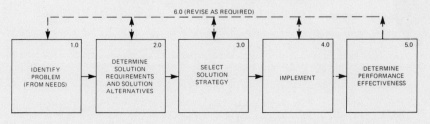

A general problem-solving process. Five of the six steps are identified and numbered; the last (revise as required) is indicated by the broken lines. Note that revision may take place at any problem-solving step (after Kaufman, 1972).

Figure 2.3

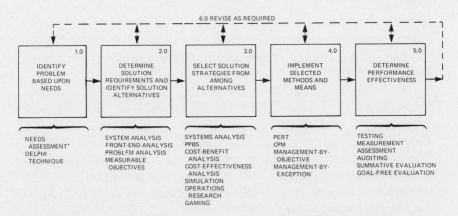

*Needs assessment in chart refers to an "alpha" mode of a needs assessment (see Chapter 3) or to an "external" type (see Chapter 4) of a needs assessment procedure.

The six-step system approach model and possible methods-means which might be associated with each of the six system approach functions. (A tool which is associated with the sixth function, 6.0 REVISE AS REQUIRED, is "formative evaluation.") (After Kaufman, 1970, 1971, 1972, 1976.)

References to each of these tools and techniques may be found in the contemporary literature—we will not go into these here.

The System Approach Model
as a Generic Tool and Process

This following point is quite subtle and is often nodded at when first presented, but real understanding frequently comes later. To accomplish any *one* of the six steps of the generic system approach process model, all of the six steps are repeated (in some form). For example, to accomplish function 1.0 (Identify Problem Based Upon Needs) one would apply the six-step model to that one function, beginning with an identification of the gaps between current status and required status, determining requirements for needs determination, and continuing until all six steps have been accomplished. Any time one wants to identify and resolve a problem, this generic system approach model is appropriate.

While this process seems to be highly similar to others in the literature today, it offers some interesting differences. This set of differences is what can supply both validity and utility to efforts being contemplated.

The first two functions of this model are concerned only with WHAT is to be accomplished—regardless of who or what externally gets it accomplished. No consideration or selection is made of the how-to-do-its other than the listing of possible methods-means. The prime emphasis is upon required ends (outcomes), so that reasonable and responsible means may be selected in function 3.0.

Thus, the first two steps are considered primary to planning and determining requirements, while the other steps are primarily concerned with accomplishment and revision. (This distinction is not altogether "clean" since planning goes on at each step, as suggested by Kaufman, (1972), in a taxonomy of planning. The concept here, however, is one of *primary* emphasis.) These first two functions are primarily concerned with WHAT, the balance is concerned with HOW.

Functions 3.0, 4.0, 5.0, and 6.0 of this system approach model are considered the basic model of what is often called a "system*s*" approach. The addition of the first two steps (and particularly the first one) makes the model a "system" approach in that it intends to build from scratch a "system" which will reduce or eliminate the identified and documented needs. The "system*s*" approach is a very useful set of tools and techniques for meeting objectives which have been previously identified and assumed or accepted as being useful and appropriate (Kaufman, 1970).

When to Apply the System Approach

A system approach is a generic, generalized process for identifying and then resolving problems. The two major "domains" within the model are:

- PROBLEM IDENTIFICATION, VERIFICATION, AND JUSTIFICATION
- PROBLEM RESOLUTION

Again, the first two functions (1.0. Identify Problem Based Upon Needs, and 2.0. Determine Solution Requirements and Identify Solution Alternatives) are primarily concerned with the first domain of PROBLEM IDENTIFICATION, VERIFICATION, AND JUSTIFICATION. Also included in this first domain (but extending to the other as well) is the ever-present sixth step: 6.0. Revise as Required.

The balance of the system approach model: 3.0. Select Solution Strategies from Among Alternatives, 4.0. Implement, 5.0. Determine Performance Effectiveness, and 6.0. Revise as Required is concerned with the second domain, PROBLEM RESOLUTION.

Reviewing, to perform any one function, simply apply the six-step model to the desired function. The six-step model will always be useful when one wants to *identify* as well as resolve problems.

Most extant models are concerned primarily with problem resolution; thus, they tend to optimize the given goals and objectives of a given problem situation. It might be seen, therefore, that "systems" approach process models will start with the given goals and objectives of an organization (such as a school district, a set of school board policies, or the operational policies of a corporation or military service) and operate as if there can be no challenge or modification to those organizational "givens."

It should be noted that regardless of what the starting problem situation might be, there still is a requirement to perform all six steps: (a) identify the gaps between current outcomes and desired (or required) outcomes (generic system approach step 1.0) and then (b) determine solution requirements and solution alternatives to close those gaps for the given step (or function) so that alternatives might be later selected (generic step 2.0); (c) select the alternative methods and means for resolution and closing of the gaps for that particular function (or step) so that later application might be accomplished (generic step 3.0); (d) identify actual making, buying, or obtaining of the how-to-do-its for that function which are to be accomplished, and put into action (generic step 4.0); (e) perform a summative evaluation (generic step 5.0); and (f) continuously, through all of the functions, revise as required (generic step 6.0). These functions are appropriate whether one is designing a new organization "from the bottom up" or a computer-managed course in map reading for military personnel.

A Planning Taxonomy

The basic difference between the application of a system approach and a systems approach is based upon the starting assumptions for the problem, not upon the generic strategy model employed.

In an earlier set of works (Kaufman, 1971, 1972), a taxonomy of planning was suggested—a starting place which would correspond to each step of the generic system approach model. Using this planning taxonomy, if we were to start with a no-assumptions beginning (similar to a 1.0 start), we would be using "Alpha-type" planning. If the starting place corresponded with the second step (where we were given the overall goals and objectives and we were to only analyze those goals and objectives into subordinate goals and objectives), we would have a "Beta-type" planning approach.

In similar fashion, the starting place and assumptions associated with each of the six steps determine if the planning approach is "gamma," "delta," "epsilon," or "zeta." There are no correct or incorrect planning approaches, only those which have differing degrees of existing, documented, and reliable data to justify our confidence in them, or differing degrees of assumptions we are willing to make relative to the selected starting place.

Of course, one risk is that planning may start at a particular point in the planning taxonomy based upon ignorance of alternatives or even implications of not selecting a different starting place. One set of results which is possible from such a defective selection of starting place for planning is that desired results are not achieved. For instance, if one assumes that a particular type of reading materials is "given," regardless of who the learners are or what they require, then one will start planning reading programs at the "delta" level. This runs the risk of developing programs of "remedial reading" or "reading improvement" which might not work well because the particular characteristics of both the learners and the nature of reading etiology have not been adequately considered. There will be more on this when we consider a possible taxonomy of needs assessment in the next chapter.

The starting place for planning is a critical consideration. It should be noted that whenever we start at a given point in a planning approach and do not go back to the beginning, where there are few or no assumptions about organizations, policies, and procedures, we are risking failure.

And needs assessment is a prime tool for avoiding those failures.

KEY CONCEPTS

1. Planning is a substitute for good luck.
2. Future success may be increased by improving the way in which we seek it and go toward it. Planning is a tool for improving our interaction with the future.
3. A system approach is a general, generic process for identifying and justifying as well as resolving problems.
4. The six steps of a system approach include: Identify problem based upon needs, Determine solution requirements and identify solution alternatives, Select solution strategy(ies) from among alternatives, Implement selected methods and means, Determine performance effectiveness, and Revise as required.
5. The sixth step of a system approach, "Revise as Required," is a continuous, ongoing function and may be exercised at any point during system planning and accomplishment.
6. There is an important (but often subtle) difference between a system approach and a systems approach.
7. Generally, a systems approach emphasizes problem resolution (the selection of alternatives, implementation, evaluation, and revision) aspects of a total system approach.
8. Generally, a system approach requires all of the six steps and includes a starting point outside of the organization doing the planning and doing.

9. There is a taxonomy of planning which allows that planning could start at any of the generic six steps of the system approach model.
10. By starting at any but the initial step of a system approach, one either has valid data, or is willing to assume that the selected starting point is appropriate.
11. Assumptions concerning starting at any point other than the first one of a system approach are risky unless that function has been previously accomplished.
12. There are different tools and techniques which are best used with each of the six steps of the system approach process.

REFERENCES AND BIBLIOGRAPHY

Alkin, M.C., and Bruno, J.E. System approaches to educational planning. In Piele *et al.*, Part IV of *Social and technological change: Implications for education.* Eugene, Oregon: University of Oregon, 1970.

Bloom,B.S., Hastings, J.T., and Madaus, G.F. *Handbook on formative and summative evaluation of student learning.* New York: McGraw-Hill, 1971.

Branson, R.K. *et al. Interservice procedures for instructional systems development,* Phase I, Phase II, Phase III, Phase IV, and V, and Executive Summary. U.S. Army TRADOC Pamphlet 350-30, August 1975.

Briggs, L.J. *et al. Instructional design: Principles and applications.* Englewood Cliffs, N.J.: Educational Technology Publications, 1977.

Corrigan, R.E. *System approach for education (SAFE).* Garden Grove, Calif.: R.E. Corrigan Associates, 1974.

Gagne, R.M. *Research and development objectives as derived from selected school needs.* The Center for Educational Technology and the College of Education, Florida State University, and the Leon County School District, October 1975.

Harless, J. *An ounce of analysis is worth a pound of cure.* Tysons Corners, Virginia: Harless Associates, 1972.

Hoeter, J., Fichtenau, R., and Garr, Helen L.K. *Systems, systems approaches, and the teacher.* Urbana, Ill.: National Council of Teachers of English, 1972.

Kaufman, R.A. System approaches to education—discussion and attempted integration. In Piele *et al.,* Part III of *Social and technological change: Implications for education.* Eugene, Oregon: University of Oregon, 1970.

Kaufman, R.A. A possible integrative model for the systematic and measurable improvement of education. *American Psychologist,* March 1971, *26*(3).

Kaufman, R.A. *Educational system planning.* Englewood Cliffs, N.J.: Prentice-Hall, 1972.

Kaufman, R.A. *Needs assessment.* San Diego, Calif.: University Consortium on Instructional Development and Technology, 1976.

Kaufman, R.A. *Identifying and solving problems: A system approach.* La Jolla, Calif.: University Associates Publishers, 1976.

Kaufman, R.A., and English F.W. *Needs assessment: A guide to improve school district management.* Washington, D.C.: American Association for School Administrators, 1976.

Mager, R.F. *Preparing instructional objectives.* Second Edition. Belmont, Calif.: Fearon Publishers, 1975.

Mager, R.F., and Pipe, P. *Criterion-referenced instruction: Analysis, design, and implementation.* Los Altos Hills, Calif.: Mager Associates, 1976.

Odiorne, G.S. *Management by objectives.* New York: Pitman Publishing Corporation, 1965.

Popham, J. *Educational objectives.* Los Angeles: Vimcet Associates, 1966.

Provus, M. *Discrepancy evaluation.* Berkeley, Calif.: McCutchan, 1972.

Reddin, W.J. *Managerial effectiveness.* New York: McGraw-Hill Book Company, 1970.

Rummler, Geary A. PI: Where the action is. *Educational Technology,* 1970, *10,* 31.

Salasin, S. An interview with M. Scriven. *Evaluation,* 1975, *2*(1).

Scriven, M. *The methodology of evaluation.* AERA Monograph Series on Curriculum Evaluation. Chicago: Rand McNally & Company, 1967.

Sweigert, R.L., Jr. Assessing educational needs to achieve relevancy. *Education*, April-May 1971.

Chapter 3

NEEDS ASSESSMENT

Introduction

Few topics in education are "hotter" than needs assessment. A number of models and concepts are available, but considerable confusion exists about such basic questions as: (1) what is a "need"?; (2) what is a "needs assessment"?; and (3) when should a needs assessment be made, and if it is, which of many available models should be used? This chapter defines several different kinds of needs assessments, suggests possible applications for each of the six types, and further suggests a taxonomy of needs assessments. It also defines a number of different but related assumptions that underlie each of the needs assessment models.

In attempting to define a taxonomy of needs assessments, we are saying that there are no "right" or "wrong" modes. Rather, there is an array of possible choices available to those who wish to design successful interventions without risking construction of a "solution" for which there is no related problem. This chapter further relates the several types of needs assessments to the system approach model for identifying and resolving problems.

Planning, Doing, and System Approach Tools

Planning and doing are the key elements of a system approach provided that they are combined with appropriate evaluation and

This chapter is based, in large measure, on an occasional paper published by Roger Kaufman at Florida State University and a resulting article in *Educational Technology*, November, 1977.

with provisions for revising and renewing the system. Many methods of planning have been available to practitioners and have been found useful in some contexts. Most tools (such as needs assessment, needs analysis, system analysis, systems analysis, program evaluation review technique [PERT], and the like) work well under some circumstances, not so well under others.

This differential utility of planning tools has been previously discussed and a possible taxonomy of planning reviewed. In addition, the suggestion of which tools were most appropriate with each step of the six-step system approach model was addressed.

The differences between types of planning are related to the starting point and referent for planning. A selected starting point might relate to the actual data on hand and/or the assumptions that the planner is willing to make (or in fact makes out of ignorance of alternatives) in starting at a particular system approach function. For example, a planner could start an effort with a statement of measurable behavioral objectives (cf. Mager, 1975). Such a starting point is frequently observed in education and training establishments where teachers (or instructors) prepare objectives based upon their experience or even a formal task analysis. By doing so, either knowingly or otherwise, the planner assumes that the objectives are indeed useful and correct. In other words, by starting at the second function in a system approach model, an assumption is made that a useful needs assessment has been conducted that identified valid and useful needs and determined the utility of those needs from which measurable behavioral objectives were derived. Seeing the task in this manner, the planner could begin planning at any point in the system approach model, knowing the potential risks implicit in the assumptional base of the selected starting point.

Needs Assessment—Different Types

In recent years, the initial functions of the system approach model (and indeed other system(s) models) have been given increasing emphasis. Needs assessment and front-end analysis have indeed been mentioned for quite some time, but recently there has been increasing interest in the problem identification aspects of system approaches. This has come about as a result of the failure or minimal success of many planned change efforts.

The interest in better planning and accomplishment, it is suggested, has derived from a feeling of many specialists and lay citizens alike that the "solutions" in our society have not been as responsible to the actual state of affairs as might be desired:

> During the 1960s the belief took hold that some kind of federal budgetary program or federal regulatory agency could be designed to deal with almost any social or economic problem. Now it is widely recognized that most federal programs do not work well, and consist principally of "throwing money at problems." (From the introduction to "The Public Use of Private Interest," Charles L. Schultze, *Harper's,* May, 1977.)

The situation has become increasingly acute, growing from an expenditure rate of some 8 percent of the gross national income of the federal, state, and local governments for purposes other than national defense and foreign affairs to a situation where, in 1977, such expenditures amounted to 24 percent of gross national income (Schultze, 1977). Expenditures have increased, and so has the public appetite for interventions in the society. But legislative actions in most states have indicated that there is widespread dissatisfaction with the outcomes of many of the programs. Solutions do not seem to fit well with the problems, and one hypothesis is that the solutions were not rationally matched with anything more than the presenting problems, the wrong problem, or no problem.

Needs assessment is a tool by which one may be increasingly assured that the intervention, once selected, is related to basic gaps and problems, not just to the obvious symptoms or to problems poorly defined. It is important to assure both the planner and the society that the problem attacked is real, important, and worthy of solving. The luxury of "throwing money and personnel" at each new problem or crisis is now well past.

Books and articles about problem identification have been increasing in number, and the term "needs assessment" is coming to have currency, if not vogue. Many needs assessment models have emerged, all seeming to be concerned with goal clarification, if not goal verification. Most, additionally, tend to elicit participation of partners—in education, partners might include parents, learners, community members, and educators (Witkin, 1977).

An analysis of the content of these various needs assessment models indicates varying degrees of partnership involvement and varying degrees in the extent to which the models include system performance criteria derived external to the educational system. Extant models seem to vary from one which strongly emphasizes the ability of a recipient to survive and contribute upon exit from a system, to those that call for sorting potential solutions to problems in order of priority.

Another difference among models is the definition or use of the important term "need." On the one hand, need is conceived of only as a noun—as a gap between current outcomes and desired or required outcomes. On the other, the term is used differentially, sometimes referring to an outcome gap, and at others to a process or solution gap.

A Suggested Needs Assessment Taxonomy

Perhaps there is an analogy with the previously reviewed planning taxonomy—there is no "right" or "wrong" needs assessment modes, only differences as to whether a particular mode is appropriate. There is a suggested taxonomy of needs assessments (Kaufman, 1977)—one for each of the six different functions of the system approach model: Alpha (1.0), Beta (2.0), Gamma (3.0), Delta (4.0), Epsilon (5.0), and Zeta (6.0). Each mode differentially starts at one of the six system approach steps (or functions), these differing according to the available data and/or existing restrictions placed upon the needs assessment process and subsequent change efforts. (It should be emphasized that the starting place is the only criterion for the taxonomy classification. Almost all extant models cover several of the six system approach functions.)

For example, a needs assessment mode classified as "Alpha needs assessment" (corresponding to activity 1.0 of the system approach model) would have relatively few "givens" and would be required to assume no "sacred cows" in terms of organizations, personnel, history—or even existing laws. The "floor" or "bottom line" for planning in such a mode would be the survival and contribution of people within a flexible society governed by laws that could be changed. (This type of needs assessment could be conceived of as being primarily concerned with policy *formulation,* and those that followed primarily with policy *execution.*)

An example of an "Alpha-type needs assessment" would be that undertaken for a school district willing to find out whether current policies, procedures, mores, folkways, myths, curriculum, and procedures were, in fact, related to the operational requirements of learners at the time they completed school. This starting point would require that all parties to the needs assessment—board members, teachers, administrators, parents—put aside their cherished preconceived solutions. This would then determine the operational needs (gaps between current outcomes and required and desired outcomes) and thus, empirically determine the requirements for outcomes before using existing policies and solutions. The Alpha-type is the most basic of the six proposed needs assessment modes. Also, it requires a relatively *high* degree of risk-taking behavior, and is the most direct route to the identification and achievement of "deep" change.

Other models start (perhaps more pragmatically) with more "givens" relative to the organizations that initiate the needs assessment. In this regard, it is appropriate to identify perceived needs of the partners, analyze these needs, assign them a priority, and then design programs to meet the needs. In such models, the survival of a learner upon exit from the educational agency and the learner's contribution to society are assumed, and "need" is both an outcome gap and a process gap. It is suggested that this is a "Beta-type needs assessment" mode, which best fits function 2.0 of the system approach referent. A "Beta-type needs assessment" might be implemented when a school district felt that it was sure the goals, objectives, and policies of the system were correct and immutable (or did not wish the "risk" of challenging them), and that it became appropriate to determine the gaps in current learner performance (usually relative to standardized tests and/or standard criteria of performance, such as reading test performance) as compared to desired performance.

Another type of model, "Gamma needs assessment," is available in which people are asked to order or sort existing goals and objectives (both for process and outcomes) with the purpose of obtaining a ranking of goals. Based upon the resulting list of sorted priorities, alternative programs or materials are emphasized in the school system. There are a number of needs assessment "kits" available that are seen as being of this Gamma variety (cf. Witkin, 1977). Also available for this mode of needs assessment are financial discrepancy tools, primarily those associated with budgeting, where costs begin to govern decisions, rather than behavior-change criteria being used to determine programs and results.

The fourth needs assessment type is not usually seen as such, but might be so considered, since it is a discrepancy-determination procedure. In the implementation of selected alternatives, it is necessary to manage the outcome process. When starting here, one has already decided what to do and frequently how to do it; so the major function is concerned with task management and accomplishment. Examples of such models are management by objective and management by exception (cf. Reddin, 1970, and Odiorne, 1965); or models specific for instruction, such as the Instructional Systems Development model developed by Branson *et al.* (1975) and used first in the U.S. Army and now in other services; or Mager and Pipe's criterion-referenced instruction package. This then, would be considered a "Delta-type needs assessment" and is most closely related to function 4.0 of the system approach model.

When it is appropriate to determine the extent to which required results have been accomplished, another type of discrepancy model becomes appropriate. This type of needs assessment may be related to summative evaluation, and comes in several kinds of "packages," ranging from Provus' discrepancy evaluation to Scriven's summative and goal-free evaluation models. This is "Epsilon needs assessment," which is primarily associated with function 5.0 of the system approach model.

Finally, another gap analysis is possible and necessary to provide constant and continual system change and renewal. This requires the collection and use of data at any time in system conception, analysis, design, implementation, and evaluation for the purpose of making decisions about changing, keeping, or stopping the effort or parts of the effort. Scriven's term "formative evaluation" seems appropriately descriptive, since discrepancy data concerning en-route progress and accomplishment of both means and ends can be used to modify or continue an effort. This is termed "Zeta needs assessment," referenced from function 6.0 of the system approach model.

It should also be observed that many data collection efforts, status reports, surveys, and observations frequently are dubbed needs assessments, but in actuality are not if the taxonomy discussed here is observed along with the maintenance of the rigor of the concepts and definitions which undergird it. An additional purpose of this proposed taxonomy, then, is to provide a referent for both what is as well as what is not a needs assessment.

Summary and Conclusion

Needs assessments seem to be of several different varieties. All appear to have in common the central thrust of determining discrepancies and suggesting or requiring some sort of action based upon these discrepancies—continuing whatever is happening, modifying action, or stopping it. There seems to be a difference in the extent to which the several needs assessment models have references external to the current sponsoring organization for requirements, as well as differences in the data base that they use for determining needs.

Still a third difference is in the use of the term "needs." Some use it as a gap in outcome, some as a gap in desired processes and/or solutions, and some as both.

Table 3.1 presents several types of possible needs assessment referents, varying from the one related to 1.0 of the system approach (and here termed "Alpha" needs assessment) through five additional ones, also given Greek letter designations. Thus, like the suggested taxonomy of planning (Alpha through Zeta) there are six suggested referents for a taxonomy of needs assessments (also Alpha through Zeta). Additionally, each type of needs assessment mode is presented along with the related system approach function, possible characteristics of that needs assessment mode, and finally, a possible assumptional base upon which each referent is based.

Figure 3.1

POSSIBLE NEEDS ASSESSMENT MODELS AND THEIR SUGGESTED RELATIONSHIP TO A SYSTEM APPROACH REFERENT

System Approach Functions	Needs Assessment Type	Possible Characteristics	Possible Assumption Base
1.0 IDENTIFY PROBLEM BASED UPON NEED	ALPHA	External utility plus partnership-based perceived needs referent for survival and contribution. Single emphasis upon "need" as an outcome gap.	Almost anything may be changed and questioned, there are no "sacred cows," even laws can be added, deleted, modified, organizations may be challenged, disassembled, rebuilt, or eliminated.
2.0 DETERMINE SOLUTION REQUIREMENTS AND IDENTIFY SOLUTION ALTERNATIVES	BETA	Partnership-based, analysis of output gaps of the system; analysis of process and product gaps within the system.	Work is to be conducted within a context, usually organizational, and for the most part, the rules, policies, goals and objectives of the organization, as they now exist, are the ground rules for planned change.
3.0 SELECT SOLUTION STRATEGIES FROM AMONG ALTERNATIVES	GAMMA	Ranking of solution by partners. Cost-efficiency models, cost-effectiveness models, etc. Emphasis on processes and inputs.	The existing organizational goals and objectives are useful and appropriate, and the charge is to find the most efficient and effective manner to meet the objectives. The purpose is to develop products using effective and efficient processes and inputs.
4.0 IMPLEMENT	DELTA	Determination of gaps in prespecified performances. Management-by-objectives, management-by-exception, scheduling, etc.	It is known what is to be done and how to do it, the important function here is to successfully administer the jobs to be done and manage the resources to help accomplish the overall organizational mission and identified products.
5.0 DETERMINE PERFORMANCE EFFECTIVENESS	EPSILON	Determine discrepancies between results and objectives for the end-of-term/project/program for decisioning. Gaps in outputs and outcomes evaluated.	The jobs have been done, this function is to determine the gaps between the goals and objectives, and the accomplishments.
6.0 REVISE AS REQUIRED	ZETA	En-route evaluation of both processes and progress toward outcomes, with possible changes of inputs, processes, products, and/or outputs.	While the jobs are getting done, or after we have finished any segment of one or more jobs, discrepancies between our goals and objectives (usually en-route) are determined, and corrective action is instituted, or a decision not to change is accepted and implemented.

A possible taxonomy of needs assessments. Possible needs assessment tools and strategies and their possible relationship to the system approach model. Each is concerned with discrepancies, but might define the term "need" differently.

It is suggested that they all are potentially useful. The only question facing professionals choosing among alternative models is the extent to which they (or their clients) are "locked in" to the existing organizational goals, objectives, and structure, and the starting assumptions or data that are used to begin the planning process. At any rate, there are choices, and all of them seem potentially useful for successful and valid change.

A needs assesssment is best used as the basis for useful planned change. It should be noted that the further into the taxonomy we start (e.g., the further from an Alpha mode), the possibilities for non-cosmetic ("deep") change narrow and the probability of making errors due to faulty assumptions increases.

KEY CONCEPTS

1. Any needs assessment is a gap analysis.
2. One may start planning at any of the steps of a system approach model; the only difference is the data on hand from previous study or the assumptions the planning is willing to make.
3. There is a possible taxonomy of needs assessment which, relating to the six-step system approach model, is:
   - ALPHA: Assumes few or no "givens" concerning starting conditions and ground rules for operation or resolution.
   - BETA: Assumes the validity and utility of the goals and objectives of the sponsoring or target agency. Attends to finding the gaps between current organizational outputs and required or desired outputs only.
   - GAMMA: Starts by determining discrepancies concerning methods-means for problem resolution.
   - DELTA: Gap analysis relative to implementation of selected methods-means.
   - EPSILON: Gap analysis relative to the existing objectives derived, not to any referent outside of the implementing agency.
   - ZETA: A gap analysis for the entire process, based on the entire process as given and only discrepancies relative to the system are determined.

REFERENCES AND BIBLIOGRAPHY

Alkin, M.C., and Bruno, J.E. System approaches to educational planning. In Piele *et al.*, Part IV of *Social and technological change: Implications for education.* Eugene, Oregon: University of Oregon, 1970.

Bloom, B.S., Hastings, J.T., and Madaus, G.F. *Handbook on formative and summative evaluation of student learning.* New York: McGraw-Hill, 1971.

Branson, R.L. *et al. Interservice procedures for instructional systems development,* Phase I, Phase II, Phase III, Phase IV and V, and Executive Summary. U.S. Army TRADOC Pamphlet 350-30, August 1975.

English, F.W., and Kaufman, R.A. *Needs assessment: Focus for curriculum development.* Washington, D.C.: Association for Supervision and Curriculum Development, 1975.

Gagne, R.M. *Research and development objectives as derived from selected school needs.* The Center for Educational Technology and the College of Education, Florida State University and the Leon County School District, October 1975.

Harless, J. *An ounce of analysis is worth a pound of cure.* Tysons Corners, Va.: Harless Associates, 1972.

Kaufman, R.A. System approaches to education—discussion and attempted integration. In Piele *et al.*, Part III of *Social and technological change: Implications for education.* Eugene, Oregon: University of Oregon, 1970.

Kaufman, R.A. A possible integrative model for the systematic and measurable improvement of education. *American Psychologist,* March 1971, *37*(3).

Kaufman, R.A. *Needs assessment.* San Diego, Calif: University Consortia on Instructional Development and Technology, 1976.

Kaufman, R.A. *Identifying and solving problems: A system approach.* La Jolla, Calif.: University Associates Publishers, 1976:

Kaufman, R.A. *Toward a taxonomy of needs assessments.* Instructional Systems Development Center, The Florida State University, Occasional Paper No. 1, Tallahassee, Florida, March 25, 1977. Also published in *Educational Technology,* November 1977.

Kaufman, R.A., and English, F.W. *Needs assessment—A guide to improve school district management.* Washington, D.C.: American Association for School Administrators, 1976.

Mager, R.F. *Preparing instructional objectives.* Second Edition. Belmont, Calif.: Fearon Publishers, 1975.

Mager, R.F., and Pipe, P. *CRI: Criterion-referenced instruction.* Los Altos Hills, Calif.: Mager Associates, 1976.

Odiorne, G.S. *Management by objectives.* New York: Pitman Publishing Corporation, 1965.

Provus, M. *Discrepancy evaluation.* Berkeley, Calif.: McCutchan, 1972.

Reddin, W.J. *Managerial effectiveness.* New York: McGraw-Hill Book Company, 1970.

Salasin, S. An interview with M. Scriven. *Evaluation,* 1975, *2*(1).

Scriven, M. *The methodology of evaluation.* AERA Monograph Series on Curriculum Evaluation. Chicago: Rand McNally & Company, 1967.

Shultze, C.L. The public use of private interest. *Harper's,* May 1977, 43-62.

Sweigert, R.L., Jr. Assessing educational needs to achieve relevancy. *Education,* April-May 1971.

Sweigert, R.L., Jr. Assessing learner needs with criterion-referenced tests: A working approach. *Educational Technology,* November 1977, *17*(11), 28-35.

Witkin, B.R. Needs assessment kits, models, and tools. *Educational Technology,* November 1977, *17*(11), 5-18.

Chapter 4

INTERNAL AND EXTERNAL
NEEDS ASSESSMENT

In the previous chapter, it was suggested that there were at least six varieties of needs assessment, one for each of the six steps of a system approach model. Based upon the starting assumptions of the actual data on hand, one could start a needs assessment at any one of the six steps.

One could start with an Alpha needs assessment, for instance, which had no givens or *sacred cows*, and thus could look at any presenting set of problems or any situation and not have to assume much about currently operating organizations or existing policies or regulations.

A Beta-type needs assessment starts at the second system approach step and usually assumes the validity and utility of the organizations which frequently sponsor or initiate needs assessments.

Four more possible varieties of needs assessments were identified, one for each of the remainder of the six steps of the generic system approach problem identification and problem resolution process.

This chapter is based, in part, on an invited paper presented at the Association for Educational Communications and Technology meeting, April, 1977 in Miami Beach, Florida. The symposium title was "Excellence in Instructional Development" and was sponsored by the Divisions of Instructional Development and Theory and Research. Part of this presentation was published by R. Kaufman as Occasional Paper Number 4 of the Instructional Systems Development Center of the Florida State University in 1977, and is published in Vol. I, No. 1, of the *Journal of Instructional Development,* Fall, 1977.

This taxonomy of needs assessments would allow educators, trainers, and other would-be problem-solvers to know that different varieties and possibilities for conducting needs assessment were available; and the choice would be based upon knowledge of the possible array and thus be most responsive to the problems and organizations being addressed.

This chapter deals with a possible way of separating these six modes of needs assessment into two types: internal and external.

Internal View of Education—The Way It Is

Most educators are hired, fired, and nurtured by an organization, a school, a district, or an agency which monitors or oversees them. Thus, any changes and problems which arise, naturally, tend to be viewed from the perspective of that organization. Any problem, if we are a part of a school district, for example, is seen as an "educational" problem within the context of that district. If we were in a state educational agency, for instance, that agency along with its policies, procedures, and history would usually become the frame of reference for thinking and doing. This posture toward planning and doing might be best viewed as an "inside" view of a problem or problem context, and this perspective *assumes* (knowingly or unknowingly) that the organization is the proper starting point for planning, changing, or doing. This further assumes that the organization is basic, relatively unyielding, and is the bedrock of change. It pays the salaries, makes the promotions, assigns the offices, determines success and failure—why should not that organization and those bosses and opinion leaders be the beginning and end for all activity?

External View of Education—The Way It Should Start

The simple truth is that what the schools do and what the schools accomplish are of concern to those who depend upon the schools, those who pay the bills, and those who pass the legislation. We are not in a vacuum, and our results are seen and judged by those outside of the schools—those external to it. If we, as educators, are unthreatened by the concept, we will admit that the schools are a *process,* a *means* to an *end* for survival and contribution outside of the schools upon legal exist from the

Figure 4.1

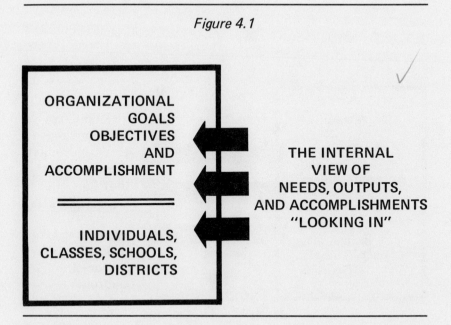

education agency. Graduates and those legally leaving our schools might well be minimally (not maximally) judged by the extent to which they are able to exhibit behaviors and attitudes which result in their being able to survive and hopefully contribute in the worlds of work, play, families, and relationship—an external view of our education and our results.

This external referent should be the basic starting place for functional and useful educational planning, design, implementation, and evaluation. If education does not allow learners to live better and contribute more, it probably is not worth doing and will probably end up being attacked and decimated by taxpayers and legislators.

Needs Assessment—Starting Off Right

There are many models, varieties, and concepts of needs assessment, as was pointed out in the previously noted taxonomy; none is either correct or incorrect—the only question is, which is most appropriate for any given application?

Figure 4.2

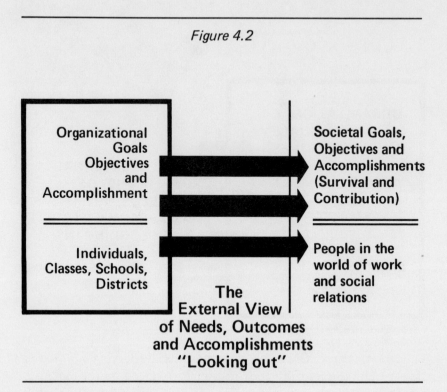

The most basic and useful form of a needs assessment determines the gaps between current outcomes and required or desired outcomes based upon external survival and contribution. It reconciles differences among the educational partners of learners, educators, and society, and places the needs (outcome gaps) in priority order to determine needs and their utility.

Since it looks at gaps in outcomes, not in processes, an Alpha-type needs assessment is critical if one wants to identify problems before trying to resolve them. It is a vital starting place for achieving educational success.

The central point is that an outcome gap analysis, which best starts at the first step in a system approach, is the way of determining the correct and justifiable problem to be addressed. The starting place, or the assumptions inherent in a selected starting place (e.g., assuming that the organization is the proper context for understanding and solving the problems, or assuming that a teaching method is correct and then trying to plan its implementation, etc.), is important in determining which problem will be addressed, and thus what the solution will look like and eventually accomplish (or not accomplish).

Internal Needs Assessment—The Way It Is Usually Done

When most educational agencies embark upon a needs assessment, they usually start with an analysis of the discrepancies between current student behaviors and accomplishments, and goals and objectives for those accomplishments. The current goals, objectives, policies, laws, rules, regulations, and procedures are seen as given, fixed, and generally unchangeable.

Gaps (needs) thus harvested are in relation to the goals and objectives of the organization, and these goals and objectives are *assumed* to be valid, valuable, and having utility and worth.

In the earlier taxonomy context, this mode of needs assessment is *beta,* since it starts with the *givens* of the organizations which sponsor it.

Gamma, Delta, Epsilon, and Zeta needs assessments, in similar fashion, are also seen as internal needs assessments, since they also operate within the context of existing organizations.

While these internal modes of needs assessment are necessary to the accomplishment of the system problem-solving approach, and indeed will eventually be performed when using the system approach to problem-solving, it should be carefully noted and understood that they begin with the acceptance and understanding of all of the assumptions associated with starting analysis and planning with preconceived goals, objectives, policies, and rules of an organization already in place and operating. This limits the degrees of freedom for revision and renewal to the borders of that organization or starting referent. Being conceptually or perceptually "locked-in" to an organization usually means that you can only change within that organization and usually cannot redirect that organization's goals and purposes.

To challenge the existing goals and objectives of an organization is perceived to be threatening to most people. So acute is this

Figure 4.3

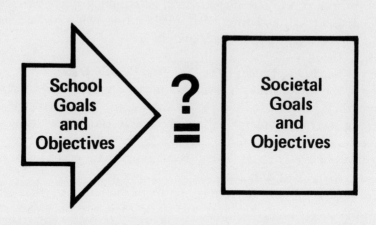

Do the objectives for learners and schools yield behaviors which are important in and for society?

problem that Reusch (1975) warned that in our society, deviations in means are considered to be only misbehaviors, while deviations in goals are considered to be subversion!

Changes to the organization other than "tinkering" with the means—the how-to-do-its—have serious consequences. The implementation of an external needs assessment, then, is a serious proposition which should be undertaken knowing that there is a distinct possibility that the people in power might not look kindly toward the results or the major changes it might suggest—or worse—accomplish.

External Needs Assessment—The Rational Starting Place

As we noted earlier, the external view of education starts with looking outside educational agencies for the "payoffs" of the education enterprise and endeavors. Do children learn anything which they can use when they go to the outside world? Are learners capable of knowing and accomplishing anything which is worthwhile when they leave the school? It is to this life outside, now and in the future, that an external needs assessment is addressed. Do the results outside of education have validity as well as utility? "Ulidity" is a term used to describe the joint set formed by the intersection of validity and utility (Kaufman, 1977).

In an external needs assessment, criteria for actual performance (now and in the future) are used as a template to design the goals and objectives of education and to then select the best methods and means for achieving these outcomes.

Thus, there is a natural, logical progression for intervention design and accomplishment which would lead us in the planning, design, implementation, evaluation, and revision of education in this manner:

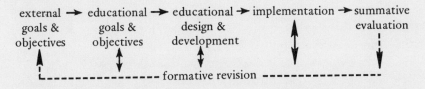

external goals & objectives → educational goals & objectives → educational design & development → implementation → summative evaluation — formative revision —

Seen in this way, the starting point for educational planning and accomplishment is the reality outside of schools and school districts.

Some Arguments Against an External (Alpha-Type) Needs Assessment

Most people feel that they can only do what they were directed to do within the confines of good sense and judgment within their organization. This is common sense in a world which, as Reusch (1975) pointed out, tends to reinforce with vigor when "necessary" the status quo. Personal survival, some argue, requires that we not "rock the boat." If one does rock the boat, then one risks losing the job, so the agrument goes.

Others feel that the world will not understand basic and major shifts and redirections, that changes should be made piece-by-piece, rather than all-at-once, which could result in what Festinger called "cognitive dissonance."

A third argument goes, "We cannot safely and completely predict the future; so it is very risky, perhaps even wrong, to go ahead and change the world and the goals and objectives of those social agencies which are now operating." Lack of predictability is seen as a reason for not changing.

There is some merit to these positions: it is not fun to get fired. Making errors, especially with large numbers of people, can be tragic. Change is usually more successful · if it is seen by those affected as appropriate and at a pace they can "handle." Let's look at these points briefly.

Is a job which is destructive, wrong, or even unproductive worth having? What are the individual job-holders' value systems relative to contributing to their fellow citizens and getting a regular paycheck? The unwillingness to recommend change, no matter how critical the change, is one which is often observed, but not often admired when seen in this light.

Moving slowly has much more merit than moving quickly and failing—if that is the choice. We do not want to change so quickly that the change attempt is abortive and never gets accomplished. But an external needs assessment, if done with skill and objectivity, will yield information relative to change requirements, including the discovery of possible blocks to change, so that the change, whenever required and necessary (but never for its own sake), may be phased and "gentled" in order for it to be valid, have utility, and be accepted.

The most troublesome argument is the one relating to the lack of predictability of the future. There are no crystal balls. Is this a reason, however, not to try to predict and control the future so that change will not be destructive? We make some predictions every day (how to drive, where to drive, what to eat and not eat—all based upon predictions of the future) and we must do so in order to survive. Change in our world is inevitable; the only question is whether we will be the masters or the victims of change. If we have a responsive and responsible method of planning, doing, and revising, then we can see where our predictions are becoming incorrect and change in mid-course. Inability to completely predict the future is not a rational reason for the maintenance of the status quo. It would make more sense to try to predict the requirements for survival and contribution in the future, and with sensitivity and analysis be willing to, when required, shift *what* we are doing as well as *how* we are doing the job. As things stand now, not using an external needs assessment referent (and thus not obtaining external validity and utility criteria) means that we will just continue that which is now going on, or only find more efficient ways and means to do what it is we are already accomplishing.*

The Question of Transfer

One concern is that what is taught in a school should have usefulness in the world outside of the schoolhouse. This applicability of skills, knowledges, and attitudes learned in an educational setting to the world outside of classrooms is called "transfer."

Design for transfer has not always been at the heart of education. Some think of school experiences as worthwhile in and of themselves and are willing to let outside performance happen as it will. While research has been conducted on transfer of training and the relationship between stimulus characteristics and response probabilities (Osgood, 1949), the educational world does not often formally consider the relationship between what is learned in schools and what is required for survival and contribution outside of school. In the next chapter, we will review a model of educational planning and accomplishment, but suffice it here to state that consideration of the external world is critical for educational success within schools.

Put as a question, "If educational experiences in school are not related or relatable to what learners do or are to do outside of schools, why bother with them?"

Schooling is a prelude to life. It is preparation for a life of change, a life of coping, and a life of success and contribution. To be less would be a waste of the learners' and educators' time and a waste of the resources that the public spends on education each year.

*In earlier works, this distinction has been referred to as one between a "system approach" (which takes the external view before progressing with the internal), and the "systems approach" (which starts with the internal view).

Figure 4.4

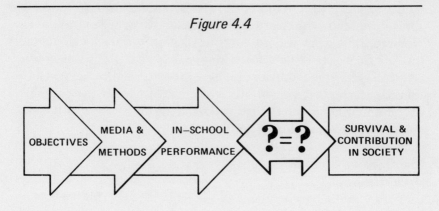

Are the objectives, media and methods, and the resulting in-school performance and outputs relevant to the requirements for individual survival and
contribution in the world outside of schools? The extent to which this
relationship exists is an indicator of "transfer."

Successful and useful transfer, in large measure, is why we have
educational experiences for learners.

Tinkering Versus Deep Change

Our world of planning and accomplishment, as we have noted
before, is one frequently based upon "polishing up" that which
existed previously. This could be likened to "tinkering" with a
system which might be failing. Making something more efficient
when it is performing an incorrect mission or a non-mission is a
waste of time, talent, dollars, and other resources. Besides, the
time and resources, whether or not they are important, do not
speak to the problem of what has *not* happened that is useful to
those people who we thought were being adequately served and
helped by the failing agency. Think of the actual cost of a failing
educational system in terms of what the students, once legally
exiting, are not able to do when they enter society: Are they able
to get and hold jobs? Survive socially? Personally? Is there a higher
crime rate among the poorly educated?

Could we not think of "costing" education in terms of "value added" to our society from successfully implementing a useful educational intervention or total program? Could we not think of pricing education in terms of "value subtracted" by a program or effort which has malfunctioned or which has wasted time or even destroyed people it attempted to serve?

It might be a compelling exercise to look at the costs of failed education in terms of additional required costs which our society spends for law enforcement, unemployment, welfare, and the host of social services which result from non-mastery during public education.

When we only re-arrange our educational activities and make them more efficient (within the understandings and confines of the agencies in which they are embedded), we are "tinkering" with our agencies. We are not looking at possible major changes. "Deep change" is a term used here to indicate a type of change which transcends the more usual type of planning and doing. It looks for major needs and requirements which are not even being currently considered, let alone served, in any agency for which planning and activity are being accomplished. Deep change is a possibility when one considers questioning and challenging the basic assumptions and ground rules under which any organization currently operates.

For example, one could question schooling (as Illich has, but we think less-than-productively), thus opening the door to: (1) seeing that there is not a need (no gap, no problem) to which this method-means, or solution, is responsive, or (2) changing the requirements for solutions and interventions which might better meet the mission objectives of the agency.

Deep change is a humanistic approach in that it considers nothing more important than people and puts their current and future welfare before the survival of an agency, school, school district, or methods-means which are in place and operating. No solutions are more important than the people which they were originally acquired to serve. Deep change questions all of the status quo in an attempt to assure the validity and utility of what it is we are currently accomplishing. Deep change involves values and valuing behavior, since it intends to go outside of the agencies which already exist, and attempts to find needs, both current and future.

An Alpha-type needs assessment (an external needs assessment) is one which affords the possibility of deep change. It is an alternative to forever "tinkering" with the status quo.

External Needs Assessment (Alpha-Type)—A Moral Decision

In educational planning, there is probably no more basic decision that one makes than whether or not one should attempt an Alpha-type needs assessment. To even suggest one is to risk, many think, being accused of disloyalty, idiocy, or worse. Again, Reusch (1975) reminds us that any questioning of goals or outcomes is frequently considered to be subversion!

In the world of educational planning, most personnel are not the presidents of school boards, superintendents, or even "gate-keepers" of senior status and power. There is commonly too much of a feeling of powerlessness and futility to even suggest a needs assessment model which is capable of eliciting a negative response. What to do?

The position, strongly taken here, is that it is critical to our society that this external reference be at least considered before expending human and fiscal resources. Human life is a shameful thing to waste.

As Carron (1977) points out, most approaches to planning, even at the federal level, amount to rearranging the deck chairs on the sinking Titanic. We often only tinker with our environments and our organizations, and we do not (at least not often enough) question the basic goals and objectives for which they were originally formed. Should organizations go on forever without modification or questioning of their utility and validity? We feel that this is not a rational position, and urge that all forms of human enterprise be continuously and rigorously subjected to proving their utility and viability in order to survive.

Ordinarily, societies delegate prized or important functions to social agencies. When they are accomplishing the job for which they were intended, these agencies are nourished. When they begin to fail (unfortunately, usually after long periods of time and money expenditures elapse), other agencies are given the tasks, or new agencies are formed. Thus, there seems to be an evolution of bureaucratic agencies brought to life to reduce or eliminate a recognized "need" situation. When they fail, new ones are found.

A contemporary response to agencies which are not performing up to par is "zero-based budgeting" where, periodically, an agency is obligated to go out of existence if its functional utility is not demonstrated and proven. But life goes on even while the budgeting process and territorial imperatives are fought about. We cannot afford the time and human waste that accrues to our society while human demands and needs are being left unmet.

Arguing about jobs and security seems to be of little solace while a society might be failing because large numbers among us fail to ask the basic question: What is it we *should* be accomplishing as compared to what it is we *are* accomplishing?

It is suggested here that there is a moral decision which must be made relating to needs assessment and planning. If all significant human planning and accomplishment are not related to survival and contribution in the external world, then one might be responsible, individually, for not being professionally ethical. Strong words! A moral question?

In our world, in recent years, we have seen massive human carnage and waste because individual people did not take the personal responsibility to ask basic questions of utility and social responsibility. What do we give and what do we get as a result of not tracking each and every major planning and doing activity back to the external referent of survival and contribution of each individual after (s)he legally exits our education agencies? Are we not preparing children (or learners) to survive and contribute in the external world? Are we not responsible to ourselves and others to begin planning and evaluating results on this basis?

It is strongly urged that all systematic, responsible, and responsive planning begin with an Alpha-type (external) needs assessment. Our humane and human society depends upon our doing so.

Summary

There are two possible overarching referents for needs assessment: one which looks at needs from a point of view outside of the organization doing the study, and one which looks at needs from within that organization. The external view is called "external needs assessment" and the other is termed "internal needs assessment." Most current activities in needs assessment are of the internal variety.

The external needs assessment is suggested as a rational and logical starting place for organizational effort (including learning design) in that it studies and identifies the skills, knowledges, and attitudes which are important outside of the school (or organization) and uses that information as the basis for educational design and effort. The internal needs assessment goes from that point forward to identify internally useful and worthy goals, objectives, methods, and means to meet those required and desired outcomes. Most current efforts in needs assessment are of the internal variety, and it is strongly urged that this referent be augmented with external needs assessment data.

KEY POINTS

1. There are at least two overall domains of needs assessments: internal and external.
2. An internal needs assessment restricts its view to the boundaries of the organization which sponsors the planning and doing activities.
3. An external needs assessment requires that the referent for planning and accomplishment relate to the world outside of schools.
4. Most needs assessment and planning efforts are of the internal variety.
5. External needs assessments are basic to societal survival and growth, since they are the basic referent for planning and doing.
6. External needs assessment is identical to Alpha-type needs assessment.
7. Challenges of organizational goals and objectives are threatening to most people, and might even be seen as subversive.
8. "Tinkering" is optimizing what is already going on in schools regardless of the impact on learners when they exit our schools and attempt to survive and contribute in the external world.
9. "Deep change" requires that the assumptions, mores, folkways, and conventional wisdom of our current efforts be challenged.

REFERENCES AND BIBLIOGRAPHY

Carron, A. Needs assessment in government: Rearranging the deck chairs on the ship of state. *Educational Technology*, November 1977, *17*(11), 27-28.

Corrigan, R.E. *System approach for education (SAFE).* Garden Grove, Calif.: R.E. Corrigan Associates, 1974.

Drucker, P.F. *Managing for results.* New York: Harper and Row, 1964.

English, F.W. *School organization and management.* Worthington, Ohio: Charles A. Jones, 1975.

Glasser, W. *Schools without failure.* New York: Harper and Row, 1969.

Greenwald, H. *Direct decision therapy.* San Diego: Robert R. Knapp, 1973.

Illich, I. *Deschooling society.* New York: Harper and Row, 1970.

Kaufman, R. *Identifying and solving problems: A system approach.* La Jolla, Calif.: University Associates Publishers, 1976.

Kaufman, R. Organizational improvement: A review of models and an attempted synthesis. *Group and Organization Studies*, December 1976, 474:494.

Kaufman, R. Needs assessment: Internal and External. *Journal of Instructional Development*, *1*(1), Fall 1977, 5-8.

Kaufman, R.A. *Educational system planning.* Englewood Cliffs, N.J.: Prentice-Hall, 1972.

Kaufman, R., Feldman, D., Snyder, E., and Coffey, W.C. *Human dimensions of school improvement.* Philadelphia: Research for Better Schools, 1975.

Kaufman, R.A., and Harsh, J.R. *Determining educational needs—An overview.* California State Department of Education, Bureau of Elementary and Secondary Education, PLEDGE Conference, October 1969.

Mager, R.F. *Preparing instructional objectives.* Second Edition. Belmont, Calif.: Fearon Publishers, 1975.

Mager, R.F., and Pipe, P. *CRI: Criterion-referenced instruction.* Los Altos Hills, Calif.: Mager Associates, 1976.

Osgood, C.E. The similarity paradox in human learning: A resolution. *Psychology Review*, 1949, *56*, 132-143.

Reusch, J. *Knowledge in action: Communication, social operations, and management.* New York: Aronson Publishers, 1975

Rogers, E.M. *Diffusion of innovations.* Glencoe, Ill.: The Free Press of Glencoe, 1962.

Tebelskis, A. *The effects of an intervention workshop on the attitude change of personnel in a school district.* Unpublished doctoral dissertation, United States International University, 1975.

Witkin, B.R. *An analysis of needs assessment techniques for educational planning at state, intermediate, and district levels.* Hayward, Calif.: Alameda County School Department, 1975.

Witkin, B.R. Needs assessment kits, models, and tools. *Educational Technology,* November 1977, *17*(11), 5-18.

Chapter 5

INPUTS, PROCESSES, PRODUCTS, OUTPUTS, OUTCOMES

In the world of behavior change planning and accomplishment, there has been much attention to classical works of general systems theorists (cf. Von Bertalanffy, Buckley, Churchman, Cleland and King, Etzioni, T. Ryan, and Weiner, to cite a few). In many of these works, the attempt has been made to determine the "system" aspect of any system or systems and to compare them in terms of their inputs, their processes, their outputs, and the extent to which they did or did not interact with their environment. This type of effort described the characteristics and similarities/differences between systems, and allowed for the possible planning of change or maintaining of that system or systems.

In this useful and productive logical model, one could determine the characteristics of one system or several systems and describe them in clear, unmistakable terms. If one wanted to, he or she could decide to change from a current mode of system operation to a different one, and thus could shift to a "solution-implementation mode" of a system approach. Finally, if one were to combine the descriptive mode with the solution-implementation mode of a system approach and also include the requirements to shift from a current system to a desired or required system, one could use an over-arching model of a system approach termed "design-process" mode. This model is presented here as a system approach, and includes both the descriptive aspects of a system model and the solution-implementation aspects.

But what about all of these "systems" words—are they just jargon which get thrown among people who have conspired to nod knowingly and never challenge each other's ignorance? Or do they actually mean something precise which is worthy of our careful consideration? We suggest the latter.

Earlier, in Chapter 3, we noted that there were different types of needs assessment, with the Alpha-type being the most basic and requiring the fewest number of assumptions. In Chapter 4, we noted that this Alpha-type needs assessment was also known as an "external" type in that it derived its basic referent from the ability to survive and contribute, external to the school system, and after the learner legally exited from that educational agency.

Outcomes. We would like to suggest that the results of any intervention or process, be they schooling, training, therapy, or the like, must be ultimately judged by their *outcomes*—how well or how poorly the recipient of the behavior change intervention was able to perform in the world external to the intervention. Thus, any ultimate result of any intervention is best viewed, measured, and evaluated in the environmental context external to the intervention (such as after graduation from a school system, completion of therapy, completion of a training program) and in the operational world within which people and organizations are required to labor and live.

Outputs. Internal operations and efforts are important, and we usually measure achievements and competencies within the organization which is responsible for the activities. We suggest that the fruits of such efforts which are measured within an organizational context be labelled *outputs.* Thus, outputs are that which a system achieves, hopefully in order to accomplish useful outcomes. The internal outputs are intended to achieve *external* outcomes.

Products. Products might be any materials, goods, or services which an organization produces and offers. They might be anything from programmed learning packages to automobiles. An internal output is hoped to contribute to useful outcome. Thus, a product is both internal and it is a result.

Processes. These are how-to-do-its, means for achieving products, outcomes, and outputs. They are solutions and solution vehicles which are selected to do a job—to accomplish things. They are best chosen on the basis of cost-efficiency, or how few "calories" are expended in order to achieve the desired outcomes, outputs, or products which the system internally selects.

Figure 5.1

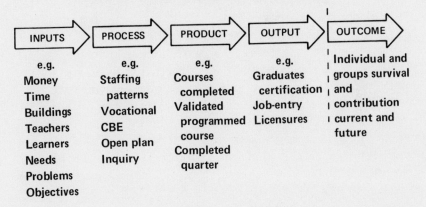

**Possible Interrelationships Among Inputs,
Processes, Products, Outputs, and Outcomes**

INPUTS	PROCESS	PRODUCT	OUTPUT	OUTCOME
e.g.	e.g.	e.g.	e.g.	Individual and
Money	Staffing	Courses	Graduates	groups survival
Time	patterns	completed	certification	and
Buildings	Vocational	Validated	Job-entry	contribution
Teachers	CBE	programmed	Licensures	current and
Learners	Open plan	course		future
Needs	Inquiry	Completed		
Problems		quarter		
Objectives				

Implied in this figure is the fact that organizations such as the military, business, and schools are "internal" agents which hopefully contribute to societal goals and objectives.

Inputs. These are the raw materials and factors of production which are available to do a job. They might be people, facilities, equipment, or dollars—the whole host of possible and available requirements, materials, and factors of production which can be selected and coordinated through processes to produce products or outputs internal to the system. Ultimately, the effectiveness of the use of inputs will (or should) be measured by the outcomes— the results external to the system.

We might look at this relationship in the manner as shown in Figure 5.1.

Another possible way of viewing this use of terms is relative to our earlier discussion of "means" and "ends."

Means are processes or how-to-do-its which will result in outcomes or results. Thus, we might use the word "means" for all things internal to an organization, and "ends" for anything relating to the external aspects—the results or outcomes.

In the context of Figure 1.1, we might add the following elements thus: MEANS and ENDS in the bottom of the figure, with "means" in the center of the *internal* box, and "ends" in the center of the *external* box.

Again we might add that schools, school systems, teachers, principals, materials, generals, sergeants, trainers, and the like are all means with the potential to achieve worthy ends. They are inputs, processes, products, and possible outputs which we hope to design and implement to achieve valued outcomes (Figure 5.2). Why all the confusion? In this field, we seem to be awash in jargon and misunderstandings. It is a new and emerging field, and new concepts are often confused with older ones; frequently there is a desire not to change, even among those of us who are lobbying for change in others.

Our field has changed from one primarily interested in designing educational systems (curriculum design and delivery to specified learners in specific surroundings) to a broader, generic set of related concerns dealing with not only "how to teach better" but also with consideration of "what should be taught, and why?" We are no longer concerned with improving just the internal (inputs, processes, products, means) aspects of operations; but we are now focusing on the overall, system aspects of presenting problems to make sure that they are treating real problems, not just the obvious symptoms.

Once a rationale has been developed (such as "systems approaches to instruction"), it is often easy to look at new concepts as being "more of the same, packaged differently."

We are suggesting that the systems approaches are indeed valuable and useful, but they should be seen in the context of an overall system approach.

A system approach (no final "s" on the word system) includes the determination of external requirements, including survival and

Figure 5.2

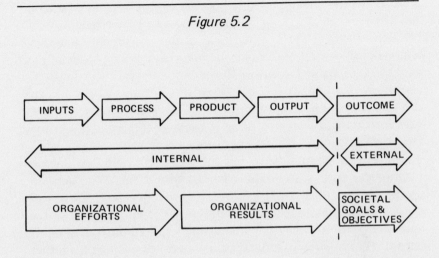

The relationship among inputs, processes, products, outputs, and outcomes, and their collective relationship to organizational activities and results, both internal and external to the organization (based in part on Kaufman, 1978).

contribution, and then moves to determine the possible means for achievement. Put into the above context, a system approach is first concerned with valid, useful, and desired outcomes and then relates possible means such as inputs, products, processes, and outputs to these. The systems approaches are generally useful when considering the attainment of desired and desirable outputs.

For many years, distinctions such as these were treated with a wide array of responses, varying from disdain for "semantic quibbling" to serious thought and discussion. We maintain that it is not semantic quibbling, nor is it jargon for jargon's sake. (One of the authors was once asked what this field would be like if one were to cut out all of the "jargon" including the "funny words" and the "little boxes and arrows?" He replied, "the same thing that would happen if you took math or chemistry and excised all of their 'funny symbols' and 'queer' words.")

There is no desire here to "cover up" through the use of

unusual words. On the other hand, we do not pretend that a new and precise field can long survive using words in common usage. "Plain English" is useful when talking about everyday things; it is nonresponsive when describing detailed and exacting phenomena and facts to others who are serious students in the field. The allegation of "semantics" and "jargon" is frequently a sign that the accuser is personally unsure or does not understand the conversation and wants to bring it back to comfortable territory. Or some of us might be hiding our own ignorance.

The central point here is that there are no "right" or "wrong" techniques; both system approaches and systems approaches are useful. As was discussed in the taxonomy of needs assessments, there are different tools for different conditions. A systems approach is useful when one knows the required outcomes and has derived the associated and necessary en-route outputs from them. Systems approach tools, usually, are ideally suited for internal organizational problems.

"Layering" of Organizations. Each person has an organizational or personal starting point for what he or she is doing and what he or she would like to accomplish. Almost invariably, this starting place is within an existing organization, and that organization finds itself within a larger organization or context; and, frequently, there are a number of organizational layers above those. We live with several layers of organizations, as shown in Figure 5.3. In planning and in needs assessment, it is necessary to relate one's starting place with other organizations in the "layers" and with the overall external societal referent (Chapter 3 and 4). It is important to understand that the referent for any organizational change, from curriculum or instructional design to policy planning and analysis, should be rooted in the external, societal referent. Without this referent, "deep" or non-cosmetic change will be difficult if not impossible.

KEY POINTS

1. A system approach differs from a systems approach in that the former uses an Alpha, or external, type of needs assessment to identify the needs and problems to which it

Figure 5.3

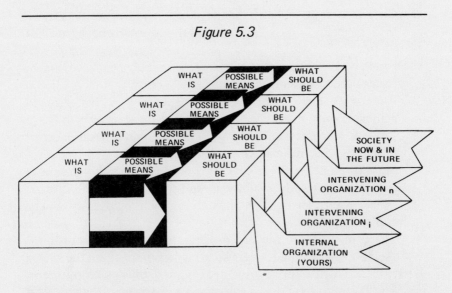

The relationship between one's starting place for planned change and intervention is usually in one of several "layers" of organizations between one's position and society. Planning should start with this "external" and societal referent (from Kaufman, 1978).

will be responsive. A system approach also has additional features usually missing in the other, such as the use of the tool of system analysis which determines requirements and alternatives based upon the external needs assessment before finding methods and means for eliminating them.

2. Systems approaches are useful and viable tools and techniques for resolving problems. A system approach is useful when one wishes to identify and justify problems before resolving them.

3. There is an important difference between the following words: outcomes, outputs, products, process, inputs.

4. Outcome is the result of the use and/or application of outputs, products, processes, inputs. It is the impact upon individual survival and contribution in the world external to the intervening agency or agent.

5. Output is that which happens as an "end" of any organization or effort. It is internal to the intervening agency or agent.
6. Products are any materials, goods, services, or packages which contribute to any output.
7. Process is any how-to-do-it of any agency or agent in achieving outputs.
8. Input is any raw material which is used in a process or set of processes to achieve products, or outputs.
9. Most of what we do in education and human interventions in general is viewed, evaluated, and stated in an "internal" frame of reference. These include inputs, processes, products, and outputs.
10. The utility of any output, process, product, or input is most usefully determined by evaluating its impact in the world external to the intervening agency, and thus as an outcome.
11. The basic referent for measuring an outcome is the change it makes on an individual's ability to survive and contribute in the world external to the intervening agency or agent.
12. Seen in this perspective, any organization, group, agency, or agent, including its inputs, processes, products, and outputs, are "means" to achieving the "ends" of survival and contribution—the outcomes.

REFERENCES AND BIBLIOGRAPHY

Buckley, W. (Ed.). *Modern systems theory for the behavioral scientist.* Chicago, Ill.: Aldine Publishing Co., 1968.

Churchman, C.W. *The systems approach.* New York: Dell Publishing Co., 1969.

Cleland, D.I., and King, W.R. *Systems analysis and project management.* New York: McGraw-Hill Book Co., 1968.

Etzioni, A. *Modern organizations.* Foundations of Modern Sociology Series. Englewood Cliffs, N.J.: Prentice-Hall, inc., 1964.

Kaufman, R.A. System approaches to education—discussion and attempted integration. Piele *et al., Part III of Social and technological changes: Implications for education.* Eugene, Oregon: University of Oregon, 1970.

Kaufman, R.A. *Educational system planning.* Englewood Cliffs, N.J.: Prentice-Hall, 1972.

Kaufman, R.A. From how to what to why. *Educational Communication and Technology Journal,* Summer 1978.

Ryan, T.A. Systems techniques for programs of counseling and counselor education. *Educational Technology,* June 1969.

Von Bertalanffy, L. General system theory: A critical review. In W. Buckley (Ed.), *Modern systems theory for the behavioral scientist.* Chicago, Ill.: Aldine Publishing Co., 1968.

Chapter 6

NEEDS ASSESSMENT AND
SCHOOL SYSTEM MANAGEMENT

The application of a system approach to educational management has been occurring in bits and pieces over the last ten years. The major impact has been the increased strength of federal requirements in the planning phases in virtually all of the various federal program titles. Originally rather weak due to fears of teacher unions, state superintendents, and other groups, increased rigor of planning and conceptualization has been incorporated into federal grant requirements as pressure has grown from Congress for "hard data" regarding results (McLaughlin, 1975).

ESEA Title III had a substantial impact upon state education agencies and local agencies when it began to mandate needs assessments at the state level as a prerequisite for local district applications. The process of transition to a system approach in which needs assessment is a requirement has not been an easy one. This has been due to the operational nature of schools and educational agencies interpreting vague public expectations, as well as the type of training given to educational administrators in the past, which did not include courses in system analysis or require the acquisition of critical planning skills.

The most essential task of management is to define the purpose or mission of the organization or enterprise. The second function of management is to acquire the resources, human and material, to realize that mission. The third function is to engage in planning by which the configuration of the resources is developed in such a way as to realize the mission in the most efficient and effective manner possible.

This process of definition, configuration, and implementation is conceptually simple. Operationally, it has presented enormous problems for educators and even for managers in the private sector (Drucker, 1973). To define the essential task of any enterprise is difficult. It is even more difficult with a social institution in which the purposes of that institution in the larger society are complex, confusing, contradictory, and vague. This is the position in which the schools find themselves today.

In many ways the situation facing educational managers, such as superintendents or major educational officers, within school systems is analogous to the role of a college president. A study of the situation facing college presidents shows that the collegiate milieu contains three characteristics closely similar to those in the public schools (Cohen and March, 1974). These characteristics are:

(1) *Problematic goals.* Goals are ill defined and do not serve as effective foci for action to initiate, review, or configure resources. There is no concrete set of objectives which is to be attained. Rhetoric is a substitute for coherence. The organization "discovers" preferences through action more often than it acts on the basis of preferences (Cohen and March, 1974).

(2) *Unclear technology.* The system does not understand its own internal processes. There is no base for maintaining records of planned activities which result in accumulated wisdom being developed. What is maintained is a loose set of records of "trial and error" facts or crash programs designed to relieve immediate crises.

(3) *Fluid participation.* The amount of time put into the system varies from participant to participant, often radically. The participants vary from one time to another. Organizational boundaries are not defined well and seem to be changing.

The public schools match almost all of the characteristics described by Cohen and March with the possible exception of fluid participation. The rise of powerful teacher unions has resulted in more uniform sets of working conditions, at least with a segment of the work force in the schools. Whereas teaching used to be characterized by a higher turnover in staff due to mobility to other sectors of the economy and to other districts, such mobility has now been drastically reduced as the number of positions has been cut back due to the national enrollment decline. Despite changes in the mobility of teachers, many systems still experience at least a ten percent reduction in positions due to turnover factors, which has allowed them to avoid more excessive layoffs (Feinberg, 1977).

The managerial climate in public school systems is ambiguous and presents a special challenge to the administrator who is desirous of bringing a more effective approach to management to the schools. Two additional reasons are offered as to why, over the past history of public education, schools have not been able to establish effective management.

Professional Independence and Ambiguity of the Superintendency

The rise of the superintendency as a role in American education was the result of board of education graft, corruption, and general inability to manage the mushrooming growth of schools in the nation's largest cities (Tyack, 1974). The first superintendency was apparently established in Buffalo, New York in 1837 (Reller, 1935). Thereafter, in quick succession most of the population centers of the nation established the role in their school systems. Yet over one hundred years later, a national survey of school superintendents in cities ranging from 200,000 or more in population to those of 2500 in population, revealed that 45 percent had no legal tenure protection of any kind, and 30 percent were serving without any written contractual basis for employment. Of the total time devoted to various functions, only 17.7 percent was spent on "general planning for the school program as a whole" (AASA, 1952).

There has been a history of antagonism by boards, teachers, and principals toward the position of the superintendency in American schools. Despite the great visibility of the position, the lack of staying power of incumbents is testimony both to the great pressures of the job as well as its insecurities. The position of superintendent has rarely been operationally defined well by boards of education. Much of the rhetoric about policy and administration found in conventions and meeting halls is totally out of touch with the great demands for action pressing upon school officials. Indeed, the separation of policy as a board function, and administration as a superintendent function, is both artificial and false and does much to cloak the real struggle, which continues into the present day (Cuban, 1976).

The ambiguity surrounding the functions of the superintendency is an impediment to the person occupying the role taking or claiming a legitimate function, perhaps because in so doing it demands the defining of the purposes of the organization. Traditional thinking says that this is the role of the board of education and a policy decision. The superintendent, however, is responsible for translating board policies into action. Therefore, the superintendent must guess what the board had in mind or wanted when it adopted often vague and conflicting goal statements. The translation of goals into objectives and then into jobs or work is a difficult process even with clear goals. In addition to the insecurity of the office, the nebulous division of labor separating the superintendent and the board, and high turnover in the position make the tenuousness of this function apparent (March and March, 1977).

Inability to Distinguish Between Solutions and Problems

In his treatise on the failure of the systems models to alleviate human problems, Gall insightfully notes that the one thing systems cannot do is solve problems. He quips, "A System represents someone's solution to a problem. The System does not *solve* the problem" (Gall, 1975). As we have noted throughout this book, there is a fundamental difference between solutions and problems, means and ends; and to confuse them runs the risk of bypassing the problem and engaging in the implementation of a "pet" solution which cannot and will not solve the problem. Hence, our reference to the "system" (no final "s") approach process, which avoids Gall's objection.

Since the mission of the system is often defined as services to be delivered or functions to be performed rather than as *results to be obtained,* school administrators have also been the victims of the inability to differentiate between solutions and problems (Young, 1966). This confusion is partly understandable given the difficulty superintendents often have with boards of education in defining the goals of the school system. However, educational management itself has too often been confused over what is a means and what represents an end or outcome.

The definition of the enterprise's mission must be rooted in the client's definiton of need, not the enterprise's (Drucker, 1973). Business does not exist to sell products to people. Rather, business exists to serve the client's definition of need with products/ services which facilitate that need. There are profound differences possible relative to exactly how one starts in defining the mission of a system. As one hardboiled teacher was overheard remarking, "School would be wonderful without the kids." Students do not exist to keep the school going. Rather, schools are means for students to obtain the necessary skills, knowledges, and attitudes required to find personal fulfillment and employment in the larger society.

Educational needs assessment begins with the client (the student) and focuses on the skills, knowledges, and attitudes that he/she should acquire. The student is involved as an integral partner in this process. The process also recognizes that parents as taxpayers and the community as a whole are clients too. The primary beneficiaries of schooling are students, and the secondary beneficiaries are parents and the larger society. However, we should not forget that the school fulfills its social function through individual students.

In the past, professionals have excluded citizens, students, and parents from meaningful involvement in the definition of the functions of schooling. The great educational commissions at the turn of the century which defined the objectives of schooling were largely professional commissions (Bureau of Education, 1918). The exclusion of citizens was partly a matter of maintaining control of the schools in the hands of an elite, and partly the result of the previous fight to rid the schools of "partisan politics" and the damage to what was considered efficient management. The continuing conflict between the public and professionals, as embodied in the move toward competency-based student perfor- mance, is one such response to ambiguous goals at the school district level. At stake is not only the argument about control, but also the definiton of functions for the schools. The accountability movement is in part a response to a century of problematic goals for the public schools.

The public school's management system developed a crude organizational scheme early in its history. Since there were no performance goals of a specific nature, histories of school accomplishments are very scarce, except as prolific superintendents wrote in journals or annual reports to sell various aspects of a new organizational plan or financial accounting system (Callahan, 1962). An examination of superintendents' annual reports may be more or less instructive depending upon the degree to which the superintendent was able to relate organizational activities to organizational goals. If the goals were means to ends, the reports will not be very helpful. For example, if the superintendent reported that the system required a junior high school because most systems were developing one, and that this goal was successful because the system now had a junior high school, it is not known what problem the implementation of the junior high school solved. The implementation of a solution sufficed as the goal.

Rarely do annual reports by superintendents map out the existing technology—the internal processes of the school system—in clear outcome-oriented objectives. School administration has been dominated by a mode of thought which expresses quality in terms of variety of means or characteristics of the "good system" or "good administrator." Only recently has there come to be a consideration of the results obtained from what school systems do.

Professional administrators can no longer sit in their offices or call meetings in their conference rooms to formulate the purposes of the results of education. Legislation, the civil rights movement, and the courts have forced open the doors to greater community and lay participation in this process. We believe that this is a healthy trend and that the involvement of clients is necessary to determine the mission and outcomes of the schools. Once the clients have been involved in determining the outcomes of the schools, it is the responsibility of the superintendent and his or her colleagues to transfer desired results into functional definitions of work to be accomplished. This requires an interlocking series of events and activities to occur.

However, the development of such goals also presents to

educators special kinds of theoretical problems. Just exactly how do goals shape or influence human behavior (Larson, 1977)? Is it possible that some planning approaches are better utilized without establishing specific mission statements for human activity? McCaskey defines certain types of situations which are not conducive to goal setting as an initial activity; rather, goals are discovered by doing. He asserts that the approach has been to set goals and then attempt to derive behavior from the goals. McCaskey believes that goals can be derived by acting upon a situation. They are then logical derivations from a set of human activities (McCaskey, 1974). McCaskey cites three aspects to organizations in which the planner or manager may not establish goals as a prerequisite to planning. These are: when it is too early in the life of the organization because its parameters have not been well defined; when the environment is unstable and uncertain; and when there is not enough trust or agreement between persons in the organization to act upon specific goals.

We believe that schools have generally not established measurable goals and objectives because there was not an appropriate technology with a precise vocabulary to permit specificity until the behavioral or performance objective movement of the late sixties. Planning models were extremely crude and lacked sensitivity to tracing the utilization of resources to outcomes; and the prevailing mood of educators to avoid asking and answering the hard questions about missions, functions, and outcomes was due to the lack of an adequate skill base within the teaching profession itself. The latter stance has been reinforced with the increasing unionization of teachers nationwide and has blunted the emergence of a senior profession within teaching, one which is firmly planted in advanced skills and expertise (Lortie, 1969).

It stands to reason that when advanced skills within an occupation are absent or nascent, there will be great resistance to being accountable for the welfare of the recipient of the services and to application of sophisticated skills. Accountability and specificity are partners. Loosely held, philosophical premises which cannot be translated into practice are inadequate guides for improving performance or professional practice in any occupation.

Public schools of the present general type have been in

existence for over one hundred years in North America; and while the environment has changed, there were certainly great periods of stability as well as ferment. Perhaps the only condition mentioned by McCaskey which relates to the problem of goal formulation is the matter of trust and agreement. This is a political problem because schools governed by school boards are often embroiled in differences which can only be subsumed by highly abstract and pious sounding statements. The problems of large educational bureaucracies indicate substantial hostility within and between the various working groups which prevents and inhibits clear work statements from being developed by which resources can be more effectively and efficiently configured (Rogers, 1968).

A close examination of most work plans developed by school systems prior to the early sixties should reveal the lack of clear bridges between philosophies of education and specific work tasks. While boards of education toiled to develop a philosophy of education, the superintendent and staff wrote job descriptions. Sometimes these became part of board policy in policy handbooks. The necessity for clear mission statements did not exist for public schools and still is not present in a majority of school systems. It is our position that the reasons for this discrepancy are not inherent within the nature of schools any more than in other types of social service agencies, and that schools cannot be substantially improved until they become more responsive to more sophisticated approaches.

The answer to the dilemma, we suggest, is to increase the skills and knowledges of educational administrators and managers about what types of planning strategies yield what kinds of results, and to help boards of education in asking more pointed questions which remove the pressures for "instant" solutions. Actions alone cannot raise the standards of the teaching profession, improve learner performance, or make schools safer or more humane places. Actions are infinite in scope and variety. Repetitious acts embedded in conventional wisdom reflect as much failure as success. The development of goals and objectives that define, configure, and shape action can produce descriptions of success and failure which will enable the schools to shed strategies which produce mediocrity, failure, and discontent.

We do not agree that research proves that they are unamenable to change. Research reflects what exists in the culture of the schools. While such studies may be instructive from the point of view of describing what is now practice, we disagree that they should necessarily be the description of what should exist in the future. We do not believe that research descriptions of the status quo define some "natural" state of schools which should necessarily be extended into the future (Argyris, 1972; Sarason, 1971). Society has come to expect more of its schools than they may be able to deliver; and we believe that some societal contradictions regarding the functions of the schools have not been faced well, particularly by boards of education, legislators, and Congress (Bowles and Gintis, 1976). We believe that the culture of the school is no more difficult than that of other institutions, and that with more precision and definition, separation of means and ends, and more adequate models of development and change, schools can become more effective and efficient. Dalton (1973) has summarized the importance of goal statements in changing organizational behavior:

> The first pattern which consistently seems to characterize successful attempts to bring about behavioral and attitudinal change is a movement from generalized goals toward specific and concrete objectives . . . one of the clearest signals that a new pattern of behavior will not be established and maintained is the objectives remaining general and nonspecific.

Needs Assessment and School System Dynamics

Needs assessment as the first step in the process of applying a system approach to educational planning represents part of a process by which management is able to determine the essential mission of the enterprise. As such, it is not a reduction strategy that the organization uses to arrive at some immutable building block or kernel of truth. Rather, needs assessment is a process of successive approximation. To understand the backdrop by which the process works, it is necessary to examine the nature of school system dynamics.

A school system represents a constellation of assumptions and definitions about how students should be educated. Within classrooms and schools and sub-districts, the sum total of those assumptions and decisions operates from day to day. The school system is the total of all of its parts. While various offices within school systems are concerned primarily with the operation of a part or parts, such as a school principal at the building level or a central office supervisor concerned with a subject discipline, all are affected by the totality of the whole. Viewed as a whole, a school system acts and reacts; it is effective or not effective as a total social institution. How any individual educational manager or school officer behaves is to a great extent governed by the context of the work to be done, the reward system under which the person functions, his or her personal needs and desires, and the extent to which that person views the total organization as compatible and responsive to his or her contribution.

Those responsible for educational system management, either in part or totally, function in roles which were established in relationship to each other to perform a designated set of tasks or functions. Such tasks or functions represent a pattern of responsibilities arranged from individual roles or offices into larger work units called bureaus, divisions, or departments. These larger work units have been designed to cover a certain scope of responsibilities which is the totality of that system.

It is important to understand that there is nothing sacred about the configuration of such units in educational system. An Alpha needs assessment would challenge the existing configuration. These units are the result of a series of human judgments about how to organize the work of the system. Such decisions rest upon stated and unstated assumptions about what the essential work of the system is or ought to be, how to motivate people to do the work, and how that work is subsequently valued and rewarded or not rewarded. Such work is *configured,* that is, arranged, sometimes deliberately with forethought and sometimes by default. This fact would be more apparent if school systems differed radically from each other in terms of organizational patterns and/or shape (they obviously differ in size). The fact that they all look pretty much alike obscures the fallibility of the decisions and assumptions and gives the appearance that there is more to support their structure or configuration than may be merited. Reformers, critics, and even defenders of the school system then typically move into proposals and programs to change some part or function of the system and assume that the totality should (or can) be left intact because the current shape is the most effective one possible and must have evolved with some sort of systematic abandonment of earlier and less effective models. Needs assessment models which make the assumption that the current goals, objectives, and shapes are valid begin at the "Beta" stage.

Even if the educational manager has no intention of changing the current configuration of the parts of a system, the manager should understand how it has been put together, its history of development, and what political compromises were made by which the divisions of the system are held together to form and maintain the whole. Those involved with educational management have the responsibility to *conceptualize alternatives,* for without that ability they have no way of behaving towards change. One of the essential tasks of educational management is to shape the organization most effectively, given what the system must accomplish. Not knowing what other ways the same set of tasks could be accomplished is to leave an institution without any definition of success or effectiveness. In the words of a former board of education member (Clement, 1975) of the Chicago Public Schools:

> There's a difference between a successful public school system that accomplishes objectives and one that just survives. I imagine that the Chicago Public Schools will survive in the sense that the buildings will be standing and teachers and students will still be in the classrooms, but they won't be doing the job they should be doing. The school system will survive in the minimal sense, but unless it's greatly improved, it's not going to do the job it should be doing.

To conceptualize alternatives of configuring the organization requires some knowledge of the role the organization plays within the larger social context, its objectives and the backdrop of reality upon and within which the school system must exist. How does the educational manager view reality?

A View of Reality for the Educational Manager

Reality is seen to be fluid and infinite. Such delineations as

past, present, and future are impositions of our ability to exist
within a set of moving phenomena upon which we impose
definitions and categories to make sense of that which is
overwhelming in its totality. Totality, in a human sense, is merely
the innate limitations of perception to grasp all that is occurring at
any given time. In order to make sense of reality, we construct
categories and re-examine what is seen. From the re-examination,
we construct patterns and theories which become explanations
that can be tested. Such tests lead to predictability and improvement of life by forming guidelines for subsequent human action.
With the creation of such categories and constructs upon a
limitless data base, we find a niche in the universe. Civilizations
grow and the organizations within those civilizations expand; they
define and add new dimensions to social guidelines. No matter
how complicated such civilizations are, from primitive to complex,
they all rest upon human constructs, definitions, and assumptions
at the core.

While any human organization may be huge and appear
implacable, it is in reality a limited set of definitions and
constructs which rest upon a very fluid base.

A human organization is at the simplest level a group of people
who have been arranged to perform a limited set of functions
which relate to each other and which attempt to accomplish the
objectives for which the organization was established. Organizations are really people who exist only in relationship to other
people, and all must consent to confine what is essentially a
limitless range of possible actions to a relatively small range of
actions to be performed in a repetitive manner. While job scope
and depth (Filley and House, 1969) may vary from the superintendent to the custodian, each has a range of responsibilities and
possible actions which are primarily repetitive. Since organizations
are restraints, deliberate decisions must be made about the
limitations of all possible actions that could be performed within
them.

A social organization or social system must relate to its
environment to be effective. It must exercise control and direction
over its parts and internal functioning to be able to accomplish its
objectives. It must be concerned with internal problems and

conflict, because it can never be more effective than the least effective and smallest part. To the individual parent, the school system is no more effective than the teacher's success in relating to a son or daughter in a classroom.

Critical Managerial Assumptions

Reality is fluid. It is timeless. It is all at once and everywhere. It is total happening all the time and includes past, present, and future within its scope. Management which does not recognize the limitations of the system and the assumptions which hold it together to perform a limited range of functions is incapable of re-examining those assumptions and limitations. Such management deprives the organization of a future as a viable social organism. Survival and viability are ultimately linked when a new institution is created.

In order to come to grips with reality as fluid and timeless, it is the function of management to create constructs and definitions which continually probe the effectiveness of the organization within its social milieu. It is management's function to structure the organization and its resources and re-structure if necessary. Any such decision or levels of decision filter out segments of reality. Since this is what an organization essentially does, that is, impose limitations upon reality, it must know what it is NOT doing as well as what it IS doing.

Management, by selecting what it does over what it will NOT do, limits the system's resources to perceived essential purposes. This is a top-level decision or series of decisions. It begins with dividing all that is reality into the knowable and the unknowable or unknown. The line between the two is constantly shifting. Organizations may exist over time without any substantial rethinking about what is known and unknown, or what the objectives of the organization might be or should be. The imposition of constructs and categories by which an organization is formed should be periodically and deeply examined (by an "Alpha" assessment). This is a primary function of responsible educational management.

An educational manager functioning in a school system should be aware of the limitations of the enterprise. Since it is a managerial decision as to how resources are to be utilized, it is vital to understand the limited scope of human concentration set within the structuring of time. Management and needs assessment represent human imposition upon infinite choice and possibilities. The criteria for choice, the possible types of choices, and the consequences and effectiveness of any given choice are the repetitive tasks which comprise the primary managerial activity within any given level of a school system. In the words of Kurt Lewin, who attempted to define what is known and unknown to an individual and to a society, the principle of *contemporaneity* underlies all that is known (Lewin, 1936). It is the ultimate perceptual boundary of all possible relationships. Within the scope of those boundaries are contained all possible causes and effects, and within the same boundaries lie an explanation of how a person behaves and how a school system functions. To understand the actions of a school system, it is important to know what the system sees and what it does not see. Any range of choice is limited to what is deemed possible and what exists. Lewin defines what is real as what has effects or consequences for a person or a system. What is possible as a solution to a problem is only possible within the range of vision or perception of the system. For this reason, it is vital to know if any of the initial constructs, definitions, and/or assumptions by which the organization was formed or operates on a daily basis have tended to obscure what is possible or not possible for it to perceive. To rephrase the answer as a question, "Is the way we have organized ourselves to accomplish our objectives part of the reason we have not been able to reach those objectives?" An organization can become blind to its effectiveness, if in the process of being shaped, what is possible is not ever considered fully because of the way the problem was defined, to *exclude* something which was within the grasp of the system to know or to believe was possible.

In order for management to decide how the system should undertake its responsibilities, it must first know what the organization should be accomplishing. It cannot reasonably know this if it does not have some idea of what it should not be accomplishing. To answer that question requires knowledge of all the possible things that could be outputs. It is in the fundamental division of what is possible and not possible which forms the first data base for all subsequent managerial decisions. Management must always be aware that what is possible is never static and that sometimes removal of the assumptions, definitions, and constructs which the system has been using for some time (as in an "Alpha" assessment) will open up a new field of vision of what is actually required as well as that which is possible.

To understand the criticality of this activity is paramount. It is the periodic removal of the prescription lenses by which any organization perceives its environment and itself. The problems which we are able to solve are ultimately testimony to what was considered possible. The fact that so many educational problems are unsolved supplies the impetus to re-examine what is possible and to ask the question, "What should we be doing?" We can no longer assume that what we are now doing is adequate, in order to increase educational system effectiveness. This cannot be done if we fail to ask the questions which remove the necessity to re-examine the shape of our current school system and its internal dynamics.

Facing Up to the Bureaucratic Challenge

Every school system officer, from superintendent to principal, and all of the intermediate offices, division executives, coordinators, supervisors, directors, and teachers find themselves a part of an organization which is inhibitory of solving actual and important educational problems. The literature is filled with diatribes against bureaucracy (Katz, 1971) and its deadening impact upon the failure of large and middle-sized school systems to educate children, but particularly children of minority groups (Greer, 1972). The sum total of judgment is that school systems have been organized to protect themselves and the performance of various officers of the system; particularly various administrators have been rewarded for and thus transformed into bureaucrats who care more about their own positions and benefits than the performance of the system itself. On the face of the evidence, school systems have been organized into a configuration which prevents them from being optimally effective in terms of the utility of outcomes to which they contribute. Somehow the implication is left that this was part of a plot or that well meaning but blundering educators duped the public into believing bureaucracy was a better way; or if not that, once the bureaucrats got their collective feet into the door, all the ills of education thereafter followed.

Bureaucracy in a sociological sense refers to a type of organization and the way it is shaped. Max Weber, the German sociologist who coined the term, delineated the earmarks of a bureaucracy as follows:

(1) Areas of the organization are designated or set apart from each other, and rules, laws, or regulations are developed to determine proper jurisdiction between them.

(2) Offices or roles are developed within the organization and established into hierarchical relationships. This determines higher and lower authorities.

(3) Written communication becomes the major means of official activity and a system of records or files is developed.

(4) Encumbents holding various roles or offices do so on the basis of their previous training and expertise to fulfill the position.

(5) Encumbents perform their roles full time no matter how restricted the particular role might be.

(6) The management of each office is based upon rules which are regarded as fairly stable over a period of time (Gerth and Mills, 1946).

Weber pointed out that bureaucracies have existed long before modern democratic states. Large bureaucracies existed in Egypt during the period of the New Empire, in Ancient Rome and the Byzantine Empire, in the Roman Catholic Church since the thirteenth century, and in China for many centuries. Weber accounted for the rise of bureaucracy as a specific type or organizational configuration on the basis of its "purely technical superiority over any other form of organization." No other type of organization can compete with a bureaucracy for predictability, continuity, and impartial application of the services which it may render to a society. According to Weber, the major forces which led to the rise of bureaucracy were the development of a money economy, the necessity to maintain large standing armies composed of troops who were not land holders, and the necessity of administering public services such as telephone, railroads, and waterways impartially without regard to wealth or status. Weber also observed that, once entrenched, bureaucracy was one of the types of social structures most difficult to destroy. It was a power instrument of the first order.

In education, there has been a battle for hegemony over the public schools, in which professionals have argued that those with responsibilities for control of the school system should have the necessary expertise and that favoritism should be eliminated in terms of personnel appointment and patronage. As systems grew larger, board standing committees were replaced with a variety of officials in the school system as paid full-time employees. The evolution of assistant superintendents for business, personnel, instruction, and later in the sixties planning and evaluation followed the exodus of lay control over the day-to-day affairs of the school system.

It should be recalled that bureaucratization of the nation's school systems was actively pursued by professional educators in the field and by universities, colleges, and leading citizens. The advantages of bureaucratization were stated over and over as increased efficiency, greater expertise in the daily affairs of the system, elimination of favoritism and bias in hiring teachers and principals, elimination of machine politics in the selection of board members, and the necessity of having a superintendent who minded the store every day through a cadre of subordinates. Painted against the evils of the past, bureaucratization was clearly a more technically efficient form of organization and it did serve to eliminate some problems. It was in this battle that the concept of limiting the board of education's function purely to legislative or matters of "policy" was born. The confinement of the role of a board of education to this theoretical ground represented an expansion of the professional administrator's responsibilities, chiefly the superintendent and his or her immediate delegates.

The Dysfunctions of Bureaucracy

Bureaucracy may have solved problems but it certainly created others. Bennis (1966) indicates that bureaucracy creates a system of "group think" in which individual creativity is not welcome. Perhaps the largest inhibiting factor against bureaucracy is its penchant for categories and categorization as a necessity to engage in problem-solving. In the words of Merton, "The generality of the rules requires the constant use of categorization, whereby individual problems and cases are classified on the basis of designated criteria and are treated accordingly" (Merton, 1968).

If this is true, then the division between what is possible and impossible in Lewin's terms is limited to the categories constructed by the bureaucracy itself. The result is that a bureaucratic organization is frozen into a response, and any given problem must fall within its division of labor—or it will not be approached. Figure 6.1 shows the organizational table of a large city school system. Now, take a hypothetical problem facing the school bureaucracy, such as a decline in reading scores on some standardized reading test. Where does the problem go? What officer or division of the school system is assigned the problem? Would the problem be assigned to the assistant superintendent for instruction, who in turn assigns it to the director of elementary education, who in turn delegates it to a supervisor at the elementary level? Or would the problem be referred to the director of staff development, who is responsible for testing? Perhaps the problem should be referred to the assistant superintendent of planning and evaluation, who in turn would include it as a responsibility of the director of Title I.

The reading program does not fit neatly into any line of the table of organization. The problem obviously cuts across several divisions of the school system. It cannot be located precisely and involves many people and functions. To give the problem to one division may be to enhance that division's power and stature, and so some superintendents would avoid assigning it exclusively to one. Some might organize a cross-divisional committee, but who would head the committee? And which division would implement the recommendations from the committee? For this reason, assigning a problem to a committee is often a way to avoid confronting the problem.

School system bureaucracies are not problem oriented; they are scaled from high to low within units or divisions whose broad functions are organizational in scope. The table of organization was not shaped to deal with field problems which involve two or

*Figure 6.1. Hypothetical Division of Labor in
Large City School System (Partial).*

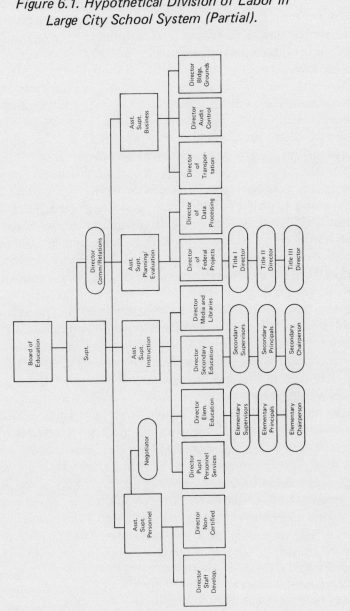

more divisions and which do not fall neatly into any one area of responsibility. Since very few problems do fall the way the table of organization has been constructed, very few are addressed with the proper allocation of resources. Problems often fall through the "cracks" of the table of organization. Either no single division is given the authority to attack a problem, or there is no one responsible for making sure it is addressed, if it involves more than one area of the table of organization. Sometimes the various units or areas will organize to make sure that no other division or area is able to work on a problem to the point that existing power relationships are effectively mobilized or changed.

As Merton so accurately described, the construction of response categories inhibits the school system from an adequate reply to any problem which is multi-dimensional in nature. Since these are often the "gut" or "survival" issues for the school system itself, the bureaucracy attempts to subvert them rather than deal with them, as the case study by David Rogers of the attempted integration of the New York City Schools demonstrates (Rogers, 1968). In much earlier times, the rejection of the supervisor's role by the Boston City Schools as an attempt by the board to remove power from the school masters is another example (Katz, 1971). Whenever an organizational response is required which demands total concentration upon an issue, there are usually vested power interests within the bureaucratic school system which will coalesce to prevent a response on any other basis than that which already exists. For a bureaucratic system, what is possible or impossible must be understood in terms of its own structure rather than in what resources can be organized to solve actual system problems. What is virtually impossible is a response which would require a different kind of organization. This also accounts for the difficulty in getting bureaucrats to consider an Alpha or external type needs assessment because of the perceived threat to the status quo. When the alternative is suggested, it is likely greeted with misunderstanding or immediate long and intense discussions of philosophy. Both reactions connote fear.

The internal problems of bureaucratic structure are further illustrated in Figure 6.2. This represents an attempt to clarify the cycle of inaction and inability of a middle-sized school system

Figure 6.2. Administrative Dilemmas Cause/Effect Matrix.

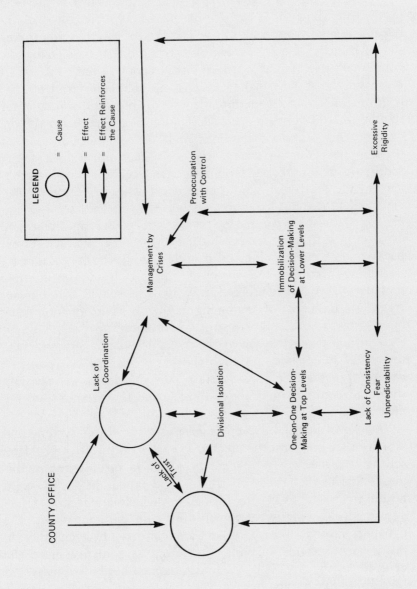

(25,000 students) to be responsive to the demand for change. The system is represented by problems within the central administrative complex, or county office, and its relationships to the field participants (English, 1973). Within the county office the divisions remain isolated from each other. The lack of coordination among the divisions is fed by a lack of trust among them and by the continued crises which permeate the school system. Instead of organizing cross-divisional task forces to solve the problems, the divisions came to the superintendent or the board of education for resolution. This "one-on-one" decision-making style reinforced the lack of trust between divisions and led to immobilization of decision-making at the school level. Principals, not wanting to get caught up in intra-organizational warfare, avoided bringing problems to the county office until they were ready to explode or had exploded. This reinforced the pattern of "one-on-one" decision-making because a committee could not render an immediate decision in such a situation. This led to further crises. The system became more rigid, preoccupied with maintaining its balance by instituting narrower and narrower ranges of responses to field problems. This also reinforced the crisis atmosphere. The bureaucracy was incapable of examining its own behavior or mobilizing its efforts towards any constructive or innovative responses to system-wide problems. Given the dynamics of the system, it was impossible to consider any real innovation. All that was posssible was to perpetuate in "steady state" the existing power relationships and continue to react to the demand for a response to the next crisis.

This set of internal dynamics governs many school systems and inhibits their response to creatively engage in effective problem-solving. We have an *iatrogenic problem.* In medical terms, this means that in the process of treating the patient, he/she is caused by the treatment to become worse. In such situations an "Alpha" assessment is usually extremely difficult or impossible. The dynamics involved feed upon and are reinforced by each other. In many such systems, planning is viewed as a luxury given the demands of the day. It is not uncommon to hear such phrases as "We would like to plan but we don't have time."

Teachers as Part of the Problem

So far the discussion has dealt with problems of schools and the central or "downtown" offices. Bureaucracy may be thought of as the cork in the neck of the bottle of the school system. "If only we could get rid of the bureaucrats on the hill!" is an echo heard in more than one faculty room in some school systems. The response appears to leave teachers and classrooms apart from the malaise. This picture is false from two perspectives.

Classroom Structure Is Bureaucratic

The structure of the school classroom is the basic bureaucratic underpinning of the downtown office. A division of labor encapsulated within four walls and which is essentially cellular in scope and organized within the age grading of school children is bureaucratic. The age grading is mirrored in the structure of the central office and in a variety of roles throughout the school system, including department chairpersons and subject area supervisors.

Lortie's intensive study of the sociology of the classroom teacher supports his thesis that the cellular structure of the schools reinforces the major reward patterns of teaching (Lortie, 1975). Lortie also shows that organizational goals and goals of classroom teachers are not the same. Teachers most definitely feel that basic improvement can come in the schools *within* the status quo. This means, in their terms, *leaving them alone,* i.e., less interference from the administration and parents in the conduct of daily affairs of teaching.

Teachers have exhibited a paralysis in responding to the calls for accountability because they do not know how to respond as a group, i.e., collectively. The isolation of teachers from each other has been a significant barrier to the full professionalization of teaching as an occupation; but it also is a major barrier to improvement of the schools, because any improvement in the organizational effectiveness of the schools must depend upon movement away from the dominant cellular composition of classrooms and the current definition of the role of "teacher." Changes at the central level to promote more responsive and responsible management cannot be isolated from the classroom.

Organic Growth as an Alternative to
Needs Assessment Is a Fallacy

The assumption that merely "freeing" people to "do their thing" will result in a sudden uplift of learning in the schools has its roots in the eighteenth century ideas of Rousseau. There is little pragmatic evidence to support this concept of "organic growth" in practice (Moore, 1972). Even the extreme view advocated by some free-school thinkers that there is no formal curriculum has been disputed as false (English, 1972). Such schools do indeed possess a curriculum, if only in the limited range of experience that the teacher carries in his or her head to the classroom or learning environment. Even the selection of a learning environment outside of the school is a *curricular* decision.

Drucker also notes in his analysis of the responsible worker that what constitutes "the proper structure of work—of any work—is not intuitively obvious" (Drucker, 1973). Analysis must precede the establishment of work and work patterns. The argument is not "structure versus no structure"; rather, it should be what kind of structure to reach what kind of outcomes? In American education we built the structure before the outcomes were clearly defined. We now find that our structure inhibits the kind of outcomes for the schools we had expected. Freeing teachers of any obligation to question the structure in which they work will not release a wellspring of untapped energy. All the evidence points towards a re-establishment of the same old norms as before. The classroom and the bureaucracy are one and the same in almost all of our public school systems.

Exploding the Alternative to Successive Approximation:
The Myth of the One Right Decision

It has been stated that needs assessment and system planning are a process of successive approximation. School administrators pursuing needs assessment will not be troubled by searching for the one "right decision." This is the "one" which will be the best of all possible alternatives to any given problem. What may be forgotten is that there may be several "best" solutions, or that none of the solutions listed as "best" will be responsive. What organizational dynamics account for this? Some of the factors are listed below.

(1) Few Educational Problems Are Unidimensional

Most problems cut across several layers of any school system. Because of the nature of the interconnectedness of the system, a problem cannot be solved by any one division, office, or bureau. Solutions are usually series of responses interwoven and highly interdependent. What is a proper "solution" from one layer may be inappropriate for another. A solution is thus not a response to a stimulus; it is many responses to many stimuli.

(2) Problems Represent "Filtered Reality"

What the school system admits is a problem may correspond to its ability to perceive it and cope with it through its existing division of labor. Problems are screened into the system and follow the division of labor. Problems are thus redefined many times before solutions become apparent. In many cases, problems are merely redefined to "fit" existing solutions or resources in order to become "manageable." This is not functional management, it is the avoidance of managerial responsibility of the first order. Forcing problems to fit into the division of labor as represented in the table of organization overloads some offices and avoids others. One result is overstaffing. The degree to which a problem has been severely reshaped before solutions are considered may be the degree to which none of the solutions considered by the system will actually be adequate. All may be terribly poor. Unfortunately, the frequent solution to any problem in most bureaucracies is to "throw more money and more people at it."

(3) Problem Identification May Threaten
a Change of Internal Power Coalitions

Cyert and March (1963) postulate that organizational goals may be defined by consensus of various coalitions within a system. While consensus may be possible at one level of abstraction (at the goal level), this consensus may disappear when the goals become objectives, that is, more specific. To agree upon objectives, it is necessary for the internal groups within an organization to enter into some form of bargaining over priorities. An organization is therefore a coalition of groups in more or less constant dialogue and communication which vie for position and authority in the decision-making process. Consensual work goals are the result of broad coalitions of agreement within the organization. Frequently, agreement by consensus only happens when the specificity of the problem is generalized and "loosened" in language until all can agree. Usually this amounts to an "ink blot" test mentality, since the statement of the goal or problem is so unclear that *all* can be pleased with it; each sees in it what he or she wishes to see. As Cyert and March indicate, much is made of precedents and policies because this preserves the past level of consensus into the future and avoids fighting previous battles over again. Bureaucracies have long memories.

As a problem is made more specific, it may become apparent that the organization is working at cross purposes, that is, many objectives are incompatible. Also, problem assignment may increase the resources of one group and alter the existing relationships with any given coalition. Problems may be ignored, fought over, kept at a harmless level of abstraction, or split into so many pieces as to become submerged in the system.

For this reason, much more emphasis must be placed on problem definition outside of the existing coalitions before applying the resources of the organization to any range of possible solutions. The only "right" decision may be deciding that there is no "right" decision and spending the energies of the system defining the problem in such a way as to be amenable to a number of approaches which will reduce or eliminate the needs. Then the problem should be assigned the proper resources with an appropriate balance of power, or in a conscious decision to create a new balance without letting the forces within the organization re-shape the problem prior to its definition.

Can Needs Assessment Help Change a Bureaucratic Structure?

Despite the fact that a bureaucratic structure once firmly entrenched is extremely difficult to change, alteration of the structure *is* possible. While bureaucratic systems often respond only to outside mandates from larger bodies and then may subvert those mandates (Jones and Doherty, 1975), change is possible both from an internal and external point of view. Internal change can be approached with strategies of organization development

(OD) (English, 1975). External change may be invoked with requests for outside evaluation involving organizational effectiveness on such criteria as the measurableness of system objectives and whether or not the identification of such tasks lead to permanent or "temporary" staffing arrangements (English, 1974).

Bureaucratic staffing without precise objectives leads to the creation of nebulous "coordinator" type positions, such as the coordinator of human relations, coordinator of personnel, etc. Such offices are sometimes established to promote better relationships between the major linkages or linking pins (Likert, 1961) within the overlapping levels of bureaucratic organization. Unless such jobs have at their core specific and time-conditioned statements as to when the job is done, the system will have created additional permanent appendages. The continuing public complaint about the growth of bureaucracies is justified. The layer upon layer of new middle-management positions in large bureaucracies is an attempt to fill in the "cracks" lacking in the formal table of organization, or to cope with various internal problems created by a rigid layering of authority within the existing divisions. Such roles do not always have happy endings unless they are coupled with several other organizational strategies, such as the institution of structural changes and the movement towards identifying specific work objectives for each role which are measurable. Only then do such interventions or additional jobs appear to have a chance to be effective. The other contention may be equally true, that is, as the tasks of the organization are made discernible and assessable, it may be possible to eliminate much of the overlapping and duplication of labor. For this and other reasons, such efforts will find no shortage of resistance.

There is no one method for the de-bureaucratization of the public schools; however, some approaches are more powerful than others. At the center of the effort will be the continuing battle for the control of the schools, now joined by another force, the teachers unions. There is evidence that the general public is awakening to the fact that control has slipped from their hands and must be restored. The inability of the public to find an effective voice in board of education and union contract disputes while the children are not in school due to strikes has apparently become the mobilizing force. If educators continue to resist efforts to make the current structure of school organization a battle ground for resistance to change, the trend towards alternative schools, financing, and private schools funded at public expenses will expand.

Understanding the internal system dynamics of the educational bureaucracy and how needs assessment can help alleviate bureaucratic problems is the first step towards regaining public confidence in public education (English, 1977). By so doing, educators will redefine the known and the unknown, and form a clearer picture of some of the strictures which have heretofore bound school leaders from solving real problems.

It is from this perspective that the educational manager engages in the essential task of defining the mission of the organization. Depending upon the courage of the manager, the nature of the political system, the state of internal dynamics, and the interchange between all of the interacting parts, the selection of a needs assessment model may range from the most fundamental and "radical," i.e., the "Alpha" (external) assessment, to the more conventional and conservative "Beta" or internal designs. Needs assessment is the basic step towards assisting the educational manager with this critical job. It is a job which is never really accomplished, but one of a series of efforts towards approximating a moving reality (Kaufman and English, 1976).

KEY CONCEPTS

1. A system approach has been growing in use in educational administration for years, much through federal funding requirements.
2. The most essential tasks of management are to: define the purpose or mission of the organization; acquire the resources necessary to achieve the mission plan; and achieve the mission in the most effective and efficient manner.
3. Successful management relies upon the ability, conceptually and in practice, to separate means and ends.
4. School management often fails to realize that the prime

consumers of their goods and services are learners and that the secondary consumers are parents and taxpayers in the community.

5. Frequently, for political reasons, a needs assessment procedure is done in stages. While an Alpha-type needs assessment is primary, it might not be done during the first attempt at introducing and using needs assessment in an operational district.

6. Bureaucracy is often a "shock absorber" for successful management and change, and provides a consistency and resistance which has to be overcome.

7. Alternative structures are possible: schools can change.

8. Effective and efficient are two different terms, not synonyms. Effective refers to the degree to which mission objectives are obtained. Efficient refers to the least costly method to reach the objectives.

9. The ambiguity of the superintendency refers to the lack of clarity of the role within school systems in terms of functions and power compared to the historic role of boards of education.

10. The translation of goals refers to the process of making work more specific, from goals stated on a nominal and ordinal scale to those stated on a ratio or interval scale.

11. The culture of the schools is that unique series of norms and behavior which characterize schools as different than other kinds of work climates or norms.

12. The limitations of the enterprise are those things from the mission statement and assumptions that the organization will not be or not attempt to undertake.

13. The proper structure of work refers to the way in which tasks are arranged, divided, and assigned to be performed. Propriety is determined by factors belonging to the worker and whether the objectives of the work are realized.

14. The division of labor means the way or manner in which tasks are assigned and grouped to offices, bureaus, or persons.

REFERENCES AND BIBLIOGRAPHY

American Association of School Administrators. *The American school superintendency.* Washington, D.C., 1952.

Anderson, J.G. *Bureaucracy in education.* Baltimore: John Hopkins Press, 1968.

Argyris, C. *The applicability of organizational sociology.* Cambridge, Mass.: Harvard University Press, 1972.

Bennis, W.G. *Changing organizations.* New York: McGraw-Hill, 1966.

Bowles, S., and Gintis, H. *Schooling in capitalist America.* New York: Basic Books, 1976.

Callahan, R.E. *Education and the cult of efficiency.* Chicago: University of Chicago Press, 1962.

Clement, J. as quoted in *The orientation and training of school board members.* A Position Paper prepared by the Recruitment and Leadership and Training Institute, United States Office of Education, July 1975, 31-32.

Cohen, M.D., and March, J.G. *Leadership and ambiguity.* New York: McGraw-Hill, 1974.

Commission on the Reorganization of Secondary Education. *The cardinal principles of secondary education.* Washington, D.C.: Bureau of Education, Government Printing Office, 1918.

Cuban, L. *Urban school chiefs under fire.* Chicago: University of Chicago Press, 1976.

Cubberley, E.P. *Public school administration.* New York: Houghton Mifflin, 1929.

Cyert, R.M., and March, J.G. *A behavioral theory of the firm.* Englewood Cliffs, N.J.: Prentice-Hall, 1963.

Dalton, G.W. Influence and organizational change. In A.R. Negandhi (Ed.), *Modern organizational theory.* Kent, Ohio: Kent State University Press, 1973, 314-342.

Drucker, P. *Management.* New York: Harper and Row, 1973.

Drucker, P. Conversation with Peter F. Drucker. *Organizational Dynamics,* Spring 1974, *2*(4), 34-53.

English, F. Can spontaneity serve as a curriculum base? *Educational Technology,* January 1972, *12*(1), 59-60.

English, F. *Position paper on current dilemmas of the administra-*

tion of the Sarasota county schools. The School Board of Sarasota County, Sarasota, Florida, May 31, 1973. 7 pp.

English, F. *A report regarding recommended reorganization of the bureau of curriculum and instruction of the Department of Education of the State of West Virginia,* April 1974. 12 pp.

English, F. *School organization and management.* Worthington, Ohio: Charles A. Jones Publishing Company, 1975.

English, F. Matrix management in education: Breaking down school bureaucracy. *Educational Technology,* January 1977, *17*(1), 19-26.

Feinberg, L. 70 teachers lose jobs in D.C. cutback. *Washington Post,* September 2, 1977.

Filley, A.C., and House, R.J. *Managerial process and organizational behavior.* Glenview, Illinois: Scott Foresman, 1969.

Gall, J. *Systematics: How systems work and especially how they fail.* New York: Oxford University Press, 1975.

Gerth, H.H., and Mills, C.W. *From Max Weber: Essays in sociology.* New York: Oxford University Press, 1946.

Greer, C. *The great school legend.* New York: Basic Books, 1972.

Jones, A., and Doherty, W.F. Garrity asks Fahey to appear in court on personnel changes. *Boston Globe,* August 15, 1975.

Katz, M.B. *Class, bureaucracy, and schools.* New York: Praeger, 1971.

Kaufman, R., and English, F. *Needs assessment: A guide to improving school district management.* Arlington, Va.: American Association of School Administrators, 1976. 63 pp.

Larson, R. *Goal setting in planning: Myths and realities.* Unpublished paper presented to the 31st Annual National Conference of Professors of Educational Administration, Eugene, Oregon, August 1977. 49 pp.

Lewin, K. *Principles of topological psychology.* New York: McGraw-Hill, 1936. From a 1969 reprint from Johnson Reprint Corporation, New York, 14-17.

Likert, R. *New patterns of management.* New York: McGraw-Hill, 1961.

Lortie, D.C. The balance of control and autonomy in elementary school teaching. In A. Etzioni, *The semi-professions and their organization.* New York: The Free Press, 1969.

Lortie, D.C. *Schoolteacher.* Chicago: University of Chicago Press, 1975.

March, J.G., and March, J.C. Almost random careers: The Wisconsin school superintendency, 1940-1972. *Administrative Science Quarterly,* September 1977, *22*(3), 377-409.

McCaskey, M.B. A contingency appoach to planning: Planning with goals and planning without goals. *Academy of Management Journal,* June 1974, *17*(2), 281-291.

McLaughlin, M.W. *Evaluation and reform: The elementary and secondary education act of 1965/Title I.* Cambridge, Mass.: Ballinger Publishing Company, 1975.

Merton, R.K. *Social theory and social structure.* New York: The Free Press, 1968.

Moore, D.R. Strengthening alternative high schools. *Harvard Educational Review,* August 1972, *42*(3), 313-350.

Reller, T.L. The development of the city superintendency of schools in the United States. In American Association of School Administrators, *The American school superintendency.* Washington, D.C.: AASA, 1935, 81-82.

Rogers, D. *110 Livingston Street.* New York: Random House, 1968.

Sarason, S.B. *The culture of the school and the problem of change.* Boston: Allyn and Bacon, 1971.

Tyack, D. *The one best system.* Cambridge, Mass.: Harvard University Press, 1974.

Young, R.C. Goals and goal-setting. *Journal of American Institute of Planning,* March 1966, 76-85. In A.P. Johnson and J.F. McNamara, *Planning perspectives for education.* New York: MSS Information Corporation, 1975, 97-109.

Chapter 7

THE CURRICULUM FOCUS

Curriculum development and its application as a vehicle for school system improvement is one of the most widely discussed but least understood processes in the schools. This is probably because the focus for curriculum development has had multiple sources of origination, little real consensus among school people about its appropriate functions, no precise vocabulary, and has emanated from an imprecise theory base (Schaffarzick and Sykes, 1977).

The schools have not suffered from a lack of "experts" or expert advice in this area. Philosophers have proposed grandiose plans for the curriculum based upon the values and assumptions of social utility (Dewey, 1962; Illich, 1970) or coming from the assumptions regarding study in the classical fields and notions of the "educated person" (Hutchins, 1953; Phenix, 1964). Still others denigrate curriculum study as an activity in which the schools limit human creativity and stifle the "natural impulses" of the organic human being (Kohl, 1969). Some notions of the curriculum are viewed as a straightjacket which is antithetical to effective teaching and pupil spontaneity (Kliebard, 1970). Varied conceptions of curriculum are described by Schiro (1978).

Needs assessment,* properly done, imposes upon the curriculum development process a theoretical and practical base which

*When used without a descriptor (such as "Alpha," "Beta," "internal," "external"), the term "needs assessment" here refers to the Alpha or external variety.

123

has already been explored in some detail in earlier chapters. A defined theoretical base is crucial to understanding variables at work in the real world and to utilizing feedback of results when a process has been applied. Feedback is only meaningful if it can be related to an overall framework provided by a theory and results in improved system success. The development of an adequate theory base begins with the exploration of critical assumptions and limitations as well as explication regarding how a process works or is supposed to work. The development of theory, far from being an esoteric venture, is essential to the practitioner. Little sense can be made of application without it, nor may future change be realistic without a base which serves as a referent for change and evaluation.

Curriculum development in the schools has generally been a disparate development. It has been loosely conceptualized as creating course descriptions for catalogs and lesson plans, writing behavioral objectives, publishing scope and sequence charts, using instructional kits to individualize or personalize instruction, or writing various "modularized" curricular pieces. The latter activity is simply the straining of the curriculum into smaller parts around skills, knowledges, or concepts. These are then arranged like beads by level of difficulty or presentation. While these activities are based upon assumptions and involve a variety of approaches to curriculum development, their wholesale use in schools and school districts has generally served to confuse rather than clarify the role of curriculum in the schools.

Clarification of Terms

Words, words. What they mean to us and what they mean to others is of critical importance. Many "good" words have been reduced to glittering generalities due to imprecise use and the warping of meaning to fit situational expediencies. To make sure of our words and referents, the following definitions are offered: input, process (or means), outputs, and outcomes. A useful relationship between these terms is presented in Figure 7.1.

Inputs. Those factors which are used to develop, support, and maintain education, including: money, time, learners (including their entry skills, knowledges, and attitudes), teachers, admini-

Figure 7.1. A Utility Model for Education.

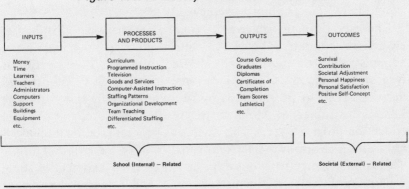

strators, computers, teaching machines, dollars, buildings, equipment, etc.

Processes and Products. The tools, techniques, strategies, and methods which intervene with the learner or staff to change behavior and develop necessary skills, knowledges, and attitudes necessary for success in school and later in society. These include: curriculum, programmed instruction, television, computer-assisted instruction, staffing patterns, organizational development, team teaching, differentiated staffing, etc.

Outputs. The results of the application of inputs and processes in terms of in-school performance, as indicated by course grades, graduates, diplomas, certificates of completion, team scores (athletics), etc.

Outcomes. The ultimate referent for any agency dealing with interventions: the survival and contribution of learners in society. Included here would be indicators such as: survival, contribution, societal adjustment, personal happiness, personal satisfaction, positive self-concept, etc.

The dimensions of "inputs," "processes," and "outputs" are considered to be "internal" or school-based considerations, while "outcomes" are related to "external" considerations. Seen in this manner, the utility of the schools, including their inputs, their methods, and procedures, and their outputs, are meaningfully understood in terms of their impact or "value added" in society. It is to this "external" societally-related referent that education should move and attempt to achieve success.

The establishment of goals is usually the responsibility of the elected or appointed board of education. It is the role of the administration to *translate* the desired outcomes into a series of measurable objectives and allocational decisions. Such allocational decisions tend to be clustered by function, specific task, or in the schools by subject disciplines (the reading program, the physical education program, etc.). The clustering process establishes boundaries and areas of authority and responsibility for administrators. This is an attempt to avoid duplication of labor and realize some economy of scale in the procurement and retention of highly specialized and costly personnel. (Such clustering, however, might be based upon historical precedence rather than upon functional utility.)

The school administration is usually arranged in the form of a hierarchy with the fewest members at the top and the most at the bottom. Intended results statements, often called *goals,* are translated into objectives and then into tasks to be accomplished. The responsibility of coordination becomes larger with bigger school systems.

The process of translating the goals of the board of education at the policy level into specific administrative objectives occupies a vague boundary between the policy-making responsibility of the board and the allocation/managerial responsibilities of the school administration.

While a rigid delineation is probably not possible nor desirable (some latitude permits flexibility of response), administrators sometimes find themselves at a loss to translate vague organizational statements regarding desired outcomes into specific types of managerial decisions. This vagueness results from unclear statements of intended outcomes and thus a poor roadmap for progress. Sometimes board goals represent little more than platitudes of loosely held statements of belief. Larson's (1977) follow-up study of four school districts in Vermont utilizing the Phi Delta Kappa goal ranking kits revealed that the exercise had no impact upon the school program. "No formal linkage was made between PDK level goals and program and instructional level objectives," reported Larson. This might be due, in part, to the fact that such goal ranking kits and so-called needs assessment "packages" are "internal" at best and do not allow for old and inappropriate goals and objectives to be eliminated and new ones added.

Some boards of education find themselves developing administrative objectives regarding means or processes dealing with *outputs* rather than *outcomes.* The mixup causes considerable confusion at the top levels of school systems and leads a board to enter into and become a part of curriculum development or school operation per se. As a result, the board loses a good deal of objectivity about the correctness or adequacy of the system's administrative responses in carrying out policy directives (Raoul-Duval, 1977). The nebulous area of translation has been called *transformational* by Pedersen (1977). It represents the interfaces between the school system and its clients and between the administration and the board of education.

Organizations are a collection of individuals bound together to attain common goals desired by a funding agency. Some analysts of organizations have wondered precisely how people use such goals to carry out their activities. One of the critical assumptions is that the administration must bring the goals of the system's sub-divisions into harmony with the outcomes desired by the policy-making body. It is possible for an administrator to be given goals and to be held accountable for conflicting goals. In this situation, breakdown may occur among the outcomes desired by the policy-making body, the activities of the individual administrator, and the actual results obtained by that administrator. In such circumstances, there has been a breakdown in the transformational areas of the system. Various kinds of remedies have been proposed. They range from increasing an emphasis upon group decision-making as a check on any one individual, to creating more visible decision-making channels, such as instituting management-by-objectives (Odiorne, 1965) or using such techniques as PERT (Program Evaluation Review Technique) (Cook, 1966). We take the position that internal goals and objectives are not usually clearly related to external goals and objectives (outcomes). This incompatibility results in an optimization of school efforts to achieve internal results (outputs) which do not contribute meaningfully to survival and contribution outside or external to schools.

Linkages in the transformational areas are difficult to specify precisely, and most school systems have difficulty in dealing with them. One method to cope with the problem has been the creation of a common language in these areas, which often consists of ratios of inputs to clients or outputs to clients. Input ratios are costs per pupil or other ways of specifying services allocated per pupil. Such ratios have sufficed in the past but are now being criticized by taxpayers as inadequate since they appear to have little relationship to outcomes or valued societal results. A school system may be striving to lower class size as an input variable, but may also have no way of knowing whether or not outputs (such as learning) are affected by that investment (Summers and Wolfe, 1975). Or, put another way, the results of the efforts of schools and their resources may be evaluated to determine if there has been any "value added" to the individual and society as a result of this educational investment. If there are no useful changes as a result of our educational investment of time and resources (including the learner's) there should be some changes in the processes utilized. The ultimate yardstick of value added should be applied in society, not in the schools.

The Curriculum as a Causal Chain

The vehicle which is the *means* to produce what students learn is the curriculum. However, much current curriculum development is merely the reallocation or reassignment of categories within the existing curriculum. This is a paper exercise which usually changes little. The reasons why curriculum in schools is so difficult to change include:

(1) curriculum has been incorrectly perceived as an end or result in and of itself rather than as a means to an end;

(2) curriculum has not been defined well, nor has there been an adequate theoretical base for curriculum development by which it can be empirically tested; and

(3) teachers are trained as quasi-curriculum developers and not as curriculum consumers or curriculum managers.

The Means/Ends Dilemma

To most educators and lay persons the curriculum is a collection of subjects, i.e., science, math, geography, industrial arts, which should be presented to students in some predetermined order. The function of curriculum is to set forth the order and scope of what is to be taught so that learning may be enhanced. Some curriculum writers have said that the curriculum is every- thing that goes on in school, planned or unplanned; it is thus the sum of all experiences in the school.

For our purposes in explaining the application of needs assessment, the definition of curriculum is of a linear expression, a causal chain between the procurement of resources and the elicitation of outputs. The curriculum is a planned series of interventions in which the resources of the school system are configured in such a way that goods and services (processes) are utilized to produce the desired results. If the outputs are useful, they will bring about valued outcomes (Figure 7.1). It has been argued by some curriculum theorists that linear expressions must exclude one or more foci for curriculum development. For example, if the curriculum designer begins with subject matter, learners or other types of social phenomena must be neglected because they must at least follow in a pattern. Therefore, subject matter values would be the dominant set of values (MacDonald, 1971). The needs assessment model developed by Kaufman (1972) avoids this problem by utilizing learners, society, and professionals *simultaneously* in the development of value (goal) statements for the schools. Subject matter would not predominate because "subjects" are means to obtain the values.

A fortuitous circumstance in a school which results in desired learning is not the curriculum any more than an automobile accident is part of a highway. Accidents happen on highways and learning occurs without formal planning. The term which ex- presses the concept is *luck,* or bad luck, as the case may be. The function of a curriculum is to increase the probability that desired learning (outputs) will occur. Otherwise, unsystematic behavior would be acceptable. If unsystematic learning were acceptable by society and the odds were that such behavior could be learned in a variety of places more cheaply than in schools, schools could and probably would be abolished. As Sechrest (1977) has noted, mediocrity is so easily achieved, there is no point in planning for it.

However, schools are the social mechanisms for societal reproduction, and the curriculum is the plan by which the school utilizes its resources to ensure that replication. The curriculum must therefore be capable of being described, configured, changed, and reapplied many times so as to define the optimal pattern of goods and services necessary to obtain the desired results.

Learning outputs are best understood and evaluated for utility external to the curriculum. The desired outcomes should be determined outside of schools and should be integral to the policy-making directives of the school system. Administrative activity is concerned with developing plans and strategies to obtain or realize the policy directives. If the desired outcomes are not obtained, then a different blend of managerial decisions can be developed in order to achieve different outputs. Goods and services can be redesigned and the curriculum modified accordingly. The curriculum is therefore the conscious and planned intervention of organized goods and services to optimize specified learning. The sum total of learning is the output of the school and should lead to improved survival and contribution in society.

The Inadequate Theoretical Base

Curriculum writing has been concerned with matters of scope and sequence, debates about the narrowness or inclusiveness of various subject disciplines, the fusion of subjects, the substitution of process and/or inquiry or inductive modes of learning as outputs per se rather than as "things" to be learned (Parker and Rubin, 1966), and various ways subject matter can be organized and modularized (Walker and Schaffarzick, 1974). One group of curriculum theorists has largely abandoned empirical methods as productive means to improve curriculum (Pinar, 1977).

For classroom teachers, curriculum development frequently consists of writing lesson plans, course descriptions, or following an arrangement of topics in a textbook or course/grade-level curriculum guide prescribed by the school district. Rarely is curriculum in this sense something which is well-defined to the point where it could be replicated and compared to desired outcomes (Blalock, 1969). In fact, outcomes (or even outputs) are not part of traditional curriculum development. The typical kind of curriculum development process moves from a global outcome statement such as, "students will acquire a knowledge of the humanities, social sciences, and natural sciences in order to be able to participate in a complex world" (New York Regents, 1977) to a lesson plan which states, "read pages 61-67 in the text and answer the questions at the end of the chapter. Quiz Friday."

What is usually missing from traditional curriculum development is a whole series of activities in which outputs are separated from outcomes, and both outputs and outcomes are described in sufficient detail so that decisions can be made about any given curricular configuration's utility, validity, and efficiency.

We suggest that needs assessment and its assumptions can supply the theoretical base for curriculum development. If the steps of the needs assessment process are followed, the gap between generalized outcome statements and curriculum building can be a public, verifiable, and valid method for making decisions and selecting any given curriculum configuration or series of configurations with confidence.

At least two assumptions are crucial to needs assessment as applied to curriculum development. The first is that as part of a larger progressive process, means and ends ыл be separated accordingly. A progressive approach is a step-by-step method to define and proceed from means to ends. It begins by defining the ends desired. Then the means are selected to best obtain those identified and selected ends. By a series of approximations involving the definition and utilization of feedback, the process is correctable and is improved with each successive application.

Some educators have grouped curriculum building into two distinct camps, *preactive* and *interactive* (Jackson, 1966). The *preactive* curriculum is prepared prior to instruction. The interactive curriculum *emerges* as the result of group process. Our view is that neither camp is precluded in the application of a needs assessment, so long as curriculum is viewed as a means to achieve *ranges* rather than fixed points of pupil achievement. The mere fact that instruction occurs within classrooms and schools imposes limitations on the parameters of acceptable interaction. These parameters or ranges can be specified prior to instruction, and those which are not productive can be precluded from occurring. Because instruction occurs within a specified societal place and within specified settings, it can never be totally spontaneous. The place for spontaneity is a relative, not an absolute, factor in curriculum planning (English, 1972).

It is recognized that the world is not always amenable to such progressive processes; therefore, such models must represent certain limitations upon a moving reality. Planning is a process for coding and then shaping reality so that people can cope with what would otherwise be overwhelming. Thus, while in one sense logical, progressive models severly restrict the quantity and quality of information capable of being processed by people, they are absolutely necessary to enable people to confront that same reality.

The difference between empirical, progressive-based approaches, such as embodied in a system approach, and other approaches frequently used in education is that the former is quantifiable and verifiable. There is a built-in correction process. There is also a method for information gathering, coding, de-coding, re-coding, and incorporating the knowledge base utilized for decision making. Non-empirical based approaches are considerably less correctable and have a difficult time being challenged by data obtained in an empirical sense. Such non-empirical systems may screen out or homogenize data, which is then difficult to trace or to develop an audit trail; thus, accountability and "fixability" are removed. Empirical procedures provide both an idea of error and some degree of the relative magnitude of error. They provide directions for correction.

All human conceptual systems represent a series of assumptions, decisions, and impositions upon a vast reality. We believe, first, that those systems which can be challenged and tested in a rigorous fashion are much preferable to those which resist such methods or cannot be defined sufficiently to be put to the test. A theory base identifies the assumptions, decisions, and impositions used. It is only from such a theory base that empirical testing can be performed. The process is rarely absolute, most always relative.

To date, curriculum development has lacked such a definitive base, and rigorous examination of the results have not always been possible (Steeves and English, 1978).

The second assumption crucial to needs assessment involves learning. How human beings learn is still somewhat unclear. The factors of intelligence and human ability reveal a broad spectrum (Meeker, 1969), but some success may be obtained by deliberate and appropriate design (Popham, 1971). Needs assessment is based upon the assumption that the probability of learning any given skill, knowledge, or attitude is so wide as to make a study of *process* per se not a definable place to begin a curriculum development (Schwab, 1964).

Needs assessment, especially the external mode, is more concerned about identifying the "what" to be learned (including more processes) and assumes that if adequate pupil diagnosis occurs and if presented properly by the teacher, appropriate, useful, worthwhile learning can and will occur.

It is logical for a physician to assume that if a patient is treated properly, the human body will heal itself. Based upon proper professional diagnosis, learning has to be assumed in the same way that healing has to be assumed. Both processes are generic to life and both are virtually infinitely complex.

Teacher Training

During their pre-service training, teachers are taught to develop lesson plans and write course descriptions. Sometimes they are given formal coursework in writing a curriculum unit. However, traditional curriculum development has not trained the teacher to be a consumer of packaged curricula, with the exception of some rudimentary instruction in selecting a textbook. Today's variety of curricula move far beyond applying the lessons of a textbook. Few teachers know how to adopt, adapt, or change such materials in systematic ways for further empirical investigation or follow-up.

No curriculum is teacher-proof that depends upon teacher/pupil interaction. As long as schools depend upon teachers to implement the curriculum, the essence and quality of that interaction will be a major variable in the translation of a curriculum into an applied good or service to a client or group of clients.

Very few teacher preparatory institutions provide instruction to prospective teachers in the comparison and selection of curricula. Such institutions would provide criteria for possible selection, an evaluation model to utilize in setting up a limited classroom empirical study, and ways to analyze the data produced from a study. To provide teachers in training with the skills to adapt a highly sophisticated curriculum poses still another problem.

The major reasons why curriculum is still "developed" in the traditional sense that we have earlier described appear to be these:

(1) The Pre-eminence of Localism. Many teachers apparently believe that only locally produced curricula are most appropriate for their work situation (Dreeben, 1973). A curriculum writer or subject area expert at some university or think-tank just could not know or fully understand the local situation. Teachers as a group tend to be "here and now" people (Lortie, 1975). They desire immediate kinds of day-to-day gratification. The adoption of a curriculum developed externally to their work situation contradicts their notion of immediacy. Many teachers believe that their work situations cannot really be understood without having full and first-hand knowledge of their classroom work and what they think and feel should be going on. Teachers appear to believe that their work is so idiosyncratic that few sets of generalized principles developed externally could possibly include all of the important facets in their classrooms.

Most supervisors of teachers know that this is simply not true. The reason this appears to be the case may be merely a matter of perspective. Most teachers work in physical isolation from each other. They do not normally observe other teachers working and are unable to effectively discriminate between those aspects peculiar to their own style and those unique to their colleagues. Many supervisors can and do group teaching styles, approaches, and methods into various kinds of categories. Some teachers simply refuse to believe that any categorical system can adequately include them. However, few fail to categorize children in a variety of ways. That this represents a contradiction does not apparently occur to many of them.

(2) Professional and Teacher Union Power. Pre-packaged curricula which require only adaptation pose a perceived threat to the

prerogatives of both the teacher and the teachers union. A locally defined and controlled curriculum, safeguarded by union contractual clauses, assures teachers of the ability to nullify or modify threatening changes. Curricular changes which also influence job security and other working conditions will be stoutly resisted.

Many teachers unions are now making sustained drives to capture control of the decision-making process about curriculum adoption and development in the schools (Braun, 1972). Teacher curriculum advisory committees, through which any proposed innovation or change must successfully pass, are becoming more and more commonplace in union demands. This is an unfortunate development. Teachers unions/associations exist first and foremost to serve the interests of their members. Unions are not client centered, but member or mutual benefit associations (Blau and Scott, 1962).

A curriculum design which required fused subject disciplines and resulted in fewer department chairpersons or supporting teachers would be opposed by unions in hard times. Coupled with the impact of staff layoffs due to enrollment decline, the prospects for getting a fused curriculum through a union-dominated curriculum committee would be remote regardless of the soundness of the rationale. The interests of unions and those of the school system are not always parallel, and what is good for teachers is not always good for students (Vecsey, 1977). Perhaps future years will bring learner lobbies or learner unions which will insist upon outputs which will improve societal survival and contribution.

The issue of control and curricular origination are important ones in adopting a predesigned, non-locally developed curriculum. Newer curricula also tend to be more specific about the responsibilities of the teacher for diagnosis, testing, and teaching the identified content. The accountability factor is considerably increased in many of these nationally developed packages. Some teachers may find this very uncomfortable, especially when the old curriculum allowed for much more variation in approach and content and the results were more broadly defined. With broad parameters, the types of acceptable student responses were much wider and looser. The individual classroom teacher has considerably less responsibility in formulating precise teacher strategies that "deliver" the intended range of outcomes. If, however, the parameters are specifically defined along with the types of requisite outputs and outcomes, the teacher must be far more careful in determining the proper intervention and use of materials to reach the desired results.

The Curriculum

The curriculum of a school system is the sum total of the planned utilization of goods and services necessary to most effectively and efficiently produce or approximate a desired set of learner outputs.

The curriculum includes a design, which is itself a series of decisions about the production of goods and services and their timely application within defined school or school-related settings. The curriculum has boundaries and limitations. The boundaries are represented by a political consensus about what is desired to be learned in the schools, by ways in which global *curriculumless goals* are translated into specific content areas, by specific types of school schedules and organizational patterns, and by the level of financial support accorded to it by a funding agency (Kirst and Walker, 1971). Curricula-related decisions are therefore made by a variety of officials in a number of capacities and at varying levels of abstraction.

The curriculum is primarily a globally-related array of linear sequential expressions and concomitant decision-making points. Linearity may be represented by a stair step analogy or by a spider web construct (Kohl, 1969). The former symbol is that of the traditional curriculum, i.e., to set forth in some logical sequence the content to be taught. Such content allocation may have nothing to do with learning, as studies of scope and sequence optimization have often proven. The designation of content is necessary for the curriculum to be an effective causal chain between inputs, outputs, and outcomes (Figure 7.2). Management is impossible without some designation of sequence, and sound resource allocational decisions are dependent upon a determination of sequence. Without such roadmaps it is impossible to backtrack with performance data into the curriculum and give intelligent directions to teachers about what to change if the results are not effective. The notion of feedback is dependent upon knowing what to do with information to improve pupil learning and performance. Scope and sequence decisions, when clearly marked, provide the school system with the ability to pinpoint sub-system ineffectiveness and to use feedback in a positive sense to change.

A spider web analogy to the curriculum refers to the way the curriculum may be organized by themes or strands. Learners may begin anywhere but by the time they have traversed the curriculum, the important and unifying strands, concepts, attitudes, or skills have been learned. This too can be the subject of linear expression but in a different format. Sequence in a curriculum identifies the paths or trails which should be followed. If such a sequence represents a series of proven "optimal" ways, the desired outputs may be acquired by students. The function of a curriculum is to improve upon the unplanned chance that a desired set of outputs will indeed be acquired. The purpose of a curriculum is to raise the probability that a set of designated outcomes will be learned. If the results are valued and useful, the results are even more appropriate.

Making Curriculum Useful

It is our hypothesis that curriculum has not been an adequate delivery vehicle in the schools because the transformational areas between inputs and the application of outputs have not been defined so as to know who was precisely responsible, nor has the translation of goals been adequately accomplished to provide the criteria for the selection of curriculum. This is the advantage of utilizing needs assessment as a strategy to build useful, successful curriculum. Needs assessment provides a mechanism for developing, defining, and validating curriculumless goals and the "bridge" by which curriculum is subsequently selected, shaped, implemented, evaluated, and improved.

Needs assessment is therefore "soft technology" in that it represents a traceable method for bridging the transformational areas. After employing the needs assessment procedures, it should be possible to audit the types and kinds of decisions made, to understand the situational variables present and the choices selected or not selected, and to revamp the process and criteria if the outcomes did not materialize. This presents a considerable advantage to current models where outcomes are vague and organizations move quickly to output statements as substitutes for outcome realization. For example, in spelling out the Regents Program Priorities in New York, the outcome goal of "ability to maintain one's mental, physical, and emotional health," is cited. Then the Regents cite increases in drug and tobacco use as well as increases in teenage pregnancies and adolescent suicides. They then propose that the health program develop "more mature approaches to major personal health decisions" (New York Regents, 1977).

The first difficulty is that the "ability to maintain one's mental, physical, and emotional health," has not been sufficiently defined to know when it is being maintained in terms of observable student behaviors. Vague references to teenage pregnancies or suicide rates do not establish a linkage between goods and services (outputs) and outcomes desired. How school curriculum should be changed to "deliver" unknown or unspecified outcomes is equally perplexing. The outcomes are so vague that almost any combination of goods and services could be called "adequate" or "inadequate" if being evaluated by those antagonistic to the system, and it will never be known if the goods and services applied really attained the desired outcomes. A funding agency would have enormous difficulty knowing if hiring more health teachers, instituting a new course on teenage problems, or altering existing sex education courses is the most appropriate solution. How many more health teachers to do what? What happens if the teachers are hired and the teenage pregnancy rate still increases? What if the rate is reduced? Could some other solution be more effective or less costly than the one selected? Unfortunately, the usual bureaucratic solution to most contemporary problems consists of throwing more money or more people at it. No wonder our efforts are characterized more by failure, or no change, than by success.

Needs assessment is a method which allows the decision-maker to set forth the major assumptions regarding curriculum to become the bridge between *inputs,* associated *outputs,* and eventually valued *products* and valuable *outcomes.* We believe that curriculum development has occurred in isolation from outcomes because of the lack of such a "soft" technology.

While needs assessment is a "soft technology," it is dependent upon a value system within which to translate generic goals into operational or performance objectives. It is the goals at the policy level that provide the framework for enhancing the value system supporting those goals. Needs assessment is not merely an analytical tool which can provide management with data for decisions, or curriculum developers with feedback to reconfigure goods and services. It is the application of a technology *within* a desired set of goals or values. The value laden goals represent assumptions about the good life, the purpose of living, ideas about the individual, the function of government, the role of the state, and the ability of a culture to provide a basic set of freedoms for its people.

Some typical goals might be as follows:
- Upon graduation from high school, the student will:
- *Goal 1:* Possess competence in the process of developing values which are life sustaining in the spiritual, ethical, religious domains and which preserve individual dignity and a humane culture (New York Regents, 1977).
- *Goal 2:* Understand the processes of effective citizenship in order to participate in and contribute to the government of our society, or "to gain the knowledge and acquire the attitudes . . . for active participation in Canadian society" (Ministry of Education, Canada, 1975).

In goal one, the outcome desired at the global level is for a student to have acquired the ability to form a set of values which are life sustaining in the domains/areas specified. These values must in turn preserve individual dignity and perpetuate a culture which advances those same values.

A culture which did not espouse individual dignity or place value upon an individual's developing the ability to deal with spiritual, ethical, and religious problems would not select this as an outcome for clients of the educational system. Such a culture may espouse amoral, non-religious, or non-spiritual values and place heavier emphasis upon adherence to official dogma, group norms, or the political apparatus. Here the individual would be important, but as a tool to enhance the identified dogma or existing party line. Individual dignity may only be important in the light of being an exemplar of official state concepts which define individualism as sacrificing for the good of the state or the group.

These are gross differences. Actual differences may be far more subtle. The translation process from goals to objectives also illuminates what is really meant by outcomes. In a totalitarian nation, "effective citizenship" may be not questioning the party line, voting for approved party officials, non-resistance to government policy, not joining unions or reading the wrong books. It is when global, policy-type outcome statements are translated that the actual and operational differences become more clearly manifest.

Dealing with Value Questions

Needs assessments present the curriculum developer with consensual tools to deal with value questions. Questions of value represent political and philosophical areas which are part of the function of the board of education to resolve. The usual philosophy of education, which consumes vast amounts of board and staff time, makes little actual difference upon internal, operational affairs and curriculum development because the translation into practice, or from outcome to output, is lacking. Just how an administrator makes managerial decisions about outcomes desired depends upon the level of specificity of the outcome statements. Very broad goals demand little more than the maintenance of the status quo. More specific goals or objectives considerably reduce the tolerance of the system for "anything goes" and demand a more selective and careful analysis of how resources (inputs) are arranged to provide goods and services (products).

At the policy level, a board of education must decide what to stress of all the outcomes that the schools could embrace. The assumptions underlying the search and selection of outcomes can be translated into output statements, embedded in the curriculum, and acquired by learners. There is nothing antithetical about individualization and this approach. With the development of a standard, individualization is a requirement because all learners simply cannot acquire any skill, knowledge, or attitude without the professional staff's taking into account the fact that learners are different in ability, motivation, background, and learning style.

The utilization of standards correctly applied should lead to greater emphasis upon diagnosis and a variety of teaching approaches in the schools. It is only the vague and undefined standards that allow rigidity because rigidity can pass without precise specification of the outcome desired. The usual objection to precise performance objectives is that they will lead to unnecessary rigidity and uniformity and therefore are contrary to an emphasis upon the individual child (Combs, 1972). This may occur on two counts: first, if the global goals do not stress individualism and individual competence in valuing, and uniformity is really desired as an outcome; second, if global goals are not translated into more specific learner objectives.

Psychology and research provide ample evidence regarding differences among and between learners in the schools. A system with only vague philosophical reference to individual dignity will often sacrifice that philosophy on the alter of pragmatism by resorting to processing students in batches, exposing them to uniform textbook lessons, and grading them "on the curve." Technology did not produce that system (which is certainly a description of many school systems), nor did precise objectives which required individualization as an implementing strategy, but the very opposite conditions. If instructional individualization is desired, it must be specified, translated into operational objectives and standards, and traced into the curriculum to be sure it is happening. The curriculum must be shaped to produce the outcomes desired. This will not occur unless the outcomes desired are specific and the curriculum can be tested as an appropriate delivery vehicle.

There are also those who disagree that any group of learners should be held to anything in common in the schools. Common learnings are viewed first as impossible, given the literature on human growth and development they say; secondly, they are undemocratic. If this were the case, there would be no reason to have schools except as institutions of containment to hold children until the proper releasing age for entry to the labor market. That schools are now places of containment has been the subject of passionate attacks from the romantic critics of education (Holt, 1964; Postman and Weingartner, 1969).

Common learnings have been the cornerstone of schooling in this country since 1647 with the passage of the Deluder-Satan Act, which viewed children's ability to read as essential so as to learn from the Bible the ways to avoid a life of sin (Duggan, 1948). Schools are rarely neutral places where any value is taught. Schools are socially selective instruments in which a given range of values is crystallized and passed onto each succeeding generation. That schools indeed possessed less than egalitarian values in a pluralistic society has been well documented by the manner in which immigrants to the United States were viewed by school people (Tyack, 1974).

There can be no valueless or "value free" school. Even a decision to present no values is a value decision itself (Greenwald, 1973). We argue that the lack of specified and operational sets of values allows schools to be accused by our society of having failed. The public's concern about the lack of discipline in the schools and the clamor for a return to the "basics" are evidence that the public does believe that the schools should be accomplishing something (Fiske, 1977).

It is only with a common set of values that a democracy can survive because the value of a democracy must be taught in order for all to participate in it. Appropriate and sensible common learnings are therefore not undemocratic. A democracy or democratic society places heavy emphasis upon the individual and individual responsibility. The selection of occupations, marriage partners, children, and life styles are individual choices within the existing cultural fabric. A common value supports that society. To make choices, individuals must support a society that enables them to make choices. To possess the ability to make choices, a democratic society denies the choice of not allowing others to make choices, that is, the selection of a form of government which would deny choice as an option. There can be no choice about a democracy per se, but democracy is simply one set of assumptions about life and the role of the individual in human affairs and the state. Totalitarianism represents another set of assumptions. Some of the same options may exist to people in both types of cultures, but there are differences as each way of life imposes a set of assumptions and decisions upon reality.

Needs assessment is a conceptual tool that is dependent upon (and includes) a value system to provide it with meaning. For instance, the Alpha mode values individual survival and contribution and puts them as the central focus of planning. In fact, one must value learner success, human worth and dignity, effectiveness, and reduced waste in order to decide to use any needs assessment in education or training. If the tool enhances the ability of the school system to perpetuate the way of life of a given culture more effectively, then the schools are made more effective social maintenance instruments. Needs assessment provides the board of education and administration with a way to become more effective. We believe that the schools can more effectively teach democratic values if they employ more precise managerial tools. The meaning of a technology must be measured not only by costs, but also by results. Results always involve questions of values, meaning, and choice. A decision to select an internal mode of needs assessment is a value decision—one has chosen to assume the external utility of the current system and is interested in optimizing whatever currently exists.

The Procedures for Applying Needs Assessment to Curriculum Development

Step 1: Selecting Educational Outcomes

The first step at the policy-making level is to define or select the kinds of educational goals desired by the school system. Usually these are statements about what the policy-making body believes should be the results of the educational system upon the application of a given level of goods and services. The policy-making body should be concerned with behavioral change or the growth of its clients.

A common mistake at this step is for policy-making bodies to bypass educational goals or outcomes and deal with *outputs*, or even processes and products. Boards may frame goals in terms of tests to be administered, curricula to be developed, programs to be implemented, or procedures to be considered, such as:

(1) each child should have access to the services of a full-time counselor;

(2) within two years each student will pass a minimum competency test in composition and survival math;

(3) to work with the Division of Criminal Justice in reducing youthful criminal activity;

(4) to expand and improve multicultural curricula; and

(5) to develop a program to better acquaint the young with occupational choices at an earlier age (New York Regents, 1977).

All of these are process or product objectives. Such objectives are properly the province of the administration, not the board of education, the policy-making body for the school system.

Programs, testing, and curriculum development are all means to ends. They represent goods and services. Boards which confuse policy statements with administrative objectives are fairly common. Cross activity in transformational areas serves to blur which group is accountable for the failure to achieve either output or outcome objectives. Both the board and the administration can deny being responsible, since neither can claim sole jurisdiction. Statements of policy are *curriculumless* or "out of discipline" (English and Kaufman, 1975).

Few boards of education have developed the sophistication to articulate and define a clear set of outputs or outcome statements in terms of desired learner objectives. Either the job falls upon the administration as part of implementing vague policy goals, or it is simply not undertaken.

The procedures for policy development or output statements begin with the board indicating what the results should be after a student spends a given number of years in the school system, or at some exit point, what skills, knowledges, and attitudes (i.e., behaviors) he or she should reasonably have been expected to acquire. The board does not have to develop them from scratch, since most state education departments have published recommended lists of goals. The board should be interested in obtaining the broadest scope of goals possible with the least duplication or overlap among the goals themselves. Then the board must determine the relative degree of importance or priority of the goals. It can do this as a governing body alone, or it can use some consensual method. We strongly recommend the consensual approach for reasons which are explored in greater detail in a later chapter.

The first step in a functional needs assessment is to obtain commitment to the purposes of allowing learners, upon legal exit, to survive and hopefully contribute in the external world (Kaufman, 1972). Upon commitment to this overall outcome (and thus an Alpha, or external mode), en-route subsidiary goals and objectives may be derived, either from a set of possible outcomes or from the partnership of learners, community, and educators. These may be deductive, inductive, and/or classical. The classical mode will not be considered, for it is merely a perpetuation of the status quo. The deductive starts with given goals and objectives and derives subsidiary outcome statements from these "givens." The inductive requires that goals and objectives be obtained "from scratch" from the partnership of learners, educators, and society and thus serves as the basis for further educational activity and curriculum determination. Given that the overall mission objective of education is the survival and contribution of the learners when they legally enter society from the schools (a value judgment), then inductive or deductive progression from that point can use the survival and contribution of the learners in society as a "template" or pattern for deleting, adding, or augmenting goals and objectives (Kaufman, 1972).

Step 2: Establishing Outcome Priorities

Many boards, teachers, students, and/or administrators find trouble in determining outcome priorities for school systems. "Aren't they all important?" they say. The answer is affirmative. While most outcome statements are important, that is, they represent worthy endeavors for the design and development of goods and services, they are not equally important. Indeed, there is now in all school systems a priority in terms of what is allocated fiscally for goods and services to various system activities. Some activities appear to be more important because they demand and receive a higher level of support than others. Whether that level of support has been rationally selected in light of emerging requirements is another question. Boards find themselves confronted with such priority questions all the time. Questions as to whether a full program of athletics should be continued in view of the increasing demand to differentiate instruction in special education and to mainstream students is but one example. When resources are not keeping pace with expansion of demands for goods and services, the determination of priorities becomes even more crucial.

If a school system had all the money it required, it would not have to establish priorities for the delivery of goods and services. If this requirement were somehow met, however, a second limitation would always be present: time. If human beings lived forever and they were always in school, then no decisions would have to be made about what should be learned or taught in schools. All that was knowable could be learned. However, both human life and schooling are finite. Schools therefore have a limited time period in which to prepare clients to live and work in the real world. The mere fact that time limitations exist and that there is more to learn than can be learned requires choice. If students cannot learn all that there is to learn while they are in school, what *must* they learn? The imposition of such limitations requires organization and planning for the most expeditious delivery of critical goods and services.

Boards of education may find the prospect of declaring priorities uncomfortable. At stake may be the perpetuation of a society which contains fundamental inequities. Schools make determinations about clients and they sort their clients in a variety of ways. That the sorting process often has been racist and sexist has been fairly well established (Bowles and Gintis, 1976). While these maladies appear to be on the way towards some remediation, there are more manifest problems in the maintenance of schools in a society in which the fruits of the society as a whole are distributed unequally among the population. Some boards would rather leave these issues unbroached, since a public discussion might have damaging impact upon the school system or result in a change in board membership.

Another reason boards may be unwilling to spend time translating their policy goals into ranked priority objectives is that they do not envision the goals as being relative to one another. Instead, they are conceived as absolute. It is very difficult to rank absolute values. Imagine trying to rank the Ten Commandments as a comparable exercise! One way that some superintendents have countered this problem is to reinforce the concept that such priorities are already relative. This can be done by a simple summation of the current expenditures of the existing school budget by curricular discipline or subject/skill area. A sample listing is shown below for a hypothetical school district of 4500 pupils.

Hypothetical List of Expenditures by Curricular Area

Program	Budgeted Amount	Pupils Served	Cost Per Pupil
1. Music, K-12	$259,000	381	$679.79
2. Reading, K-8	$163,000	1291	$126.26
3. Athletics, 9-12	$ 81,000	453	$178.81
4. Guidance, K-12	$130,000	4500	$ 28.29
5. Science, K-12	$ 73,500	4500	$ 16.33

Boards have been shocked at what they are really spending on various curricular areas when shown the actual figures. Did the hypothetical board make a conscious decision to evaluate music to the highest level of expenditure? Was the role of the athletic program more important per pupil than the science program? Ratios such as dollars spent per pupil by designated category can also be misleading. While athletics may not be as important as science, the costs of an athletic program may be higher despite a board decision that science was more important. An indicator of what a society values may be seen in where they allocate their resources—people *do* put dollars where their values lie!

Nonetheless, such summaries can be useful methods for pointing out to boards of education that program priorities are not presently equal in importance. Often what may be at work are "hidden priorities" which are painful subjects to discuss in public.

If a winning football team does cost more than an entire curricular area, does the board really want to consider the implications in the face of a large and well organized parents' football booster club? In one school district, it was revealed that the cost of maintaining several computers in the math department was about equal to the cost of suiting up one football player; yet, the computers were eliminated from the math program while no cuts were made in the football program. The board considered the computers a "frill."

The establishment of priorities is essential in order to provide policy directives to the school administration. The administration must make endless choices in order to transform the board's directions into program decisions. The quality, direction, and weight of various administrative decisions will be (or should be) in proportion to the perceived and stated importance and priority of the educational goals. On an operational level, all decisions are not equally difficult or complex. Areas where more people are involved in specialized work requiring extensive preparation are more difficult to manage simply because specialization and complexity carry with them an increased propensity for interpersonal and intergroup conflict.

As policy-making bodies, boards of education are also faced with their own peculiar problems. Turnover of board members means that rapid policy shifts can occur, and this introduces an element of uncertainty in developing programs and curricula to carry out stated board priorities. Administrators who suspect that any given board of education does not represent the will of the majority may be reluctant to devote extensive time and energies on developing procedures and curricula which may be overturned or changed in the immediate future (English, 1976).

To combat problems of representation on a political and policy level and to provide for greater stability of directions to the administration, boards have turned to a broader involvement in ranking educational goals. There are a variety of techniques and approaches for securing consensual judgments about educational goal priorities. These will be covered in more detail later. At the conclusion of the goal-ranking step, the board will have defined a list of broad educational goals that are inclusive but non-overlapping. They should follow the principle of parsimony, that is, explain as much as possible in the most concise manner possible.

One criterion set which has been found useful in actually ranking a number of alternative possible objectives is to ask representative partner members to rank order each of the possible outcomes by asking two simultaneous questions (Kaufman, 1972):

- What does it "cost" to meet the need?
- What does it "cost" to ignore the need?

Cost, in this case, is used in the usual economic sense of opportunity lost. For example, what did it "cost" the people of the country not to adhere to the constitutional tenets of desegregation right after the Civil War? What did it cost to delay having each child be able to get and keep a job when he or she exits our schools when measured against human failure, wrecked self-concept, and welfare and unemployment monies required to support our "failures?" What does it mean when we fail to prepare learners for the external world when we measure this failure by costs of prison, law enforcement, social welfare, and social reform which might not be necessary or as demanding if the schools were funded to perform, and actually accomplished, worthwhile and functional learning outcomes.

While these kinds of decisions are not easy to make, they are critical in order to keep in perspective the fact that our schools represent optional ways in which we may spend the dollars of our taxpayers, the time of our learners and educators, and determine the future of our society. Schools must become more than the parking lots for our failures and the waiting lines for our unemployment offices. These are tough decisions and tough alternatives. What it costs to meet needs and what it costs to ignore needs will serve as priority-determination bases for turning identified needs into useful and successful curriculum.

Step 3: Translating Educational Goals into Objectives

This step is most often left undone by policy-making bodies. It is the translation of broad learner goals into specific performance objectives. The policy-making performance objective is not the same as the classroom performance objective because, although they adhere to the same format, the function of each is different. The purpose of a policy-making performance objective is to serve as a system-wide index for determining whether the school district or school unit is effective in establishing clear, causal linkages from curriculum design and development (process) to learning and performance (outputs). The difference between a goal (or aim or purpose) and an objective is one of degree. A goal is measurable on a nominal or ordinal scale of measurement and an objective on an interval or ratio scale (Kaufman, 1972).

The function of a classroom performance objective is to establish learner outputs within a program or curriculum which are intermediate indices of pupil growth. An eighth grade English teacher may have a set of pupil objectives for the class which represent skills, knowledges, and attitudes to be learned. However, eighth grade English is only a piece of the total K-12 English program for which twelfth grade exit objectives have been established by the board of education as part of its policy-making function. There may be some overlap if the eighth grade performance objectives are in fact the desired level of minimum proficiency for graduation four years later.

The process of writing a performance or behavioral objective is the same at both the policy-making level and the operational or classroom level; that is, the elements which qualify it as a performance objective are the same. A performance objective sets forth the specific *behavior* which is to be observed as evidence of learning, the *criteria* for desired proficiency or degree of competency, and the *situation* in which the behavior is to be exhibited by the student. Inasmuch as there are countless manifestations of possible performance objectives in moving from a global policy level to the specific operational level, boards may be advised to clarify their intentions in specific terms.

It is not necessary that a board of education actually write each and every performance objective, as it was not required that it write the more global goals. The board may assign such duties to the administration, groups of teachers and/or citizens, consultants, or some combination of working task forces or committees. At the end of the developmental process, however, the board must choose which performance objectives are the ones that most nearly represent or approximate the global goals earlier adopted.

This is an admittedly cumbersome and somewhat onerous chore. Board interest in the project may waiver at this step, particularly if the school system is being nagged by a variety of problems requiring attention at the process level, i.e., goods and services. This may also be a state where some additional consensual input may be required or advisable. The translation process adopted in many places has included a middle step between global goals and performance objectives. We have called this step the development of "performance indicators." Performance indicators are merely "half-way" performance objectives, since they indicate a total possible array of appropriate performances. They have been called "prototype objectives" for this reason. Such indicators are merely benchmarks or "exemplars" of what is described at a more abstract, goal level.

Example of Performance Indicators

Global Policy Learner Goal: At the end of the twelfth grade, the student will be able to comprehend and comply with essential societal materials in order to secure and retain gainful employment.

Goal Indicator 1: The student will be able to read and comply with essential job-related materials, such as want ads in the newspaper, determination of qualifications which pertain to his or her application, application forms or letters of interest or of reference.

Goal Indicator 2: The student will understand the basic principles of engaging in a successful job-related interview.

Goal Indicator 3: The student will be able to read and complete job-related materials, such as a W-2 form, health insurance applications, union pension fund forms, salary schedules, and union/firm contractual provisions relating to job advancement.

Goal indicators are not performance objectives. The indicators shown in the example fail to define in performance terms *how* the student will demonstrate compliance with a want ad, or what *standard* will be made to judge if a letter of interest or reference has been adequately developed. However, the examples do indicate what is meant at the global policy goal level by "essential societal materials."

To further define the first goal indicator into performance objectives, one might state:

- When provided with several sample want ads from *The New York Times,* the student will be able to list all those past training experiences which apply and areas in which he or she may be deficient, as certified correct by his or her guidance counselor.

- When given a standard, written application form in class, the student will be able to answer all questions legibly, using proper grammar, spelling, and punctuation as judged correct by the English teacher.
- When provided with a description from a written job analysis in a semester or final exam, together with related job requirements, the student will be able to compose a letter of application which follows correct form, with no spelling, grammatical, or punctuation errors and which indicates his or her interest in the position and in which the following is cited: past and related job experiences, application rationale, names of character references (at least two), and return address and telephone number. Accuracy and form to be judged by a personnel officer of a company to which the letter is addressed.
- At least 90% of the students who successfully complete the course will be offered a job when applying for a job for which they are trained and certified.

As the performance objectives come to be defined, the length of the definition of outcomes and the specificity, usually from ordinal to interval scale terms, will markedly increase. While the global goals may occupy one to two pages, and performance indicators perhaps eight to ten pages, a completed list of performance objectives may be fifty to one hundred pages in length.

Few citizens have the patience to be involved either in ranking or critiquing documents of this magnitude. This is nonetheless one of the most important and strategic works of the board of education. The detailed list of outcome statements in priority order comprise the policy directives to the school administration to implement programs which are combinations of goods and services to obtain the desired results. Furthermore, the board has a method and criteria for determining if the administrative decisions made have any impact upon learner growth, the ultimate criterion of system effectiveness.

Before leaving this step, we should mention an important word about citizen involvement in general. While citizens have been more active and militant in recent years about being involved in decisions regarding the schools, many find it enormously difficult to separate means and ends. Citizens deal easily with teacher salaries, class size indicators, costs per pupil, and other traditional ratios. They can separate various curricular sub-programs and determine their importance (Herschkowitz and Shami, 1976). There is evidence that citizens do not see the relationship between inputs, processes, outputs, and outcomes as having much to do with schools. Instead, citizens envision what should go on in schools as the key to whether or not they are "effective" (Greenfield, 1973). Schools are judged ineffective if they are run poorly (Florida Department of Education, 1970) or if there is a lack of discipline (Phi Delta Kappa, 1969-73). With the increased publication of state achievement tests, there is an emerging notion that schools may look good but may not be teaching students to read or to compute properly. Publication of the National Assessment of Educational Progress data is creating more public awareness of this problem (Maeroff, 1976).

Boards of education are sometimes dismayed when they are first criticized for the lack of community involvement in decision-making, but then equally lambasted for trying to involve citizens at the policy-making levels. Mann (1974) has noted that most citizen interest in the schools is idiosyncratic and personal rather than abstract. Citizens will react to costs and taxes, student appearance or behavior, losing football teams, class size, unpopular teachers or administrators, or perceived deviant courses or library books.

A board's problem is that while it is supposed to act at the policy-making level, the board's constituency does not so act. When the board involves its constituency at the appropriate level, it is criticized for carrying on a meaningless exercise when that same constituency wants to cut out frills, fire an administrator or perceived incompetent teacher, or remove something offensive from a class reading list. As Mann notes, citizen insistence on highly personal complaints tends to rob them of any real impact at the policy-making levels (Mann, 1974).

Boards are presented with a dilemma in this respect. Nonetheless, both moral and legal responsibilities for the school system should be served. Total school system improvement cannot occur if boards do not insist upon clear bridges across the transformational areas in which outcome and derivative output objectives provide the basis for effective and efficient management of the school district, and a vehicle for evaluating and improving the curriculum.

Step 4: Mapping the Existing School System Curriculum

In most school systems, curriculum guides are plentiful. However, unless such materials have been the subject of intensive and careful preparation, they rarely indicate anything more than a superficial analysis of what is really being taught. Few such guides contain specific learner outputs required at the conclusion of a period of instruction.

One of the difficulties in using information provided by a needs assessment in the curriculum area is that descriptions of existing curricula tend to be excessively vague. In order to know what is really going on in the school system from written references, the following questions should be answerable from existing curricular descriptions:

1. What precisely is being taught/learned (skills, knowledges, attitudes) at each demarcation (grade level) of the school system?
2. What rationale is offered for the selection/inclusion of certain content while other content is excluded? What are the unifying strands of the content selected?
3. How would "gaps" or deficits in student performance be identified?
4. If students or groups of students were found deficient in certain skill or knowledge areas after testing, would it be possible to locate where in the existing curriculum such skills, knowledges, or attitudes should have been taught/learned?
5. If deficits are revealed from test data, can specific instructions be given to the professional staff which will result in reduction or removal of the deficits in pupil performance?

In order for a school system to utilize feedback from test data, tests must adequately assess the existing curriculum and also be valid indicators of the needs and derivative goals and objectives. Most school systems simply do not know the degree to which any particular test or test batteries assess their curriculum. In too many cases the test *is* the curriculum. Many teachers, on the other hand, view test data as irrelevant to teaching because the information cannot be related to the existing curriculum in any specific way. A teacher selecting curriculum or lesson content from a textbook with no precise guidelines will find it extremely difficult to envision item analysis from standardized tests as helpful. If, however, the curriculum has been broken into specific performance objectives, item analysis can provide a base for the productive utilization of test data.

The problem is that with a too general picture of the existing curriculum, test information can "slip through the holes." Let us suppose that the sixth grade social studies curriculum indicates that "students will understand the significance of various geographical features upon countries in Latin America," or the "geography of Latin America will be studied in the sixth grade." Let us suppose that hypothetical data from a standardized test shows that 34 percent of the students did not know the difference between a river delta and a plateau. To a sixth grade teacher who presents the unique features of each Latin American country and requires only that students memorize the separate features, the test item is not helpful in shaping future lessons or units. With each teacher permitted to read into a vague curriculum guide the meaning and interpretation of the content to be included for study, test information of a specific nature may be considered extraneous.

This is also a problem with curricular coordination. While in one sense all sixth grade teachers may be teaching the geography of Latin America, what they really may be teaching is a disjointed and haphazard study of the continent. Such vague curricular guidelines merely serve to notify the teacher that a study of Europe or Africa is considered inappropriate, but almost anything else would be permissible unless the guide further delineates expectations. Multiply this condition hundreds of times in

classrooms across a school system and the weaknesses of traditional curriculum guides is multiplied. A school system cannot be
coordinated properly if it does not explain precisely what is being
taught and what method is being used to organize the program of
instruction or divide the curriculum. Alternative variations in
content, method, or presentation cannot be compared to the
existing program because there are greater differences in that
program than to the alternative. This has been a classic problem in
conducting rigorous field studies of alternatives in teaching
methods, curricula, or staffing (Provus, 1971).

Leaving such decisions to classroom teachers negates any effort
by the school system to maximize its resources or to control its
destiny. Arguing that teachers alone can uplift a curriculum to
levels of higher application is not borne from an analysis of what
they test. Burns conducted a study of fifty teacher-made tests and
concluded that eight of ten measured knowledge acquisition only.
He noted that fewer than one percent of some 2010 items assessed
such skills as summarization, discrimination, hypothesis formulation, generalization, estimation, integration, prediction, or sequencing (Burns, 1968). Traditional curriculum guides tend to
leave a school district without any way to improve either teaching
or learning.

Mapping the existing curriculum is necessary if needs assessment
data are to have a positive and useful impact upon curriculum
improvement. Mapping operations should indicate the following
information, in writing or in schematic/chart form:

1. What specifically is being taught and when in a sequence of
   activities?
2. What are the minimum expectations for the student at the
   conclusion of the unit or period of teaching/study? What
   specifically will students be able to do?
3. What resources are available to utilize in creating teaching
   (intervention) strategies to produce the desired outputs?
4. What evaluation methods are recommended by the system?
5. What part of the curriculum is required and what is open
   to the teacher for interpretation or choice? The curriculum
   should always be flexible about methods, but do some

appear to be more productive than others in certain situations? Are they specified?

A curriculum guide which maps the curriculum must indicate with some clarity the degree of planned and desirable overlap between grades, areas of enrichment, and the degrees to which the teacher may deviate, either in content or approach. In the sixth grade, can a teacher eliminate all of Latin American geography? In what context is Latin American geography expected to be learned and how is it applied? Mapping the curriculum means that the school system identifies the degree of tolerance for individual teacher judgment in adapting or adopting system-produced curricula. It is only with some idea as to the degree of variation that the degree of conformity can be known. The known aspect of a curriculum can be coordinated. The unknown is absorbed or contained, unless the system takes steps to make it knowable, that is, bring it to the conscious attention of the staff and administrative authorities.

When this requirement for more adequately coordinating a curriculum is discussed, the "horror story" of rigidity is recalled about the minister of education in a European country who glanced at his watch and remarked, "Ah, it is 9:15 and ten million children are learning their spelling." This is not the kind of coordination referred to as the function of a curriculum guide. As Drucker (1974) has so succinctly put it, "We undermanage work and overmanage workers." We are not suggesting that individual teacher responsibilities for decision-making within classrooms be removed. We believe that a good deal of curricular effectiveness lies with intelligent diagnosis and decision-making by teachers in classrooms. We do feel strongly, though, that the latitude for such decisions be specified; this is a prerequisite for any claim to adequate curricular coordination. Unless the elements which comprise a curriculum are knowable and capable of being changed, there can be no optimal use of resources to reach an identified optimum state.

The degree to which deviation may occur represents a "blind" part of the school curriculum. Specifying the time spelling will be taught deals with only one variable, time spent on instruction. From a system-management point of view, all the other kinds of decisions teachers may make within the existing curricular guidelines may not be conveniently identified. The deviation actually contained in the curriculum is the degree of "slack" present. Slack represents underutilized and unspecified resources. If 40 percent of the social studies curriculum is "slack," then the system should decide whether such slack should be more or less present in order to reach the desired outcomes. The system can also specify the types and/or kinds and ranges of deviations which are appropriate in the "slack" part of the curriculum. These are teacher options. The system may also decide that "slack" should vary according to some criterion, such as age or maturity of the learner. System slack in social studies may follow an hourglass pattern where the primary grades are 80 percent slack and open to interpretation and significant content or procedural deviations by teachers. This may drop to 15 percent slack at the middle grades where requirements are met in basic skills and to 75 percent at the junior and senior years in high school where elective courses or independent study options comprise most of the curriculum. Such determinations should be logical and planned. They should and must be knowable in order to be effectively coordinated and improved. Improvement is dependent upon accurate information regarding the status quo; thus, improvement implies control. We know of few school systems in which the existing curriculum is accurately described and capable of being adequately coordinated. It is a step which should be taken to utilize the data from a needs assessment.

Step 5: Compare Outcome Statements to Existing Curricula

Once the curriculum has been mapped with accuracy, the outcome statements developed at the policy level by the board of education can be compared to the curriculum map and the output objectives. This requires that decisions be made about the location of the output statements within the existing delineation of curricular organization. Outputs must be located because they were "curriculumless," i.e., not part of any particular subject matter or content area.

This comparison is necessary because it will reveal the degree to which the existing curricular scope and depth includes the outputs statements and will also determine the degree of repetition present in the curriculum. Let us assume that from a list of 280 statements of policy, outputs are located as follows:

Curricular Delineation	Elementary	-Level- Junior High	Senior High
Social Studies	12%	11%	14%
English	4%	13%	25%
Business	0	9%	7%
Physical Education	0	2%	7%
Science	4%	4%	19%
Art	1%	4%	6%
etc.			

By locating each output statement on the existing curricular map, we find that 37 percent fall into the subject area delineated in the curriculum as social studies and 42 percent are in the English delineation. An analysis of the objectives shows that there is a 12 percent overlap (not shown in the above table), that is, 12 percent are now taught or included in both the English and social studies areas. Locating the percentage of inclusion/exclusion of the existing curriculum by level allows some consideration of balance on a K-12 basis and can take into account the unique mission of the elementary, middle or junior high, and high school organizational patterns.

Some outputs will not be able to be located anywhere, which means that the existing curriculum does not include them. They may be included by chance in the "slack" curriculum. Test analysis would yield some answer to this location problem. From the table it can be shown that 63% of the social studies curriculum (excluding slack) does not now include the desired outputs or is not comprised of the outputs. Several types of adjustments can be made if gaps or "needs" are revealed in the subsequent needs assessment. The first is to reduce the known curriculum to include more of the desired outcomes. The second is to reduce the amount of slack present in the social studies curriculum to include more of the desired outcomes. The third would be a combination of options one and two.

Step 6: Selection/Development/Implementation
of Testing Instruments

A Beta needs assessment is a gap discrepancy assessment. It is the difference or gap between desired levels of pupil performance (outputs) and the actual level of pupil performance at any given point or time in the school system. Having taken steps 1-5, the district is now ready to ascertain what the gaps really are.

Once the outputs are specifically known at the policy level and the existing curriculum mapped accurately, tests can be selected or developed which (1) possess a high degree of overlap with both outputs desired, and (2) include as much as possible of the existing curriculum. These two criteria deal with test content validity. With each test the school system should be able to discover the percentage of outputs that are assessed by a particular test and what percentage of the existing curriculum is likewise assessed. Tests can be selected which include the greatest scope of both the outputs and the existing curriculum. Areas which are left unassessed can be the subject of specially designed tests which are at least locally validated as to content inclusion. Most often such testing or assessment may be in the affective areas and involve items only at the nominal or ordinal measurement levels.

The purpose of testing is to determine the degree to which the desired output statements are being delivered by the current curriculum and the existing allocation of instructional goods and services. The results of the testing present a composite picture of "gaps" or discrepancies present.

Step 7: Development of Initial Gaps or Needs List

Test collation should include the degree to which each output statement is being realized and the nature of any "gap" or "need." In order for the needs to be located on the existing curricular map, the following questions should be broached:

1. Where in the existing curriculum is the gap revealed?
2. Is the gap manifested at any lower level?
3. Is the gap or need part of the identified curriculum? If not, what evidence is there to suggest it may be part of the "slack" curriculum?
4. Does the same gap occur in more than one subject/curricular area? Which ones?

Let us assume that the preliminary assessment reveals that 29 percent of the graduating class lack certain math skills to be able to perform at required levels of proficiency. The curriculum map reveals that the skills required to do the problems should have been learned by grade six. While the gap is located at grade twelve, the *real* gap may be much lower than even the sixth grade. Professionals should examine carefully item analyses from test data in math at the sixth grade to ascertain if the breakdown in the learning of the skills began there or simply was manifested there. This procedure also underscores again the importance of having an accurate description of existing curriculum from which to identify ranges of responsibility in the school system.

If the current curriculum does include a gap, several decisions can flow from this discovery. The skill or concept to be acquired *to reduce or eliminate the gap* can be included at designated curricular levels so as to fix the range of time in which most of the learners should acquire it. If the evidence shows a very uneven trend, that is, some children have acquired it and some have not, then it may be part of the "slack" curriculum. It should then be made part of the formal curriculum.

Step 8: Examine the Adequacy of the Current Curriculum Configuration

The needs assessment process usually ends with the delineation of the gaps per se, but one final step is necessary in the application of the process for the practitioner in curriculum development. The original focus of needs assessment may have been to determine if the current curriculum configuration was "adequate." The configuration included not only the content part of the curriculum, the planned and coordinated part, but also the unplanned or "slack" aspect of the curriculum.

The curriculum is the causal chain between inputs and outputs. It is the center around which instructional goods and services are organized. There are an infinite number of ways curriculum as a causal chain may be organized. There is the usual subject-centered curriculum, core curriculum, fused curriculum, or thematic curriculum (Taba, 1962). We hypothesize that after the analytical process described in this chapter has been implemented, the effectiveness and efficiency of the current curricular organization will be indicated. We suspect that the traditional subject-centered curriculum is too narrow and reiterative and that an analysis should serve as an impetus for a search for alternatives in curricular organization. The measure of adequacy is the degree to which the current curriculum is defined and includes the application of goods and services to "deliver" the range of desired outputs.

A curriculum configuration which is effective (delivers the majority of the desired outputs and thus the required outcomes) may not be efficient (the least costly way to produce the results). Neither effectiveness nor efficiency are known in most school systems as they relate to the question of the existing curricular configuration. The application of needs assessment to curriculum development promises neither revolutionary nor traditional configuration patterns, although both remain possibilities.

Step 9: Make Changes in the Configuration/Content of the Curriculum as Required

The curriculum as a causal chain contains both a content or substantive aspect, and an organizational or design aspect. Too often questions about content are forgotten in organizational or design debates. The impact of one upon the other is not always totally clear. We have indicated an approach which should clarify the rigor of the content both of an existing curriculum and a desired curriculum. We have shown how a curriculum developer would determine whether the existing curriculum rigorously adhered to the performance outputs developed by a board of education, or was weak in one or more areas.

Substantive determinations of an existing curriculum tend to be questions of effectiveness, while questions of design tend to be questions of efficiency. If the curriculum does not include required outputs and relating outcomes, it cannot be effective. If the curriculum does include the outputs, but a different pattern or design (fusing subjects, emphasizing more process or inductive approaches, etc.) produces the outputs at less cost, then these answer concerns regarding efficiency (Chamber of Commerce, 1971).

As the data is gathered, collated, and analyzed, it should become clearer what contextual and content areas of the existing pattern are necessary and/or what design solutions are required. A design solution may be the degree to which content is repeated to obtain or retain desired levels of mastery or performance by students.

Step 10: Implement Changes and Compare Feedback to Solutions Selected

As the curriculum configuration is altered in keeping with the data gathered from the needs assessment, there must be constant monitoring to ascertain if it has become more effective and efficient. The presence of the policy outcome statements by the board of education serve as a constant set of criteria for a determination of both effectiveness and efficiency.

Curriculum development is a constant process of approximation of a hypothetical "optimal configuration" which is a mix of content and design considerations. We believe that the needs assessment process produces a public and open approach to defining both the state of the art and an optimal curricular configuration standard that is capable of replication in most school systems today.

In retrospect, curriculum development has been considered a primary and important activity of the school system. Much about it can be improved, and we believe that the application of a more rigorous and quantifiable procedure as embodied in needs assessment is a critical starting point in that quest.

Curriculum Overlap and External Reality

In setting objectives from a needs assessment, it is frequently noted that much of current curriculum coverage is redundant or unnecessary. For example, in one college it was noted that many of the stated intentions of the instructors were to allow the graduates to be decision-makers in a situation where the future was not completely predictable. Their current choice was to teach general content, using the "great works" of the past and hoping that future graduates would use this wisdom of the ages in making useful decisions. They did not know what else to do.

One possible outcome, if supported by the needs assessment data and a determination that future behavior of graduates would require identification and resolution of problems, would be to include a curriculum area on identification, justification, and resolution of problems. Frequently, the synthesis of curriculum areas is left to chance, instead of being the subject of purposive and responsible design. While, in this case, many of the teachers wanted their learners to be able to identify and solve problems, they did not look across classical curriculum boundaries to see the extent of overlap, redundancy, or integration. The data from a needs assessment will allow the curriculum planner and developer the opportunities to modify, fuse, integrate, and eliminate curriculum content. It is an opportunity to achieve effectiveness as well as efficiency.

Implications of Needs Assessment-Based Curriculum Change!

When the current curriculum (methods-means for achieving desired and required change in learners skills, knowledges, and attitudes) and required curriculum are compared, gaps will be noted. This suggests functional change, and functional change usually brings threat. Be ready. Old ways die with difficulty, and fear and apprehension will abound. The advantage of having conducted a needs assessment is that there will be a data base for suggested change; and the logical, rational educator will have an easier time resolving change requirements and resulting change. The illogical and irrational educator is another case, and there are no ready-made answers to this dilemma, although each curriculum change situation will ignite these people. We have no magic.

Group dynamics will usually help this deviant behavior, and hope springs external that rational, logical arguments and information will endure the persevere. Patience, persistence, and understanding will help the threatened persons move to a point of attempted change. Threats and shame rarely work; but understanding, compassion, firmness, and reasonable, responsible data help.

Be ready for the "heat" of change. Be ready with frame of mind, with solid evidence for change (not moving for change-for-change's sake, which has been altogether too frequent), with confidence that learners will be helped in their quest to survive and contribute when they legally exit from our schools.

KEY CONCEPTS

1. Curriculum is a prime vehicle for schools to achieve their mission.
2. The terms input, process, product, output, and outcome are abundant in the literature.
3. Input refers to the raw materials which can be used by schools, such as time, people, money, facilities, equipment.
4. Process refers to those things which utilize inputs in order to meet the objectives of the school, and may include curriculum, programmed instruction, television, staffing patterns, etc.
5. Product refers to things developed along the way to achieving the goals and objectives of schools, and might include instructional packages and materials, tests, etc.
6. Outputs are the goals and objectives achieved by the schools using inputs, processes, and products.
7. Outcomes are the achievement external to the schools, and are each individual's ability to survive and contribute, currently and in the future, in society.
8. Inputs, processes, products, and outputs are related to the "internal world" of the schools. Outputs relate to school-based activities and ends.
9. Outcomes are achieved efficiently to the extent to which there is a compatibility and "transfer" between the internal goals and activities of schools and society.
10. Needs assessment may provide the data to design a successful curriculum so that the outputs and outcomes will be positively related.
11. Curriculum is the sum total of the planned utilization of goods and services necessary to achieve desired and required outputs.
12. Curriculum is successful to the extent to which outputs and outcomes are highly and positively correlated.

13. A defined theoretical base means that the assumptions and biases of the developer are stated prior to any specific call for curriculum being developed.

14. Modularized curricular pieces refer to the way the curriculum is broken down into units or parts for implementation at various levels in the school or school system.

15. The transformational areas of curriculum development are the areas in which policy decisions are interpreted and subsequent allocational decisions are framed.

16. Management by objectives is the practice of stating objectives in a collaborative sense with one's immediate superior or work group and then setting out to accomplish them. Subsequent evaluation is promulgated on the degree to which the objectives have been obtained.

17. The function of a curriculum is to increase the probability that desired learning occurs in the schools. As such it represents an "economy of scale" of possible actions by the system itself.

18. A progressive approach in developing curriculum from a system approach is a step-by-step method to proceed from the definitions of ends to the development of means to obtain the ends. Each step is retraceable and self-correcting.

20. The idea of something being idiosyncratic is another way of saying it is peculiar or unique to a situation and may not be generalizable from one problem to the next.

21. Pre-packaged curricula are curricula that are developed outside of the school environment, as in business or industry, for use in the schools. Such items as instructional "kits" would fall into this category as well as texts.

22. Scope and sequence is the manner in which a curriculum is ordered, set forth for utilization in the schools in some developmental manner. Sometimes this may be in degree of complexity, difficulty, or both.

REFERENCES AND BIBLIOGRAPHY

Blalock, H.M., Jr. *Theory construction.* Englewood Cliffs, N.J.: Prentice-Hall, 1969.

Blau, P.M., and Scott, W.R. *Formal organizations.* San Francisco: Chandler Publishing Company, 1962.

Bowles, S., and Gintis, H. *Schooling in capitalist America.* New York: Basic Books, 1976.

Braun, B.J. *Teachers and power.* New York: Simon and Schuster, 1972.

Burns, R.W. Objectives and content validity of tests. *Educational Technology,* December 15, 1968, *8*(23), 17-19.

Chamber of Commerce of the United States, *The neglected imperatives in education: Cost effectiveness, productivity, accountability.* Washington, D.C., 1971.

Combs, A.W. *Educational accountability: Beyond behavioral objectives.* Washington, D.C.: Association for Supervision and Curriculum Development, 1972.

Cook, D.L. *Program evaluation and review technique: Applications in education.* OE-12024, Cooperative Research Monograph Number 17. Washington, D.C.: Department of Health, Education, and Welfare, Office of Education, 1966.

Dewey, J. *The child and the curriculum.* Chicago: University of Chicago Press, 1962.

Dreeben, R. The school as a workplace. In R.M.W. Travers, *Second handbook of research on teaching.* Chicago: Rand McNally, 1973.

Drucker, P.F. Conversation with Peter F. Drucker. *Organization Dynamics,* Spring 1974, 34-53.

Duggan, S. *A student's textbook in the history of education.* New York: Appleton-Century-Crofts, 1948.

English, F. Can spontaneity serve as a curriculum base? *Educational Technology,* January 1972, *12*(1), 59-60.

English, F., and Kaufman, R. *Needs assessment: Focus for curriculum development.* Washington, D.C.: Association for Supervision and Curriculum Development, 1975. 65 pp.

English, R. Statement made on the panel of critical issues: Needs assessment conference. *Educational Planning,* October 1976, *3*(2), 16-19.

Fiske, E.B. Suburban schools are evolving "basic" curriculum geared to 70's. *New York Times,* June 15, 1977, 1 and B.11.

Florida Department of Education. *Florida educational opinion survey.* Tallahassee, Florida, 1970.

Greenfield, T.B. Organizations as social inventions: Rethinking assumptions about change. *Journal of Applied Behavioral Science,* September-October 1973, *9*(5), 551-574.

Greenwald, H. *Direct decision therapy.* San Diego: EDITS, 1973.

Hershkowitz, M., and Shami, M.A. A note on the relative importance of subject matter goals and higher order goals. *Educational Planning,* October 1976, *3*(2), 24-29.

Holt, J. *How children fail.* New York: Dell Books, 1964.

Hutchins, R.M. *The conflict in education.* New York: Harper and Row, 1953.

Illich, I. *Deschooling society.* New York: Harper and Row, 1970.

Jackson, P.W. The way teaching is. Washington, D.C.: Association for Supervision and Curriculum Development, 1966.

Kaufman, R.A. *Educational system planning.* Englewood Cliffs, N.J.: Prentice-Hall, 1972.

Kirst, M.W., and Walker, D.F. An analysis of curriculum policy-making. *Review of Educational Research,* December 1971, *41*(5), 479-510.

Kliebard, H.M. Reappraisal: The Tyler rationale. *School Review,* February 1970, 259-272. As cited in *Curriculum Theorizing.* W. Pinar (Ed.). Berkeley, Calif.: McCutchan Publishing Corporation, 1975, 70-83.

Kohl, H.R. *The open classroom.* New York: Vintage Books, 1969.

Larson, R. *Goal setting in planning: Myths and realities.* Unpublished paper presented to the 31st Annual Conference of Professors of Educational Administration, University of Oregon, August 15, 1977. 49 pp.

Lewin, K. *Principles of topological psychology.* New York: McGraw-Hill, 1936.

Lortie, D.C. *Schoolteacher.* Chicago: University of Chicago Press, 1975.

MacDonald, J. Curriculum theory. *Journal of Educational Research,* January 1971, *64*(5), 196-200. As cited in *Curriculum theorizing.* W. Pinar (Ed.). Berkeley, Calif.: McCutchan Publishing Corporation, 1975, 5-13.

Maeroff, G.I. Differences persist in career education. *New York Times,* Nobember 11, 1976.

Mann, D. Public understanding and education decision-making.

Educational Administration Quarterly, Spring 1974, *10*(2), 1-18.

Meeker, M.N. *The structure of intellect: Its interpretation and uses.* Columbus, Ohio: Charles E. Merrill, 1969.

Ministry of Education, Ontario, Canada. *The formative years. Provincial Curriculum Policy for the Primary and Junior Divisions of the Public and Separate Schools of Ontario,* 1975.

New York Regents. *Regents program priorities for fiscal year 1978-79.* Albany, N.Y.: State Education Department, June 1977. 28 pp.

Odiorne, G.S. *Management by objectives.* New York: Pitman Publishing Company, 1965.

Parker, J.C., and Rubin, L.J. *Process as content: Curriculum design and the application of knowledge.* Chicago: Rand McNally, 1966.

Pedersen, K.M. A proposed model for evaluation studies. *Administrative Science Quarterly,* June 1977, *22*(2), 306-317.

Phenix, P.H. *Realms of meaning.* New York: McGraw-Hill, 1964.

Phi Delta Kappa. *The Gallup polls of attitudes toward education, 1969-73.* Bloomington, Indiana: Phi Delta Kappa, 1969-73.

Pinar, W.P. *The reconceptualization of curriculum studies.* Unpublished paper presented at the Annual Meeting of the American Educational Research Association, April 1977, New York City. 15 pp.

Popham, W.J. Performance tests of teaching proficiency: Rationale, development, and validation. *American Educational Research Journal,* 1971, *8*, 105-117.

Posner, G.J., and Strike, K.A. A categorization scheme for principles of sequencing content. *Review of Educational Research,* Fall 1976, *46*(4), 665-690.

Postman, N., and Weingartner, C. *Teaching as a subversive activity.* New York: Dell, 1969.

Provus, M. *Discrepancy evaluation.* Berkeley, Calif.: McCutchan Publishing Corporation, 1971.

Raoul-Duval, M. The intelligence agencies: What is to be done? *New York Times,* July 1, 1977, p. A-33.

Schaffarzick, J., and Sykes, G. *NIE's role in curriculum development: Findings, policy options, and recommendations.* Unpublished paper submitted by H.L. Hodgkinson, Director of the National Institute of Education, to the National Council on Educational Research, February 8, 1977. 125 pp.

Schiro, Michael. *Curriculum for better schools: The great ideological debate.* Englewood Cliffs, N.J.: Educational Technology Publications, 1978.

Schwab, J.J. Structure of the disciplines: Meanings and significances. In G.W. Ford and L. Pugno (Eds.), *The structure of knowledge and the curriculum.* Chicago: Rand McNally, 1964, pp. 1-30.

Sechrest, L. Personal communication, June 1977.

Steeves, F.L., and English, F.W. *Secondary curriculum in a changing world.* Columbus, Ohio: Charles E. Merrill, 1978.

Summers, A.A., and Wolfe, B.L. Which school resources help learning? Efficiency and equity in Philadelphia public schools. *Business Review,* Federal Reserve Bank of Philadelphia, 1975. 29 pp.

Taba, H. *Curriculum development.* New York: Harcourt, Brace, and World, 1962.

Tyack, D.B. *The one best system.* Cambridge, Mass.: Harvard University Press, 1974.

Vecsey, G. Schism grows between suburban taxpayers and teachers. *New York Times,* June 14, 1977, p. 70.

Section Two

THE APPLICATION OF
NEEDS ASSESSMENT

INTRODUCTION TO SECTION TWO

The previous seven chapters have defined and identified the "whats" of needs assessment, the terms and concepts, and set the stage for applications.

In this section we will deal with the most basic variety of needs assessment, the "Alpha" or "external" variety, and then shift to a discussion of conducting a "Beta" or one of several "internal" needs assessments.

Not all applications of needs assessment will be the same. One must adapt and adopt those concepts and models to the unique situation present in each educational context. These chapters serve as guide-posts only.

In most applications of needs assessment, consensus must be sought; and usually requirements for project, program, and staff development are energized simply by changing from the "reaction" mode of the process-orientation to the "action" mode of a system approach where needs assessment defines and justifies problems before solutions are selected and implemented. Considerations for these changes are presented in Chapters 11 and 12.

Chapter 8

CONDUCTING A NEEDS ASSESSMENT-
GETTING GOING

Usually, the most difficult part of conducting a needs assessment is obtaining commitment to the concept and obtaining the approvals and resources to get the job done: *getting going.*

Communicating with Others

Once a decision is made to conduct a needs assessment, the first task is to get the personnel and resources committed to the same objective—measurable improvement of our school(s), regardless of whether or not it happens to include the present treasured, protected ways of doing things.

There will be a number of blocks to commitment, most of them arising from a lack of awareness of what the future might hold. While this concern may hardly ever overtly surface, most people do have a concern for their future; and anchoring points in their lives should be understood (Ausubel, 1963). Change should proceed with the intention of identifying current concerns and points of personal stability and reference, and attempting to help the individuals find new anchoring points.

Kurt Lewin spoke of a change process which involved "unfreezing," "moving" and "refreezing" attitudes and behaviors. Change is one of the most painful things a person can be asked to endure. People are not stubborn merely for the sake of being stubborn but are expressing genuine concern and apprehension. The built-in desire to survive is very strong; and needs assessment strikes many as a threat to existence, stability, and the known and comfortable, rather than as a growthful experience where positive and salutary

175

change can occur to the benefit of all who care about other humans.

Successfully eliciting the aid and support of others is a critical step and is one which has been addressed by others in some detail. For a detailed study of the etiology of change, it is advisable to review the works of Getzels and Guba, Everett Rogers, Maslow, Greenwald, Frankl, Carl Rogers, Hersey and Blanchard, and Drucker to get some understanding of the anatomy of change and the techniques for human intervention into the lives and careers of others. This issue has also been dealt with, in part, specifically with reference to planning and planned change (Kaufman, 1970, 1972; and Kaufman, Feldman, Snyder and Coffey, 1975).

Several general approaches to get others committed and involved in change are discussed as follows.

The Scare Approach

This is the easiest to muster, and the one most often resorted to on the pages of our journals and by our more inspirational, "give 'em hell" speakers.

The tactic here is to parade the possible horrors of tomorrow if change is not imminent. Included in these are:

1. Each year, voucher plans seem to be getting increased support in many states. These are schemes whereby parents are not required to send their learners to specified schools, but may send their children to any school and are presented with "scrip" which allows the private school to obtain money from the state government for services rendered. If we don't change, the argument continues, we will be out of work because the learners will go elsewhere and we will have empty classrooms.

2. Private industry, which can be hired, fired, or renewed based upon their successes and failures, will be invited to bid to conduct education in failing districts (especially in urban centers) to provide an accountable vehicle for getting learning accomplished. This is often a reaction to increased salary schedules which give raises without accounting for the skills, talents, and abilities of the teachers, whether individually or collectively, to do what they were hired to accomplish. If this eventually occurs, the argument continues, all teachers will be out of work or applying to work with an industrial organization which will "make us change."

3. Legislators are cutting us off—each year they seem to get angrier and angrier, and we get lesser raises, and they supply fewer resources for teaching and learning. Local bond elections and tax overrides fail at great rates, and citizens and lawmakers alike seem to have "written off" education in terms of new dollars or even dollars to keep up with erosion caused by inflation. If we don't start delivering better and more visible results, this argument continues, we will be down to a substandard wage without dignity and ability to conduct even minimal educational experiences. To fuel this one argument, it is only necessary to remind listeners that our society tends to put dollars where its values lie: witness the salaries of streetsweepers in San Francisco, plumbers in your home town, electricians in New York, bus drivers in Los Angeles. There are plenty of examples to show that the starting (and continuing) salaries of teachers rank among the lowest of the college trained; and there are certainly many "blue collar" tradespeople who make more money than do teachers—and usually with shorter hours, fewer demands, and less education and training required.

4. Educational malpractice lawsuits are just around the corner; and if we do not start getting the kinds of results which we infer that we accomplish in schools ("education for all of the children"), start demonstrating "truth in labeling" in terms of what we do "teach children" and those with whom we cannot have success, then we will end up in court with a lawyer and start losing money. To bolster this, one has only to refer to a recent legal proceeding in San Francisco where the parents sued the school district for graduating their children from high school without the ability to read at a survival level! Get results, or get sued, this argument goes.

These are but a sample of the arguments which can be made to educators to get them moving toward accountability, productivity, and results. Lessinger defines this as "doing what you said you were going to do, and proving that it has been accomplished."

These might work in certain contexts, but we do not advocate them and we feel that a direct and positive approach is more feasible and productive.

Appealing to Human Dignity and Concern

Teachers and educators (even trainers, too) are people. They have human concerns, hopes, desires, demands, fears, apprehensions, wishes, fantasies, dreams, and nightmares. Most of them feel that there are some aspects of themselves which are defective (we call this negative self-concept), and many are concerned that they might be publicly revealed as wanting—and face shame. Most people carry around guilt and apprehension from being unable to live up to a set of parentally transmitted "scripts" or instructions which they have decided to accept (Greenwald, 1973). Most people, we feel, want to "do the right thing." Often, however, they are confused as to what constitutes the "right thing" actually. They are afraid or concerned about taking the risks for shifting from the present and known to the future and unknown.

We see this often in the classroom with the misbehaving child who continues to "cut up" even though punishment and shame are certain to result. It would seem that the child knows and moves towards the certainty of negative attention rather than changing his behavior and risking no attention. It might be possible that the teacher and educator "know" their current conditions and results, and have chosen to continue this rather than make the "risky shift" to new and different approaches and results.

Most educators, contrary to some popular beliefs, went into education to help children. Most want to be successful at helping children to be successful. Most of us want to do this, but at a very basic level we feel that both ourselves and the system fail to achieve this end.

We can attempt to deflect the blame in a number of directions: to broken homes, poor facilities and equipment, low salaries, defective learning materials, uncooperative or incompetent administrators, uncooperative parents, poorly disciplined children. All of these, however, are symptoms of problems—not the problems themselves. We know, most of us, at a very deep (and often protected) level that these are frequently just excuses, using reality as justification for perpetuating the status quo. Most people, although they do not openly admit it, know they are not doing the kind of job they want to do, and further, they do not know *how* to do it!

Most educational and training experiences for teachers have not allowed them to master the skills, knowledges, and attitudes (SKAs) of success. They have been trained in techniques and how-to-do-its without knowing how to plan and choose among alternatives, how to view the classroom as a learning laboratory where they can evaluate and change the methods-means and the objectives of learning activities. In short, they have not yet become competent in how to plan, deliver, evaluate, and revise learning success. We know it, they know it, and yet we do not offer them a helping hand in changing.

Knowing that there will be resistance, hostility, fright, and concern, we may proceed to have an open, frank discussion of our current situation and jointly decide about a common, agreed-upon future. We can together plan a more successful educational enterprise.

We have to be honest, open, objective, and leave the hidden agendas at home. Egos must be left outside of the planning and needs assessment room door. The joint focus must be improving the success of the enterprise in terms of how well the learners do when they exit schools (the external referent)—not how well our salaries look and the other hollow trappings of professional success.

Following are some possible concepts which educators will find useful in the planning and later accomplishment of a successful needs assessment.

Everything Is Measurable

In 1972, Kaufman presented a taxonomy of outcomes which proposed that everything is, in fact, measurable on some scale. This, to most people, is met with astonishment if not outright anger.

S.S. Stevens, in the *Handbook of Experimental Psychology*, noted that there are four scales of measurement:

nominal: the naming of something, such as chair, house, Janice, Jac, Lolita, Max, Molly, school, factory.

ordinal: the stipulation that something is only greater, less than, or equal to something else, such as the judgment made in beauty contests or art exhibitions.

interval: the observations of phenomena which may be
            measured in such a way that the distance between
            like points on the scale are equal, but the "zero
            point" (the origin) is arbitrarily defined, such as
            measurement of temperature on the Fahrenheit or
            centigrade scale or the so-called standardized tests
            with national norms such as in reading and math.

ratio: the observations of phenomena which may be
            measured in such a way that the distance between
            like points is equal, the "zero point" is known and
            observable, and that phenomena on the scale are
            additive, such as feet, inches, and pounds.

According to this analysis, if something is at least nameable,
then it is being measured. The simple naming of something is most
often an unreliable measure, but it *is* a measurement. Continuing,
if something is not nameable, how does one know that it even
exists? In fact, just stating that it does not exist or is not
measurable, according to this argument, *is* a measurement since it
has differentiated it from other things. This differentiation is the
basis and operational definition of nominal scale measurement. If
everything is measurable, the planning process might attempt to
identify all of the current outcomes which are desirable (or
required) to change, and then place priorities among these
discrepancies (needs) for action and resolution. This identification
of gaps in outcomes, the placement of needs in priority order for
reduction or elimination, and the selection of needs for elimination is called *needs assessment.*

Many people are concerned with needs assessment because they
have experienced incompetent measurement, and do not want to
have learners subjected to a process which is mechanical and
dehumanizing. They feel that only trivial aspects of education will
be captured and that education will be degraded into "training" or
worse.

The concern is that the really important things in education and
life in general cannot be measured and that to start this process
will begin a snowball of mediocrity and dehumanization. If sloppy
techniques and poor judgment prevail, the critics could be correct.
However, this is hardly inevitable.

First, one must show that we can measure everything which is important—if perhaps only on a nominal (naming) scale of measurement—and that anything which is important can (and must) be included in the needs assessment process. Values, valuing, feelings, attitudes, personal integrity and dignity, individual rights and responsibilities, and differential goals and achievements are possible. These considerations and factors only survive in our system (or any system) if they are considered important enough by the planners and doers to be included—included by design, not by default! If it is important in the needs assessment and the subsequent planning, include it in the process. Everything is at least nameable, and thus everything which is or could be important may be included.

One clarification process which may be used is to require that phenomena which can now only be measured on a nominal and/or ordinal scale of measurement be slated for individual group effort to increasingly define (perhaps some each year) and understand to the point of becoming measurable on an interval or ratio scale of measurement. Additionally, the measurement of important variables and phenomena which are currently beyond the means and skills of a faculty may become the research and development programs of research agencies (such as the Regional Educational Laboratories) or public and private colleges and universities.

In summary, demonstrate that important things, too, may be measured and included in a needs assessment and that each individual must participate, with the assurance that important aspects of education will be part of the process.

Goals and Objectives

In contemporary literature, there seems to be a frequent confusion between these two words, and goals and objectives are often used interchangeably. Other definitions are muddy and diffuse.

A taxonomy of outcomes provides some possible ways of viewing outcome statements (Kaufman, 1972). In the outcome taxonomy (Figure 8.1), goals and objectives are seen as being related but differentially defined by the scales of measurement used to define them. Goals are measured by nominal or ordinal

Figure 8.1

SCALE OF MEASUREMENT	OUTCOME DESCRIPTOR
NOMINAL ORDINAL	GOAL, AIM, PURPOSE
INTERVAL RATIO	OBJECTIVE, MEASURABLE OBJECTIVE, PERFORMANCE REQUIREMENT

A taxonomy of educational outcomes where there is a distinction made between outcome statements on the basis of the scale of measurement used to describe them (after Kaufman, 1972).

scales of measurement; objectives are measured by interval or ratio scales of measurement. In this way, a school or school district may see that there are several different kinds of outcome statements, some more reliable (repeatable) than others.

If a phenomenon is measurable only by naming or saying that it is "more than," "less than," or "equal to" something else, then it is a goal. If something is measurable on an interval or ratio scale, it is an objective (or measurable objective, performance requirement, or measurable performance specification—all synonymous, as we see it).

This understanding may relieve some observers about the triviality they see frequently relating to objectives and the measurability movement. Some phenomena concerning human behavior are still not defined in the experimental literature well enough to allow for interval or ratio scale measures; when this occurs, we may talk of goals. However, when there is enough known about a phenomenon to measure it on an interval or ratio scale, it would be counter-productive to use measures other than these.

"Poor" measurement could be seen as a situation in which one *could* measure using objectives but, for some reason or another, one only works with the more unreliable and diffuse goal statements.

Another type of "poor" measurement occurs when there are phenomena which can only supply nominal or ordinal scale measurements and one treats them as interval or ratio scale measurements.

Unresponsive measurement usually yields irresponsible evaluation and planning. If there are problems in the measurement of the phenomenon at the outset, things cannot get better as we progress through planning, development, and evaluation—the errors will tend to compound and increase.

Reasonable and responsive measurement of the current and intended outcomes of education is critical in needs assessment and what follows from needs assessment. The classical computer adage is well considered here: GIGO—Garbage In, Garbage Out. There is nothing about a needs assessment process or a system planning process which will compensate for "poor" measurement (except in the sixth step, which requires revision when en-route outcomes are not being accomplished); thus, the statement of outcomes in as precise and appropriate (representative) terms as possible is critical to the responsiveness and responsibleness of subsequent needs assessment, planning, and accomplishment.

Using the taxonomy of planning, the needs assessment or planning group or individuals may determine if an outcome intention is as "measurable" as possible, and strive to find ways and means for improving the reliability of measure. One method for making an important phenomenon more "measurable" is to find performance indicators for that phenomenon (see Chapter 5 for a discussion of this).

Attention to measurability and striving to move outcome specifications "up" the scale toward interval and, occasionally, ratio will improve the planning outcomes.

The Measurable Objective
The measurable objectives movement has perhaps changed education and training more than any other single recent

innovation. The impetus came from Mager's book *Preparing Objectives for Programmed Instruction* (1961) which quickly won acclaim and a newer, more generic title of *Preparing Instructional Objectives* (1962, 1975). This almost universally used book is now in a second edition.

While the data are not unanimous relative to the effectiveness of measurable objectives (Kibler and Bassett, 1977), it seems safe to move ahead with their use. Perhaps future research will note that trivial outputs, no matter how carefully and completely framed, will not have important results. Further, we suggest that a measurable objective (usually used in education as an output measure) will be useful to the extent to which the outputs are related to important outcomes. Thus, there is no equal sign between measurability and validity and usefulness, unless there is a direct relationship between the well-formed objective and useful outcomes.

A useful measurable objective has the following characteristics in that it states:

> (1) what skills, knowledge, and attitudes will be demonstrated;
> (2) who will demonstrate these skills, knowledges, and attitudes;
> (3) under what conditions these skills, knowledges, and attitudes will be demonstrated;
> (4) what criteria (best on an interval or ratio scale of measurement) will be used to measure achievement of the required skills, knowledges, and attitudes; and
> (5) all of the above in such a way that there will be no confusion between parties about what is meant.

This type of objective is useful for any output or outcome statement, and may be used any time there is a requirement for specificity of "ends." The statements to be entered into the "what is" and "what should be" cells of the needs assessment matrix will have the same characteristics as a measurable objective.

While many educators and training specialists have received training in the preparation of measurable objectives, few people have achieved competence in their definition and use. When working with individuals who have had appropriate training, it is strongly urged that review of basic principles be presented, and that the ability to write objectives be assured before moving ahead in a needs assessment activity. The ability to prepare measurable objectives is critical to a successful needs assessment, so it must be assured that the needs assessment team members have demonstrated competency in the development of objectives.

Assuring Human Survival and Contribution

An additional concern may be related to the functional utility of education. Earlier in this volume, we noted that most education is planned on the basis of internally valued outputs and achievements and not upon externally valued outcomes and achievements. In order for education to be valued and supported by legislators and citizens, we must be able to demonstrate actual "value added" to our society as a result of our efforts in education. Recently, we have been depending upon circumstantial evidence of success, and so have our detractors. We (the educators) point to the improvement of civil and personal rights, and they (society) point to the decline of test scores and increases in crime. We should increasingly attempt to provide our funding sources and our "clients" with *prima facie* evidence of the value added from our educational efforts.

In order to do this, we have to include an external referent (outcome) in our planning. The suggestion was made that an overall mission objective for education could be: by the time a learner legally exits from an educational agency, he or she will be at an "independent" survival point or beyond.

This so-called utility referent (Figure 8.2) provides three important points on a continuum:

- a zone* of dependent survival in which consumption (measured by dollars flowing out) is greater than production (measured by dollars flowing in);
- an independent survival point, set by society, where consumption exactly equals production; and

---

*The word "zone" is used to indicate that where, within a specific area or region, a case falls or occurs is not important or relevant—important only is that a case is *within* a zone.

Figure 8.2

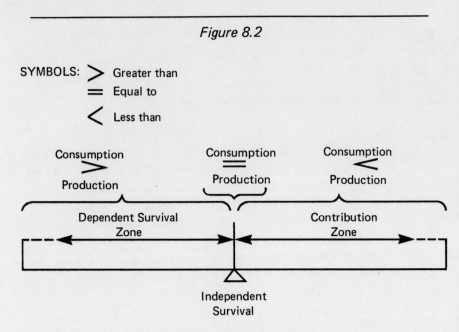

SYMBOLS: > Greater than
         = Equal to
         < Less than

Independent
Survival

Utility Continuum

The utility model suggested by Kaufman (1972) to determine the outcome requirements for education. It is suggested that this referent be used to determine the mission objective (overall minimal outcome) for education as: "By the time the learner legally exits the educational agency he/she will be at the independent survival point or beyond." Here, consumption is measured as anything requiring the surrender of money, and production is anything achieving the obtaining of money. Money, it should be emphasized, is only the medium of exchange, not an end in and of itself. (After Kaufman, 1972.)

- a survival zone where consumption is less than production.

The measurement of consumption and production in terms of dollar flow provides a ratio scale indicator for the overall mission objective of education, which is to allow learners to survive and hopefully contribute at the point of legal exit from our schools.

While it is not exactly "poetic" or "romantic" to reduce the processes and products of education to consumption and production (measured in dollars-in and dollars-out), it seems to represent an adequate *minimal* standard for an external referent for educational accomplishment.

This utility continuum provides a realistic referent for an Alpha-type or external needs assessment. It is also useful to show educational partners that we can and should plan our educational processes and outputs on the basis of measurable, demonstratable, external results.

Educational means must be related to valued and important educational ends. This referent supplies such a minimal standard. If the ends do not justify the means, what does? Our only safeguard in the process of education is the assurance of the usefulness of the ends and the involvement of all impacted people in the needs assessment process to determine valuable and valued ends.

Involving People—The Key to Success and Relevancy

Peter Drucker talks about the "transfer of ownership" of ideas from the planners to the doers if an enterprise is to be successful. Needs assessment, in order to be responsive and responsible, must be accepted by the people it intends to serve. It must involve people in the identification of needs as well as in the ultimate success of the total enterprise. Without them, it will predictably fail.

A needs assessment process, if it is to be valid and useful and if it is to be accepted and used, should include the involvement of a planning partnership: learners, educators, and community members.

In planning, these different points of view provide the opportunity for more relevant aspects of the total situation to be considered and included in the resulting educational activity. By involving those people who will be or could be impacted by the current and possible outcomes of the system, there will be a higher probability of acceptance of the results and a higher probability that all relevant aspects of the problem(s) will be identified.

At least three partners are included in an educational needs assessment effort:
- learners,
- educators, and
- community members.

Learners are included because they are the recipients of the educational process. If they do not want something to occur, they will block it. (Drop-outs and discipline problems are a possible result of *their* evaluation of the current educational scene.) By including them, you will determine their perceptions of the realities, now and in the future, of educational needs and resulting goals.

Educators are included because they are the implementers of the process. While it is quite possible (although not probable) that a thorough needs assessment could result in the diminution or even elimination of all or part of an educational system, the likelihood is that there will be a resulting educational process which will have to be implemented by existing or future educators. Their involvement is critical, for one must have their acceptance (transfer and acceptance of ownership) as well as their experience and understanding of the current and predicted educational context and requirements.

Community members are included because they pay the bills, and they receive and evaluate the products (learners) of the educational system when learners legally exit our schools. Again, they pay for what is (or is not) accomplished; they pass on changes and modifications; and they judge our results. They should have a "share" in determining needs so that future results will be acceptable and appropriate to them.

Each of the educational partners is to determine gaps between current results and desired (or required) results. This determination of gaps—gaps in *results,* not gaps in procedures or how-to-do-its—is imperative.

The partner groups should compare their perceived needs in order to find and agree upon a common set of needs—a group consensus (at least 51 percent of the group, both within and between groups) is the minimum agreement.

The needs are determined in concert in order to obtain a shared result and a reduction of "we-versus-they" confrontations which can result from factionalization.

It should be observed that three groups are defined here, but strictly speaking, all are a subset of the community group. Of course, learners and educators are citizens as well; but three partners are suggested to be sure that major forces and interested parties are involved in the needs assessment process and results. Also, for practical reasons, this partnership is a "one-person, one-vote" balance. Each partner is considered to be of equal value, so the consensus of each group (e.g., educators) is equal to one vote, as is the vote of either the community or the learners. Equality of impact and involvement is recommended here, although differing ratios might be considered and negotiated.

The General Steps for Accomplishing a Needs Assessment

As noted earlier, there is no one correct way to design and conduct a needs assessment. Each community is different and each group of people is unique, thus reducing the advisability and utility of kits, packages, and checklists of how-to-do-its. Ease of administration and application makes it tempting to use kits and packages; but this frequently amounts to having partner groups sort existing goals and objectives into piles and categories, resulting only in a ranking of current concerns. There is no way, with most extant packages, for new goals and objectives to be considered or for old ones to be eliminated.

Each needs assessment, and especially those of the Alpha or external variety, should be designed "from scratch" for each new application to ensure that it is responsive and responsible to the educational partners.

Some general steps to be taken might include the following:

1. Decide to plan systematically.

2. Obtain commitment of the initial planning group to use an external referent for planning, not just the existing goals and objectives of the agency.

3. Identify the various partnership groups and their required constituency, including representative people within each of the subgroups of learners, educators, and society/community. There should be proportional representation on the basis of at least race, religion, sex, and national origin.

4. Obtain commitment of the partnership groups to participate in the needs assessment effort and external-type planning.

5. Obtain data on current survival/contribution levels for graduates of the school system. This should include current data and data for some period in the past to provide a trend.

6. Identify the survival/contribution requirements—currently and in the future—for those who will be legally exiting from the system. A period of ten to twenty years is frequently useful, but be sure that the period will cover those learners who are in transition within the system currently.

7. Determine the present and anticipated gaps between current survival/contribution levels and desired/required levels. Make sure that these gaps are written as measurable behavioral statements which relate to outcomes, not just outputs, processes, or inputs.

8. Using the partners, place the gaps in priority order, perhaps ranked on the basis of the "cost" to close the gap *and* the "cost" to ignore the gap. "Cost" here is in societal terms, not the dollar figures to obtain the methods-means for actually closing the gaps.

9. Determine disagreements between partner groups. These may occur both within a partnership group (for instance among the educators) as well as between the partner groups. List these for action.

10. Reconcile the disagreements. Each set of disagreements is unique, so there are no sure how-to-do-its for this step. Usually, there will be a requirement to collect more data about survival and contribution levels and criteria so that an issue may be resolved. Frequently, disagreements occur over means, or how-to-do-its, rather than upon gaps in results. Take care to assure that disagreements are defined in terms of outcomes, not processes. When the item at issue is a process, a means, an input, or an output, it might be useful to re-write the need in terms of its logical consequences in the external world. After it is related to outcomes, disagreements will tend to be minimized and often go away.

11. List the agreed-upon needs and consider these and the previous agreed-upon needs (from step eight above), and re-rank.

12. If required by some additional disagreements, cycle through steps nine, ten, and eleven again.

13. List needs in priority order.

14. Select the needs for action, and list them. These needs selected for action are now the "problems" for further activity and resolution.

15. Continue the needs assessment process. The fact that a

needs assessment is never completed should be understood and serve as a basis for "institutionalizing" the process. Needs change as the external world changes. Schedule the next assessment, even if it has to be two years later.

16. Be prepared to consider new needs which might arise during the course of planning and implementation of the problems selected.

17. Be sure that the partner groups are personally and publicly thanked for their contribution, and that they are kept informed of the progress. Their job is a difficult and sensitive one, and they should not be made to feel "used" or as though they were mere "rubber stamps." They were not, and their contribution should be publicly dignified.

Again, it should be emphasized that there are very few "musts" in terms of the steps and techniques for needs assessment. It should be logical, orderly, responsive, and responsible. There is no magic, here or elsewhere. The above are general guidelines; exact tools, techniques, and procedures for their accomplishment must be determined for each unique application.

One important consideration is politics. Whenever planning for change is going on, people must be assured that there is no plot, conspiracy, or pre-selected solution or reorganization for which all of this is a coverstory. Assure people that just because a needs assessment is being conducted, there is no implication that *they* are doing something wrong . . . just that there is a formal search to find that which works and that which can and should be improved.

Change should always be functional and required on the basis of measurably improving individual abilities to survive and contribute in the external world. Change for change's sake must be avoided, and that which is sound and functional must be maintained by design and on purpose. Assurances of this must be made to the partnership groups, and then to the partners' constituencies in order for a needs assessment to be a productive contribution to children today and tomorrow.

Conducting the Needs Assessment

As the needs assessment data is collected for each of the three partner groups, the data are entered into a 2 x 3 needs statement matrix in the form of outcome statements containing the basic elements of a measurable objective: (a) what behaviors are displayed; (b) who or what displays the behaviors; (c) under what conditions are the behaviors displayed; and (d) what criteria are used to determine the existence or non-existence of the behaviors.

One set of results is currently being observed, and these results are entered under the general category of "what is." The other set of desired or required results is entered under the general category of "what should be."

There are three sets of these outcomes, one each for the partner groups of learners, implementers, and society/community. It should be carefully noted that these discrepancy statements are for the *partners,* not what the planner perceives as being the discrepancies for the partners.

The 2 x 3 needs statement matrix for needs assessment will be:

	WHAT IS (OUTCOMES)	WHAT SHOULD BE (OUTCOMES)
LEARNERS		
IMPLEMENTERS		
SOCIETY/ COMMUNITY		

There can and often will be more than one set of statements, written as measurable performance specifications, in each of the cells. A completed matrix will have at least six outcome statements within it, and often many more.

A possible sample (and strictly hypothetical) of a "first cut" of a needs assessment matrix reflecting the results of a needs assessment data collection procedure might look like the Alpha-type matrix shown in Figure 8.3.

This 2 x 3 matrix will give a summary of needs as perceived and reported by each of the three partner groups. Note that in each cell of this needs assessment matrix there are statements which describe "what is" and "what should be." Remember, this is a

Figure 8.3

	WHAT IS	WHAT SHOULD BE
LEARNERS	30% of graduates are unemployed as measured by 1977 Dept. of Employment (DOE) report X-11; Follow-up studies by Dept. of Employment (report X-11a, 1978) show 55% of graduates are below poverty level; 45% of graduates are in college, and of these 17% are in the contribution area as measured by their consumption at least being equal to their income. 58% of the graduates are white, and 56% of the total graduation group are below national reading norms as measured by the Hawaii test of reading achievement (DOE Rpt. X-11a), and 66% are below norms on math as measured by the Alaska test of Mathematic Competency (DOE Rpt. X-11a). In the sample, 95% of past graduates want higher income, and 11% have served or are serving jail sentences (DOE Rpt. X-11a). Etc.	100% of graduates should be at or beyond the independent survival point, as measured by an independent audit of income "in" and expenses "out" of a stratified random sample of those legally exiting from the school system, and certified correct by the associate superintendent for instruction. There shall be no graduates or those legally exiting who have been arrested and convicted of any crime above a $100 fine for a period of five years as measured by the certification of the associate superintendent for instruction. There will be no significant difference (.05 level of confidence or beyond) in survival and contribution of those legally exiting within five years of exit, on the basis of color, race, creed, sex, religion, or national origin as certified by an independent audit of a stratified random sample and certified correct by the associate superintendent for instruction. Etc.
IMPLEMEN-TERS	97% of teachers in the district are credentialled as certified by the State Department of Teacher Licensing (1978); 78% of them feel that minorities can perform as well as majority learners (District Study 78-2, April 1978); 55% of teachers demonstrated competencies for math and reading required by state performance criteria during the last teacher certification renewal period (Dept. of Education Report 1010, June, 1978); 83% of teachers and educators are whites, and 76% have 5 or more years of certifiable experience (Dept. of Ed. Report 1010, June, 1978). Etc.	75% feel that only 50% of the learners can reach independent survival or beyond within five years of legal exit, as measured by a survey conducted by the school district (District Study 78-2), and the same study indicates that 80% of the teachers feel that only 10% of the learners can reach contribution zone. In the same study, it was found that 91% of the educators felt that at least double the monies now spent on education is required to have any more measurable success, and 94% felt that teaching loads must be decreased at least 50% for any changes to occur. Etc.
SOCIETY/COMMUNITY	90% of stratified random sample of community members feel that too much money is spent on education, and 88% feel that the teachers are only responsible for making learners get and keep jobs after high school completion (as measured by District Study 78-2, April 1978). Etc.	100% of learners should get and keep jobs after they leave the public schools (as measured by District Study 78-2) and 88% felt (as measured by the same study) that no more public funds should be spent for public education. Etc.

sample of a first attempt at displaying the results of a needs assessment—it is not final but is an "en-route" matrix. (A "final" one is presented in Figure 8.4.)

Again, each should be written using the same content and format as any measurable objective. While the "what should be" is correctly written as an objective, one might technically argue that a "what is" statement is not. Regardless of the technical correctness, the listings under the "what is" column should have the same characteristics as an objective, with the difference being that it describes the current state of affairs in terms of outcomes.

After each partner has filled out its portion, the matrix is completed and ready for discussion and possible negotiation. Each of the three partner groups should fill out the entire matrix, inserting their perceptions (supported with data) about what should be included for each of the other partner groups. This will facilitate communication when all three groups work on deriving a common referent and an agreed-upon Need Statement Matrix.

It is not necessary to restrict the actual matrix to one page—it will take as many as necessary to complete the need statement. There is no premium on brevity. The only premium is on clarity and correctness.

This needs assessment matrix is not unusual in that it shows the perceived feelings and values of the partners. Note that in spite of efforts to keep the partners from identifying means and processes, they have been inserted and thus appear.

The insertion and listing of perceived means (how-to-do-its) are important in the needs assessment process. They show the perceived differences between the groups and allow for a dialogue to begin relative to how they can be replaced by results.

Often it is productive to ask the partner groups or their representatives to list the means in terms of outcomes or results. Frequently, asking them to "tell me what would result if we did that . . ." will help them move to listing results, not means. Another approach is to take the means, translate them into logical results yourself, and ask the partners if they do in fact represent that which they would like to have result from the application of the suggested means. In addition to this dialogue, the planner should arrange to have some of the external data collected and

Figure 8.4

	WHAT IS (OUTCOMES)	WHAT SHOULD BE (OUTCOMES)
LEARNERS	30% of graduates are currently unemployed. 55% of grads. are below poverty level. 45% of grads. are in college. 17% of grads. are in the contribution area. 48% of grads. are female. 58% of grads. are white. 56% of grads. were below norms on 11th grade reading test. 66% of grads. were below norms on 11th grade math test. 95% of grads. want more income. 11% of grads. now have jail record.	100% of learners currently in the system and all graduates and those legally exiting want to be at the independent survival point or beyond as measured by their consumption at least equalling their production; no bankruptcy for any graduates or person legally exiting, no commitments to mental institutions, no person arrested and found guilty of a felony, or misdemeanor which is punishable by a fine of greater than $250.00, a divorce rate which is significantly lower than the national divorce rate, all of the above measured by a stratified random sample certified as correct by a licensed psychometrician. There will be no significant difference between those legally exiting from the educational system on the above indicators which are attributable to color, race, creed, sex, religion, or national origin at or beyond the .05 level of confidence, as measured by a stratified random sample of legally exiting people as certified by a licensed psychometrician.
IMPLEMEN-TERS	97% of teachers are credentialled by the state for the subjects taught. 55% demonstrate the minimal competency required for certification of new teachers in the teaching areas. 83% of the teachers are white. 76% of the teachers have 5 or more years of teaching experience.	Same as above plus: 100% of the teachers will have the minimal competencies required for certification of new teachers in the teaching areas which were based upon a needs assessment conducted which identified and operationally defined the skills, knowledges, and attitudes required of learners to survive and contribute in the next twenty years, as measured by state validated criterion-referenced tests of achievement in the competency areas, as measured by State certification reports for all teachers in the system. If additional resources are required, the school board will vote to make them available, and justification will be supplied by the teachers and justified on a "value-added" basis where the additional resources will demonstrate a positive return-on-investment relative to all other possible alternatives and the consideration of no acquisition of new resources.
SOCIETY/ COMMUNITY	90% feel that too much money is currently being spent on education. 88% feel that only the teachers are responsible for making learners get and keep jobs upon exit from the schools.	Same as "what should be" for learners above, plus: Additional expenditures will be approved by a majority of the school board, and will not require any additional bond election or tax override revenues for the next five years.

available to assist in the decisions relative to the partners' perceptions of needs.

Survival/contribution data may include (but are not limited to): local, regional, and national poverty levels; employment figures for representative occupations and occupational titles; starting and experienced salary levels; current and future cost-of-living data; commitments to mental institutions and to jails; divorce and separation rates locally, regionally, and nationally; illegitimate birth rates; venereal disease rates; in short, any indicators of the successes and accomplishments of this intervention called education as it is currently being pursued.

The Needs Assessment Matrix—A Progression

The contents of the 2 x 3 matrix will change as the needs assessment process continues, as more data are collected, as means are changed to ends, as the dialogue continues in order to reach agreement among the partners, and as the external survival/contribution referent is included in the considerations and the further development of the matrix.

One change will be the reduction and ultimate elimination of means in the matrix. Other changes will frequently be reflected in one or more cells of the matrix becoming empty, especially the "what should be" cells for the implementer, and a growing agreement in the "what should be" cells for all of the partners.

It is possible to have an evolution through several matrices, each containing more and more data, and each containing increasing agreement among the three partners.

Each time there is agreement or a modification of the input, the 2 x 3 matrix may be re-written and serve as the basis for new dialogue, discussion, additional data, and modification.

Needs assessment is a process which involves data, partner perceptions, negotiation, discussion, more data, challenging of preconceived biases, stereotypes, mores, and folkways.

The process by which the partners shift from opinion and feeling to data-based statements of current outcomes and required outcomes supported by external survival and contribution data is a long, important, and sensitive job. It cannot be hurried, brute-forced, or faked. It should be an honest and sensitive effort of all the partners and planners.

A final (and still hypothetical) needs assessment matrix might be as shown in Figure 8.4.

This final 2 x 3 matrix is not without fault. It is representative of a possible "final" product based upon the introduction of external survival/contribution data, and upon open and emotion-drained dialogue between the partners or their representatives.

Note in the hypothetical example that there has been a movement toward the "what should be" for the learners, since this is a useful output for the school which will lead to a reasonable and responsible outcome in society—the survival and contribution of the learners upon exit and for the near future.

The 100% level has been chosen because it is important to strive for the best and not settle prematurely for just the possible or feasible. Using a system approach process and the "revise as required" feature, any shortfall from perfection can and should serve as diagnostic information for determining where the failures are and what might be done to improve performance. All too often in education (and in other behavior change interventions), the effort is saddled with an output or outcome which is far short of what could be achieved by not prematurely reducing the level of aspiration. The measure of aptitude and ability is *performance*, and the performance standard should be the *ideal.* One may always achieve less than the ideal, but it is rare that an effort exceeds its goals.

Needs assessment is a process for setting proper and useful goals, not for setting safe expectations. Shortfall is not the appropriate object of criticism, but rather the object of revision and rededication to achieve a measurable improvement in the survival and contribution of all learners when they legally exit our educational agencies.

Deriving the Needs—Listing the Gaps

When the needs assessment matrix has been completed, then the actual needs may be derived and listed. This derivation is a simple process of determining the gaps, or discrepancies, between the items listed in the WHAT IS column and those listed in the WHAT SHOULD BE column.

For instance, in our hypothetical example in this chapter, in the row marked "learners" the following was seen:

	WHAT IS	WHAT SHOULD BE
LEARNERS	30% of graduates are currently unemployed. 55% of grads. are below . . . etc.	100% of all graduates and those legally exiting want to be . . . etc.

By listing the gap, or discrepancy, between "what is" and "what should be" for the learners' row, it may be seen that 70% of the learners must reach the independent survival point or beyond in order to meet the need, or to eliminate the gap or discrepancy. In this manner, all of the differences between "what is" and "what should be" are listed and noted. Resulting from this process will be a summary listing of gaps, which are *not* in priority order. During this listing process, one should be careful to identify all "process" or "input" items and put them into output or outcome terms before proceeding.

What to Do with the Need Statement Matrix

When the completed matrix is available, the contents may be examined to determine the compatibility between the partner groups. If there is perfect agreement, then the needs are neatly and clearly given; and one may go on to select the highest priority needs and then to exercise the balance of educational system planning.

If there is disagreement, the differences have to be reconciled. Methods for reconciling differences have been previously identified, the chief one being to examine the statements presented to make sure that they are ends, not methods-means.

After there is substantial agreement (again, 51% of each of the three groups), the needs may be put in priority order for resolution. As discussed in Chapter 7, one method of placing needs in a priority order is to ask the dual question:

• What does it "cost" to meet the need?

• What does it "cost" to ignore the need? (Kaufman, 1972)

Again, "cost" here can be in terms of dollars (as suggested in the utility referent identified earlier), as "opportunity lost," or in a larger domain of social cost, such as the results of not having integrated after the Civil War, or denying a segment of our society minimal performance capabilities in survival skills.

Each group will have to work out its own "calculus" for pricing the results of either meeting needs or not meeting them. (Kits for doing this are available. The prime advantage of most needs assessment kits is that they require and get group interaction. The disadvantages of many of them are that they give a "pat" formula and procedure for all applications and they frequently ask partners to rank solutions, not gaps in outcomes. Some observations of this might be reviewed in "Package Paralysis," Kaufman, 1977.)

Again, the survival/contribution referent has been found useful by groups to determine the gaps between the current ability for legally exiting learners to survive and contribute and what might be required in the future. Another referent would be to determine the gap between current graduates' (or those otherwise leaving) ability to survive and contribute and an agreed-upon minimal survival level. Each need could be measured against this survival referent.

IT SHOULD BE EMPHASIZED THAT THIS CONTINUING AND BASIC REFERENCE TO EXTERNAL SURVIVAL AND CONTRIBUTION DIFFERENTIATES THE ALPHA-TYPE ASSESSMENT PROCEDURE FROM OTHER MODELS. It is suggested that this is imperative and will be the only way to identify possible significant and effective requirements for change.

After each group has obtained its ranking, the groups may be brought together to derive a common referent and ranking. One method is a sequential consensus determination technique (SCDT) where Group A (e.g., learners) is put with Group B (e.g., community members) to derive a common understanding and ranking. Then this combined Group AB is brought together with Group C (e.g., educators) and a final consensus is worked out. This SCDT methodology allows a continuous and sequential interaction of differing perspective and perceptions in relatively small groups and allows value sharing and value clarification.

Another strategy is to bring all of the groups together at one time and, there, come to an agreement. Both methods can work. Other variations might be considered, such as a Delphi technique (where group consensus is determined without convening groups).

What to do when there is disagreement. As might be expected, groups do not always agree. What is to be done? Like the first grade class who could not decide if their pet hamster was a male or female and resolved it by vote, we often try to reach agreement by voting without the benefit of outside data. This should be avoided.

Frequently, conflict comes from arguing about means, not ends. This separation of means and ends cannot be overemphasized. One strategy is to ask people to write down needs similar to this:

Current results	Possible means for resolving	Desired results
etc.	*etc.*	*etc.*

By being required to identify both "what is" and "what should be," the distinction between these outcome statements and the possible ways and means for getting from one to the other is preserved and formally required in the deliberations (Kaufman, 1976). The use of such an instrument will better help people differentiate between means and ends, and encourage the separation. When there is still conflict, an external resource person could help clarify any confusion between means and ends. Sometimes additional data is required to justify or refute a perceived gap and any disagreement concerning its existence or importance.

Another source of possible resolution is to remind each partner of the importance of the external referent in determining the existence and then the importance of a given perceived need.

There is usually a difference between "felt" (or perceived) needs and "actual" gaps. One is based upon personal observations and values; the other might have the additional component of external reality data.

In this partnership-based needs assessment model, it is suggested that both frames of reference be included.

$$\left.\begin{array}{l}\text{LEARNER-PERCEIVED NEEDS} \\ \\ \text{EDUCATOR-PERCEIVED NEEDS} \\ \\ \text{COMMUNITY-PERCEIVED NEEDS}\end{array}\right\} + \begin{array}{c}\text{SURVIVAL/CONTRIBUTION} \\ \text{REFERENT AND DATA}\end{array} = \text{NEEDS}$$

This multi-faceted effort includes both perceived needs and external reality. The probability of responsible, responsive determination of needs is increased.

This is not "perfect" methodology. There will be items which are not fully supportable, and those which will be under-represented. It is an approach to a problem, not the ultimate answer. Needs assessment should be a continuing, regular exercise, not a "one-shot" activity.

Needs change in response to a changing world. We should not lock ourselves into a single pass at the problem and the world it attempts to predict and to help.

Inductive and Deductive Aspects

In our world of science as applied to society and education, much attention is given to deductive logic and methods. Using this frame of reference, pieces of a puzzle are put together to form the whole picture. In educational planning and needs assessment, many models begin with goals and objectives which are already formulated. In this deductive mode, educational partners are required to put them in priority order and thus "complete the puzzle." This is a deductive model in that the result is deduced from an original frame of reference (the initial goals).

The model presented here suggests an *additional* (and riskier) aspect, one which has occupied sociologists and anthropologists for many years—induction. With induction, parts of the puzzle are added during the course of study and decision-making. Here the goals and objectives of education are not accepted "as is," but are only a starting point for consideration. New goals and objectives may be added, and old ones deleted or modified. With this approach, new needs may be discovered and included, and old ones reduced in priority or eliminated altogether.

Our current tendency to be preoccupied by deductive approaches to needs assessment and educational planning has led us to avoid, in some instances, the requirements for deep changes and new thrusts and directions in education. The approach presented in this book intends to include and build from the more usual deductive frame of reference by using and including induction as well.

Summary—Needs Assessment

The following are the general steps involved in getting ready for and conducting a needs assessment—regardless of the methods and means used to do each step. (Again, we are only talking about the "whats" of needs assessment, not the "hows.")

- DECIDE TO CONDUCT A NEEDS ASSESSMENT.
- IDENTIFY THE PARTNER GROUPS OF EDUCATORS, LEARNERS, AND COMMUNITY (SOCIETY).
- SELECT METHODS FOR INVOLVING THE PARTNER GROUPS.
- OBTAIN THE PARTNER GROUPS.
- HAVE EACH PARTNER GROUP IDENTIFY ITS CONCERNS WITH NEEDS ASSESSMENT AND OBTAIN COMMITMENT TO THE PROCESS.
- HAVE EACH PARTNER GROUP IDENTIFY NEEDS AS GAPS IN RESULTS, NOT GAPS IN PROCESSES OR TECHNIQUES.
- HAVE EACH PARTNER GROUP AGREE UPON NEEDS AND LIST THEM IN A NEEDS ASSESSMENT MATRIX. MAKE SURE THAT EACH GROUP FILLS IT OUT TO FAIRLY REPRESENT THE OTHER PARTNER GROUPS AS WELL.
- BRING THE GROUPS TOGETHER AND RECONCILE DIFFERENCES.
- PLACE NEEDS IN PRIORITY ORDER (USING AN EXTERNAL REFERENT SUCH AS THE SURVIVAL/ CONTRIBUTION MODEL).
- LIST NEEDS, IN PRIORITY ORDER, FOR RESOLUTION.
- BEGIN EDUCATIONAL SYSTEM PLANNING FROM THE IDENTIFIED AND AGREED-UPON NEEDS.

KEY POINTS

1. Getting people committed to a needs assessment is usually the most difficult part of doing a needs assessment.
2. The most useful common referent for a needs assessment is to results external to the agency sponsoring the assessment.

3. Most people have either overt or covert fears and apprehensions relative to a needs assessment. These are basic feelings and usually revolve around their own survival, although the concerns they voice may not be expressed in that way.
4. Helping people to help others usually is more motivating than scare tactics.
5. Everything is measurable, even if only on a nominal (naming) scale of measurement.
6. The scales of measurement are: nominal, ordinal, interval, and ratio.
7. The closer we are able to get our outcome measures to the interval scale of measurement, the more reliable and useful will be our planning.
8. Useful needs assessment will constantly relate identified needs to an external (Alpha-type) referent. A survival/contribution continuum is useful for this basic relation between organizational needs and societal ones.
9. Needs, once identified and substantiated with data, may be prioritized by asking the dual and simultaneous questions of "what does it 'cost' to meet the need?" and "what does it 'cost' to ignore the need?"
10. Disagreements among partners and partner groups usually come about over means, not ends.
11. This external type needs assessment uses both inductive *and* deductive elements. Most others are only deductive.
12. Needs may be placed in a 2 x 3 matrix (or need statement) which includes measurable outcome statements for "what is" and "what should be" for each of the educational partner groups of learners, educators, and community members.
13. Needs assessment is the critical first step in educational planning and accomplishment.
14. Needs assessment should be a continuous and on-going activity, not a one-time activity.

REFERENCES AND BIBLIOGRAPHY

Ausubel, D.P. *The psychology of meaningful verbal learning.* New York: Grune and Stratton, 1963.

Corrigan, R.E., and Associates. *System approach for education (SAFE).* Garden Grove, Calif.: Corrigan and Associates, 1974.

Drucker, P.F. *Effective executive.* New York: Harper and Row, 1967.

Drucker, P.F. *Management: Tasks, responsibilities, practices.* New York: Harper and Row, 1973.

Frankl, V.L. *Man's search for meaning: An introduction to logotherapy.* Boston: Beacon Press, 1962.

Getzels, J.W., and Guba, E.G. Role, role conflict, and effectiveness; an empirical study. *American Sociological Review,* 1957, *19,* 164-175.

Greenwald, H. *Direct decision therapy.* San Diego: EDITS, 1973.

Hersey, P., and Blanchard, K.H. *Management of organizational behavior: Utilizing human resources.* Third Edition. Englewood Cliffs, N.J.: Prentice-Hall, 1977.

Kaufman, R.A. System approaches to education—discussion and attempted integration. In Piele *et al.,* Part III of *Social and technological change: Implications for education.* Eugene, Oregon: University of Oregon, 1970.

Kaufman, R.A. *Educational system planning.* Englewood Cliffs, N.J.: Prentice-Hall, 1972.

Kaufman, R., Feldman, R., Snyder, E., and Coffey, W.C. *Human dimensions of school improvement.* Philadelphia: Research for Better Schools, 1975.

Kaufman, R.A., Corrigan, R.E., and Johnson, D.W. Toward educationa responsiveness to society's needs—A tentative utility model. *Journal of Socio-Economic Planning Sciences,* August 1969, *3.*

Kaufman, R. Package paralysis. *Educational Technology,* February 1977, *17*(2).

Kibler, R., and Bassett, R.E. In Briggs, L.E. (Ed.), *Instructional design: Principles and applications.* Englewood Cliffs, N.J.: Educational Technology Publications, 1977.

Lewin, K. Frontiers in group dynamics: Concept, methods, and reality in social science: Social equilibria and social change. *Human Relations,* June 1947, *1*(1).

Mager, R.F. *Preparing objectives for programmed instruction.* Palo Alto, Calif.: Fearon Publishers, 1961.

Mager, R.F. *Preparing instructional objectives.* Palo Alto, Calif.: Fearon Publishers, 1962. Second Edition, Belmont, California: Fearon Publishers, 1975.

Mager, R.F., and Pipe, P. *CRI: Criterion-referenced instruction.* Los Altos Hills, Calif.: Mager Associates, 1976.

Maslow, A.H. *Motivation and personality.* Second Edition. New York: Harper and Row, 1970.

Maslow, A.H. *Eupsychian management: A journal.* Homewood, Ill.: Dorsey Press, 1965.

Rogers, E.M. *Diffusion of innovations.* Glencoe, Ill.: The Free Press of Glencoe, 1962.

Rogers, C.L. *Freedom to learn.* Columbus, Ohio: Charles E. Merrill Publishing Company, 1969.

Stevens, S.S. Mathematics, measurement, and psychophysics. In Stevens, S.S. *Handbook of experimental psychology.* New York: John Wiley and Sons, 1951.

Chapter 9

NEEDS ASSESSMENT ACTIVITIES AND PROCEDURES: A GENERAL GUIDE TO THE ALPHA NEEDS ASSESSMENT

There is no one "correct" way to do a needs assessment. While it is tempting to give hard-and-fast rules and procedures, this would be a definite disservice to any who intend to do a needs assessment and who wish to use the resulting data for further educational planning and accomplishment. Each educational setting and situation is different. A kit or a set of specific guidelines and regulations is like a "one-size-fits-all" garment—it might loosely fit some or even many, but it rarely fits exactly.

If there is one thing we *do* know about human behavior, it is that there are individual differences. Each of us is different, and each of us requires at least "individually responsive education" (Kaufman, 1972). Individually responsive education is not the same as self-paced instruction. It is a process by which an individual entering an educational situation is individually diagnosed and an agreed-upon course of learning opportunities is selected. The individual then enters and exits from different learning situations based upon individual requirements and performance, not upon "administrative" requirements or managerial convenience.

So it is with a functional needs assessment—there should be a different one for each application. There might be some elements in common with other settings and applications; but the selection of tools, techniques, vehicles, instruments, and procedures should be based upon the unique characteristics and requirements of the community, schools, and mission, not upon what is available from other settings or other publishers. This is not to say that the

207

"wheel has to be reinvented" each time. Rather, one should identify the requirements for a needs assessment (even to determine first if a needs assessment is required or useful) *before* selecting the how-to-do-its. This is another instance of the usual confusion between means and ends. Before picking the needs assessment means, be sure you know the necessary ends, ideally the required outcomes.

This chapter will present some tools for and experiences with conducting a needs assessment, with particular emphasis upon the "external" variety. It will not provide a checklist or an educational recipe book for needs assessment. It will offer some guidelines and examples to help the serious individual design and conduct a needs assessment which will yield useful information.

Getting People Over the Initial Hurdle

In Chapter 8, some ways and means for helping people see the utility of conducting a needs assessment were presented, along with some conceptual models. We have found that understanding measurability and independent survival and contribution help the person who has genuine intellectual reservations about the process.

The concern about dehumanization is not an idle one, for most of us have witnessed the huckstering of some panacea or another without due consideration of the learner's present state or future requirements. The wary individual frequently wants ample assurance that this method will not be more of that same brutalization. In some cases, a seeming over-abundance of convincing will be required due to the many years of concern and experience. This is frequently the case.

There are, on the other hand, some people who will want to "charge ahead" immediately. These might be either very insightful and already convinced; they might be "early adopters" (E. Rogers); or they might represent people who will fail in the homestretch. Make sure that early supporters understand what they are supporting and why, so that they will not cause problems later in the process. Another frequently observed "type" is the one who will not even listen, let alone participate, in the needs assessment process. Greenwald (1973) typifies this type of individual as having a "differences" script—he or she has made a life decision to be different, no matter what the issue or context. You might want to point out the different types of people and the different stances they take towards life, and suggest that they might want to "decide" to change their approach in this instance—but this usually will not work. The would-be needs assessor simply has to accept a certain number of resisters as part of the problem of moving ahead, and then move ahead.

Another approach to individual involvement and group change is presented in a book by Research for Better Schools (Kaufman, Feldman, Snyder, and Coffey, 1975) which represents possible ways to encourage groups to change. There is some preliminary evidence that this approach to change in schools might be effective (Tebelskis, 1975). An introduction to this conceptual model, which is generic to organizations, may be reviewed in Kaufman (1976).

The toughest hurdle is the partner involvement, and each setting is different. The best advice is to be honest, open, trusting, and frank—and above all, be patient and non-belligerent. You are talking about change, possibly deep change, and most people are very wary of this.

Needs assessment is a good idea whose time has come. There are a number of impostors using the name, and there are surveys which charade as needs assessments. Let people know, gently and with data, what it is you are proposing, how it is different, and why you think it is better. Support your contentions with patience, understanding, rationality, and logic—and listen. It just might be that those who are interacting with you have some useful points and important objections. Needs assessment is, after all, a partnership-based, partnership-generated process. The only hard-and-fast requirements of this suggested model are that it must:

- distinguish between means and ends and focus open discrepancies in ends (outcomes); and
- use a referent external to the sponsoring or studied agency, especially referring to survival of the learners in the world to which they exit upon completion or release from the system under study.

One approach to possible partner groups is to make an initial presentation (with supplementary readings such as this work or others which carry the message you want delivered), have small groups discuss critical points, and then ask open and public questions as well as express concerns. The group and/or the leader may address these questions and concerns. This public exposure after individual and small group discussion frequently allows concerns to surface and encourages understanding of what is being proposed, and why.

Organizing into Work Groups

When the decision has been made to conduct the needs assessment, the next job is to constitute the working groups. This selection should be made only after a needs assessment plan and a set of milestones have been developed. One method for accomplishing this is to develop a system plan—a mission profile for conducting a needs assessment (see Chapter 2).

After agreeing upon a plan and a set of outcomes for that plan, representative groups should be formed. It is initially "easier" to form groups on the basis of "known friends and supporters" than to let representativeness, science, and objectivity take its course. But we recommend the latter. Groups should be formed on the basis of getting the job done *correctly,* not just expediently.

Some sort of stratified sample of each of the partner groups is recommended. Be sure that there is representation in proportion to the populations which the schools attempt to serve.

It is also tempting to form the groups of educators only, but this should also be resisted. Needs assessment is best a partnership-based effort and should include the perceptions and commitments of all the people to be served. While it is usually faster to get the needs assessment accomplished by "insiders" and let the other groups *react* to the plan, there will be a frequent confusion and breakdown when final decisions over selected needs are made. Drucker's concept of "transfer of ownership" is powerful, and transfer occurs most frequently with involvement and commitment. Include the partners in all activities; it will be worthwhile later in the process. All of the partner groups should designate leaders, and they should set for themselves a time schedule (based upon the overall program plan for the full needs assessment), along with a schedule of activities and products. They should then divide the work, including the identification of outcome gaps as well as the obtaining of data to support or reject each perceived need.

A coordinator from the school or district might be assigned to each group to be of assistance and perhaps to supply requested or required data. The coordinator should not do all of the work, or bully the group into what he or she thinks should be accomplished—the coordinator serves as a facilitator only. The coordinator might serve to remind the group of their basic commitments to needs as outcome gaps and to reference all needs to an external referent. Frequently, this might be accomplished by the coordinator's taking process-type statements and re-writing them into outcome-based statements. A possible example might be:

- Initial group-identified "need":

  Teachers do not have enough teaching resources and materials to teach English grammar effectively.

- Possible suggested substitute "need":

  Third grade performance on the criterion-referenced test on English grammar is below required levels on 19 of 33 criteria. The minimal level is 30 out of 33 as determined by analysis of skills necessary to get and keep a job in the community. Additionally, there are no learning materials available in the learning resource center or on order which will meet the criteria currently not being met.

By shifting the perceived need, initially keyed to resources and not to performance, back to (1) a measurable performance base, and (2) an external referent, the groups may see how it might be said more usefully, and learn some of the tools for framing useful need statements. A coordinator for each group can be useful and helpful if he/she does not do all the work and diminish the effectiveness of the partner-based model.

Obtaining Useful Need Statements

This has already been dealt with, partially in the previous section in terms of helping individuals in the partner groups frame need statements which are based upon outcome gaps and an external referent (outcomes).

This will be a continuing effort. Training the partners to state measurable objectives might also be useful. Mager's second edition of *Preparing Instructional Objectives* (1975) and Mager and Pipe's *Criterion-Referenced Instruction* (1976) are also useful. Additionally, Corrigan Associates' materials on *System Approach for Education (SAFE)* (1968) may be of assistance to such groups.

Help them to find themselves; do not do the work for them. One useful concept for obtaining measurable needs is that of using "indicators." Indicators are references to a domain which all will agree represents the array of desired behaviors or outcomes. An indicator of "increased love for learning" might be an increase in books taken out of the library during the period under study. An indicator of "ability to survive and contribute in the external world" might be an individual who gets and keeps a job for six months or more which would place him or her above the poverty level for that community during that period of time.

Indicators are not complete evidence of accomplishment, but are representative of the outcomes desired. By using indicators where total measures are not available, the group may settle upon needs more quickly and easily.

Additionally, indicators allow for our fallibility in identifying all of the important behaviors which constitute an educational enterprise. We cannot reasonably measure everything, so we reference those indicators which are, by agreement, important and representative.

A final suggestion in helping partners identify needs which are useful and valid is to point out that needs may first be identified in "loose" terms, and then increasingly "tightened" as more data is available. For example, one might start with a nominal scale statement (such as "Each learner will have basic skills in reading, writing, and computation") and then move into increasingly reliable measures—from nominal to ordinal ("Each learner will improve his/her mastery of reading, writing, and computation over and above the current level"), and from ordinal to interval or ratio ("Each learner will improve his/her number of criterion-referenced items by at least 30% on each of the tests of reading, writing, and computation before June first of each year").

By moving through increased reliability of measurement, the "cognitive dissonance" and stress might be lighter.

Also, be sure that each goal or outcome statement (such as the above examples) is, in fact, a *need* stated as an *outcome gap*, rather than just an objective or a status statement. Use the format suggested previously or derive one which fits the situation to which you are applying the needs assessment. Many efforts tend to omit the actual statement of the gap (the two polar positions of "what is" and "what should be") and present either one or the other.

Remind the partners that the needs assessment process is designed to identify the gaps (polar positions) so that detailed requirements and possible methods and means may be identified and selected to close those gaps. If the gaps are not identified, the educators who will be responsible for the successful planning and accomplishment will not be able to adequately build the "learning bridge" between current results and desired or required results.

Finally, encourage the groups and individuals to be their own best critics. Get the materials and statements out to the group and let them critique their work themselves—it is better to be constructively critiqued by your friends in a controlled situation than to be destructively attacked by your enemies in public.

Self-analysis and critique can be the entry door to objective and useful statements of need. Again, encourage all participants to leave pet solutions and their egos outside of the needs assessment planning room doors.

Starting Places for Outcomes

Where do goals and objectives come from? Frequently, schools and school districts have "objectives" (usually goals, using the outcome taxonomy formulation) which most groups see as being a natural starting place. Unfortunately, most of these intended outcomes take some form of the statement:

"Develop each child to his/her own capacity."

This, of course, is not much help. It does not define either "each child" or "own capacity." It does indicate, however, that the school is in the behavior change business.

A number of kits are available which supply schools and would-be needs assessors with ready-made "objectives." (Witkin, 1975 and 1977, reviewed many of the materials available at the time of this writing.) The disadvantage of the kit approach is that the objectives are frequently framed in terms of processes or how-to-do-it variables (such as "provide more art experiences" or "provide more in-service training for teachers") and are usually addressed to internal needs, not external or Alpha-type outcome indicators. Also, kits do not readily allow old goals and objectives to be easily removed (although they may be reduced in priority); and, more importantly, they do not easily allow new goals and objectives to be added. As part of this problem, new outcome requirements which might be unique to the school or school district may not be added to the considerations due to the perceptual boundary frequently put around a kit.

Pre-existing goals and objectives, once they are selected for use, tend to become static and "institutionalized." We know that our world is changing rapidly; and any needs assessment process should be open, flexible, and above all responsive to the needs of our society and community—both currently and in the future. On the other hand, the collection of new goals and objectives can be both time consuming and not fruitful.

When a community decides to derive new goals and objectives (this has been called an "inductive" needs assessment approach; Kaufman, 1972), there can be a great flurry of activity and large amounts of data collected; and the process of converting the data to information can be costly, time consuming, and often disappointing. Disappointment frequently comes when the data yield a profile which closely approximates the old seven Cardinal Principles of Education or the Pennsylvania State Department of Education-Educational Testing Service "Ten Proposed Goals of Education." Put another way, citizens, when asked about the goals of education, tend to reproduce that which they were taught.

The inductive approach does provide the salutary effect of getting the educational partners working together and communicating, so it might have a unifying and healing effect on a community—not a small dividend indeed.

So, like many other things in our lives, the deductive (taking existing goals and objectives) and the inductive (building and collecting your own) each have advantages and disadvantages. There is no clear choice between the two—each should be considered on the basis of the characteristics of the community. If community building is necessary, then the inductive might be a wise selection. If time is critical, the deductive might be the logical selection. Both methods have been used in districts throughout the United States, and there are those who are committed to either one or the other.

The deductive approach is easier to accomplish, takes less time to begin and complete, and causes less confusion among the educational partners. When this approach is utilized, several sources of preliminary goals and objectives should be reviewed and considered for inclusion, including ones from various kits from the school district involved, and from published objectives (such as the Pennsylvania/ETS goals, and perhaps the indicators supplied by Bucks County, Pennsylvania and those derived for Temple City, California by Kaufman, English, *et al.*—a review of the literature will turn up a number of possible candidates), plus the possible addition of an external survival/contribution set of criteria (see Chapter 8). When using this deductive mode, sensitivity should be maintained to the possibilities for new outcome criteria and areas and the deletion of nonfunctional ones. Also, operationally define existing outcome statements as necessary by translating them into non-process statements and writing performance criteria for them so that they are in the form of a measurable objective.

When using the "inductive" approach, keep the partners from making "process-type" statements. If necessary, take their perceived need statements and translate them into performance objectives.

A third mode might be considered, a "mixed" mode where both inductive and deductive elements are included. With this approach, a set of deduced objectives can be presented to the partner groups and then be culled for further consideration, deletion, and "gaps." When gaps occur (perhaps based upon previously collected survival/contribution data), new objectives may be generated and then included in the total array for consideration.

There are, in summary, three possible methods for harvesting objectives:

- deductive
- inductive
- mixed

The deductive mode takes existing goals and objectives and ranks them in terms of preference or criticality. The inductive mode requires that outcome requirements be generated for the school or district for ranking, and the mixed mode uses suitable portions of each.

It is suggested that the "mixed" mode has the greatest applicability to most needs assessment applications.

Taking the Role of the Other—A Key to Responsiveness

While each partner group is identifying needs, it is suggested that they also fill out need statements for each of the other partner groups as well.

Taking the role of the "other" is a key sociological concept which helps to promote mutual understanding and responsiveness. Most people tend to see themselves as the center of their own universe, and other people and other problems frequently take a secondary position. This is not appropriate for producing a functional needs assessment. In order to better assure that there is mutuality in the efforts and results, consideration of all groups is important. Thus, having each group execute the form for all groups allows for a common referent to be identified and presented.

Getting a Common Statement of Needs

After each group has completed their 2 x 3 needs assessment matrix (Chapter 8)—or the equivalent—it is time to get the groups together.

Any one of several procedures is appropriate as long as there is an atmosphere of trust, listening, and joint productivity. This is not to be a confrontation or an arguing session. It is designed for determining jointly agreed-upon needs, and it is not a contest of wills! It should be a contest of data, or rationality, and of logic.

After each group has reviewed the need statements of the other group (or groups, if it is to be other than a sequential process), then each might list agreements (matches) and disagreements (mismatches). The matches may be sorted into a single pile for later use, the mismatches into a second pile for discussion and hopeful resolution. A third category contains unique items.

First, examine the mismatches and make sure they both (1) speak to the same issue, and (2) represent gaps in outcomes which are supported by data. If they are not speaking to the same issue (or gap), then they may be treated not as a disagreement, but as an additional category for prioritization. If there is conflicting data or no data, then the approach is to supply responsive data for reconciling the differences. If one of the positions (or both) is speaking to process gaps (e.g., teaching methods, teaching aids, money, etc.), then it might be useful to translate the presented statements into outcome gap statements for consideration and possible acceptance by the partners.

A key to success here is sensitivity to what is intended to be communicated rather than what did get stated. Frequently, partner groups are trying to get to an important point, but do not know how to communicate properly. A coordinator or needs assessment manager can help by "translating" and probing for intent as well as for meaning.

Disagreements. Surely there will be areas of disagreement, and those should not allow the process to come to a halt unless it is clear to all that further progress will be destructive. Value questions are important and some people have concerns in these areas. The final arbiter of differences is the law, including the Constitution of our country. When in doubt, read the law.

Remember that most disagreements are about process, not about outcomes. Disagreements concerning outcomes may represent possible alternative paths or tracks for learners based upon individual or parental choice—if the choices are legal and not mutually destructive.

A needs assessment can identify alternative learning and performance pathways for a school system, and these opportunities should be seized upon and utilized—if the data supports them.

The final ranking of needs should be made on the basis of consensus—voting is most usual. Each individual may rank-order the perceived importance of each need and then all judgments may be pooled. Some other alternatives are covered in later chapters.

A final needs assessment summary matrix should be constructed and a report made which includes the names of all people who have participated. This summary document is the beginning of the next efforts to identify ways and means for closing the gaps—the gateway to educational success.

KEY POINTS

1. There is no one correct needs assessment model or needs assessment procedure. Let the model fit the application, rather than the other way around.
2. Be patient and not patronizing of needs assessment partner groups. They are concerned and deserve to be listened to and heard. Good suggestions should be incorporated.
3. Some participants will change right away, and some will never change. Don't strive to be perfect, and do not demand the same from them. Nothing is 100%. Do what you can and do it the best way possible.
4. Make sure that all work has the referents of external survival and possible contribution, and that needs are listed as gaps in performance (outcomes), not processes.
5. Groups should be representative of the populations involved in and impacted by the schools. Stratification should be attempted on the basis of important variables.
6. A coordinator might be assigned each group. The coordinator should not bully the group nor do all of their work.
7. Groups may be helped frequently by supplying required information and perhaps by translating process gaps into outcome gaps for the groups to consider.
8. Indicators are useful ways to represent an array of possible outcomes without listing all of the outcomes. They are agreed-upon "short-hand" which is useful in a needs assessment.
9. A needs assessment matrix should be executed by each group and include the perceived needs of each of the partner groups, not just their own.
10. Disagreements are usually related to processes, not outcomes. When conflict occurs, look first at this possibility.
11. A common need statement should result from a partnership-based needs assessment procedure.

REFERENCES AND BIBLIOGRAPHY

Corrigan, R.E. *System approach for education (SAFE).* Garden Grove, Calif.: R.E. Corrigan Associates, 1974.

Greenwald, H. *Direct decision therapy.* San Diego: EDITS, 1973.

Kaufman, R. *Educational system planning.* Englewood Cliffs, N.J.: Prentice-Hall, Inc., 1972.

Kaufman, R. Organizational improvement: A review of models and an attempted synthesis. *Group and Organization Studies,* December 1976, *1*(4).

Kaufman, R., Feldman, R., Snyder, E., and Coffey, W.C. *Human dimensions of school improvement.* Philadelphia: Research for Better Schools, 1975.

Mager, R.F. *Preparing instructional objectives.* Second Edition. Belmont, Calif.: Fearon Publishers, 1975.

Mager, R.F., and Pipe, P. *CRI: Criterion-referenced instruction.* Los Altos Hills, Calif.: Mager Associates, 1976.

Rogers, E.M. *Diffusion of innovations.* Glencoe, Ill.: The Free Press of Glencoe, 1962.

Tebelskis, A. *The effects of an intervention workshop on the attitude change of personnel in a school district.* Unpublished doctoral dissertation, United States International University, 1975.

Witkin, B.R. *An analysis of needs assessment techniques for educational planning at state, intermediate, and district levels.* Alameda County School Department, Hayward, California, May 1975.

Witkin, B.R. Needs assessment kits, models, and tools. *Educational Technology,* November 1977, *17*(11), 5-18.

Chapter 10

CONDUCTING THE BETA
NEEDS ASSESSMENT

The Beta needs assessment (see Chapter 3) has been the most common type to be used in the schools. It begins with the assumption that the current structure of the schools and the basic approaches are sound. Minor adjustments are considered possible and probably desirable; however, no radical changes are foreseen in goals or roles.

Needs assessment becomes a focusing exercise which a school system or a school staff utilizes to more fully exploit a rational approach to planning. Beta assessments are therefore less potentially threatening to the participants, since no radical swings away from current practices are anticipated, but rather "fine tuning" of the status quo.

An example of a Beta assessment is provided to assist schools in developing plans for utilizing this type of needs assessment. Schools or school systems should know, however, that much of the *power* of the Alpha assessment has been traded away and that a great deal of time and effort may be involved in "fine tuning" without major changes. On the other hand, the Beta assessment allows a staff to develop a conscious and collective group identity in addition to a classroom identity. It assists in creating a dialogue about further change that may then later involve an Alpha assessment.

The Case of Cedar Creek Elementary School
Cedar Creek Elementary School was built in the early 1970's as an open space school (but with folding doors). The original

principal was not really sure how to develop an open school
environment and left it to the teachers to discover the best
methods to make it work. Over a period of three years the
teachers went back to self-contained classrooms almost
exclusively. A few still traded classes now and then; but for the
most part, Cedar Creek was fairly traditional.

A new principal arrived with the retirement of the old and
began reading the literature about Cedar Creek published by the
school district. Her observations of the school and the literature
just didn't seem to jell. The literature described the original Cedar
Creek almost from the architect's specifications. Upon
questioning, the staff began to reveal the past history of the
school's regression and its insistence upon process objectives, such
as individualized instruction as a goal in itself. No one would
admit what was really going on at the school. Furthermore, there
was no faculty identity to speak of. Teachers were identified as
"liberal" or "conservative" by community definition or
reputation.

The new principal, Dr. Sheila Murphy, obtained permission to
hold a staff retreat away from the school. She prepared the staff
by developing some materials which described rudimentary
planning models and assumptions, as well as alternatives in
elementary staffing, organization, and instruction. With the
faculty senate, she developed a two-day agenda of what was going
to be produced as the result of the retreat. The major product was
to be the first draft of a long-range plan which ultimately would
be submitted to the superintendent for consideration.

The first day of the retreat was spent developing criteria to
describe Cedar Creek in objective terms. This proved to be
extremely trying for teachers, who had many problems describing
what they did. Finally, the following model was agreed upon as
useful.

Key Variables of Cedar Creek

Content   —the curriculum, the description of the "what"
            that was supposed to occur in classrooms.
Process   —the method or modes, "how" the what was
            translated.

Structure	—the characteristics, motivations, expectations of the students at Cedar Creek.
Faculty	—the characteristics, motivations, expectations of the faculty at Cedar Creek.

The first day the staff described the continua which seemed to be possible, eliminating a detailed list of student and faculty descriptions at that time. For the continuum of "content," they felt that the most structured aspect would be a curriculum guide which rigidly prescribed what, how, when, and where something was to be taught; at the other end of this continuum was almost "pure interaction," where the curriculum was merely the experiential base of the teacher and the student interacting together.

The teachers agreed that modes of process varied from regular teacher lecturing to pupil independent study. It was generally agreed that once a teacher was totally out of the picture, in any sense of the word, the activity involved was not the school's responsibility. Under structure, the staff felt that at one end of the continuum was the single-teacher-per-class concept or self-contained classroom, and at the other the open block.

After these indices were agreed upon, small groups were formed for each, and they attempted to describe as objectively as possible what existed at Cedar Creek. Each group then reported to the assembled group and everyone checked the group's perception. The "content" group described Cedar Creek with the following short statements:

1. There was a written guide in math but it was not too detailed.
2. Various teachers used their own guides or outlines in language arts, social studies, and science.
3. The use of basal readers constituted a curriculum.
4. The library could be considered a curriculum or examples of curricula.
5. Instructional kits in spelling and reading were also examples of curricula or "what."
6. Games, simulations, and enrichment materials were curricula.

The sum total of this description was that the curriculum of Cedar Creek was in reality a potpourri of approaches, kits, books, guidelines, and pet biases of various staff members. The staff was shocked to see that there was no "curriculum" at the school. They were clearly anxious about the degree of dispersion and duplication in the curriculum. They were unaware of the degree to which there was no real plan that instruction was to follow.

Under structure, the staff had no trouble agreeing that the dominant organizational plan was the single-teacher-per-class concept. Under process, the staff identified the lecture or teacher-directed class activity as approximately 35-40 percent of the total time spent on instruction. Between 40-50 percent was teacher-directed small group/seminar work. Five to ten percent of the total time was spent on independent study and 10-15 percent on tutorial (teacher-student) work. These figures were reached only after long dialogue. At this point, teachers were also surprised to find the tremendous variations in methodology actually present in the school.

This conclusion finished the first day's activities and the staff adjourned. The second day the staff defined where the system should be going in curriculum, methods, and structure. After prolonged debate, it was agreed that all of these things were means to ends and that the staff had spent no time defining where the school should be. How would they know what was an appropriate combination of curriculum and small group activity? When did Cedar Creek *arrive,* i.e., reach its potential or some optimum point?

Dr. Murphy put it to the staff this way:

> We have been searching for some way to know what was best. Was independent study and small-group activity superior to whole-class instruction? We read various books which extolled the virtues of pupil spontaneity without ever telling us why or how such methods were to be deemed effective or ineffective. We have spent hours in the faculty lounge and at faculty meetings debating what I would call *process* with little or no attention to outcomes. There is no way we can know what is most appropriate until we have data from two other sources. Those are outcomes, that is, results expected and information about our students. We have the information about our students, but Cedar Creek has no result-oriented statements. This series of statements would tell us what students would be expected to know, feel, and do at the

conclusion of their educational experience at Cedar Creek. Until we specify that, I don't believe we will be able to make much progress.

The staff agreed and set to work in three groups to define the required skills, knowledges, and attitudes. Recognizing that these were somewhat artificial domains, they wrote the following expected learner behaviors:

Skills

1. The student should be able to communicate effectively in writing and speaking, and should be able to engage properly in listening and reading.
2. The student should be able to communicate via creative expression in the arts.
3. The student should know where to go to obtain desired information.
4. The student should know how to make decisions by engaging in synthesis and analysis and how to follow through on such decisions.
5. The student should be able to work cooperatively and independently as the situation may require.

Knowledges

1. The student should be able to understand basic concepts in the human disciplines such as the social sciences, sciences, art, and music.
2. The student should understand and practice good health habits.
3. The student should understand how to be an active citizen in our society.
4. The student should possess awareness of different values and the components forming his or her own value system.
5. The student should know how to make aesthetic judgments and what criteria to use in making such judgments.

Attitudes

1. The student should show respect for others and the feelings and ideas of others.
2. The student should indicate an active curiosity about himself or herself and life.
3. The student should be responsible and/or assume responsibility for his or her own judgments and actions.

4. The student should be adaptive and flexible to changing conditions.
5. The student should possess a good feeling about himself/herself so that he/she believes that he/she "matters" as a person in his/her own right.

Cedar Creek staff were pleased with their work and felt that they could "get on" with the planning process. However, when it was pointed out that the goals would not provide very much direction for teachers until they became more specific, resistance was encountered to further specificity. One group of teachers felt that the remainder of the decisions should be left up to the staff and that to further delineate outcomes was dehumanizing and stultifying. Another group did not so much disagree but felt that there was not enough time to really do a good job on this and that more time and energy was necessary. The last group felt that more specific definitions were required and were apparently ready to undertake it at that time.

At this point Dr. Murphy interjected:

> Yesterday I sensed some of you were uneasy about the degree to which we as a school did not provide a more uniform and concerted push towards educating children. I thought I heard some of you express your surprise at the lack of an articulated curriculum in almost any area. How can a curriculum be coordinated effectively if we don't know what it's supposed to do? What is to be coordinated? It seems to me that all we can coordinate is the amount of time you spend on various topics and subjects. But without further delineation, we still don't know very much about what we are doing. Under these circumstances, what passes for learning and progress is subjectively and individually determined by each of you. If you were all of the same mind (heaven forbid!) we could let our case rest. But we aren't of the same mind. As a school, we have some responsibility for being sure that our students do learn and that we help them learn in the most efficient way we can. One way it seems to me we do that is to "get our act together" about what and how we go about this matter. I don't know how we'll do this if we don't get more specific.

While some were still unhappy, they did agree that it was

necessary to continue the refinement of the future-oriented learner objectives. However, more time was really necessary.

At this time the school counselor, Dr. Harry Brevard, presented some figures about the current graduating class of the system's high school. He reeled off the following statistics to a stunned group of teachers:

1. 38% of the incoming class of freshmen at the high school did not eventually graduate.
2. 18% of the girls in the incoming class of freshmen dropped out of school prior to graduation because they were pregnant. Only 2% of these were married.
3. As a result of administering the state's minimum competency exams in reading and math, the high school discovered that 37% failed the reading and 41% failed the math. Furthermore, the high school had no reading or remedial math programs.
4. The number of school suspensions rose dramatically until the eleventh grade when the dropout rate reduced it to about 2% in the senior year for boys.
5. In a recent confidential questionnaire on the use of alcohol, over 86% of the students indicated that they had had a drink of some sort. 29% indicated that they drank regularly and 14% indicated that they became intoxicated regularly; 4% indicated that they drank while in school!
6. The number of students in advanced foreign language, math, and science classes was down 21% over three years.
7. The cost to the school of vandalism was over $2000.00 in a three-month period last year.
8. According to the State Welfare Department, the number of families receiving ADC (aid to dependent children) was up by 15% in the last two years in the community.
9. Over the last three years the high school experienced its first actual suicide and there were at least four attempted suicides.
10. The number of divorced parents is up by 11% in two years.
11. Marijuana smoking in the school is rampant. Restrooms are clogged between periods with smokers.
12. Four teachers have been assaulted in the last year. One was in a hospital for two weeks recovering from a scuffle with a violent student.

Dr. Brevard then commented:

I've sat listening to your discussion about the good things you do for your pupils. But let me tell you that by the time your

students get into high school, it's too late. I've worked at the high
school and I know. Where are those good health habits? Where
are the positive self-concepts? Where is the respect for each other
and the teachers? Where are the basic understandings in communication skills? Without being condemnatory, I think the deficits
are cumulative; that is, they start here. Maybe we don't see them,
maybe we don't create them, but they start here.

Dr. Brevard's comments evoked a heated response which was
very defensive in tone. Finally, however, the staff began to focus
on their outcomes again. Said one teacher, "I guess after hearing
Dr. Brevard's comments I'd like to go back and look at what we
really mean when we say the students should be able to
communicate effectively in reading or writing. What are the real
standards we use? I gather from some of the comments that we
really don't know. Are some of our students being shortchanged? I
find this matter unpleasant, but it demands an answer!"

Dr. Murphy indicated that the use of anecdotal data was fairly
common to get a staff to examine some of its own behavior and
that some of the data was suspect for one reason or another.
Furthermore, the use of standardized tests was somewhat controversial and had built-in assumptions about failure which she found
personally offensive. Nonetheless, the data should be examined.
While the staff did not disagree, one elementary teacher was
overheard remarking, "It's those secondary teachers who are more
interested in their *subjects* than in the kids. When we have them,
they perform. When they get to that high school, they get turned
off and they tune out."

To this Dr. Brevard responded, "You know I've heard that so
often that I began to believe it. But if you work at a high school,
don't tell the teachers there they don't care about kids. Don't tell
the teachers there that kids don't count or what they think or feel
isn't important. We have as much rigidity in our curriculum at the
high school as at Cedar Creek. We just don't have the kids go to
separate teachers, that's all."

Dr. Murphy also commented, "Those kinds of simplistic
responses don't help us much. They excuse us from any
responsibility. The crux of this matter is, it seems to me, how can
we shape our objectives so that we don't reinforce those trends
and perhaps reverse some of them."

Another teacher remarked, "I'm as concerned as anybody here about what we're doing and what the data Dr. Brevard has presented really says about us. But I don't know how to plug this data into current practice. It doesn't help me make decisions everyday. What can I do differently? What should I do differently?

Dr. Murphy responded:

> I think as a staff we've got to do a number of things simultaneously. First, we have to engage in some systematic effort to define our school outcomes. These must reflect the data sources that Dr. Brevard has mentioned; otherwise, we can't even claim to be in the same school system and we might as well have our own. Second, we've got to further define what we're doing in the various areas in this school. I'd call that an exercise in curriculum mapping. Then after we make our outcome statements more specific and we really know where we are, then I think we can make the bridge between what we are now doing and what we should be doing. We ought to be able to make some adjustments in the content as well as in the process, though I think everybody is agreed that we will stay self-contained, at least for the next several years.

"When do we find time to map the curriculum?" asked one teacher. "What if the grade level chairpersons met each day with their teams to discuss what they were doing in each subject area of the curriculum until they finished it?" said Dr. Murphy. "Since our curriculum is literally all over the wall, it's going to take some time to find out what it really is."

Said one teacher, "That will take too long. It will take us over a year to find out what the curriculum is."

"Maybe with a little imagination about the format and some division of labor we could cut the time down," said Dr. Murphy. "I think what we have to do is decide the level of specificity required and then design a format which produces only that level of information. By doing that, we follow the idea of parsimony, covering the most ground with the least effort."

"I would volunteer to work on a format, Sheila," said Dr. Brevard. The staff felt that that would be an excellent approach and that as soon as the format was devised, they would proceed with mapping the existing curriculum as content and also work on refining the objectives or products of instruction. Somewhere in the future the two would be brought together, the desired outcomes with the actual scope of things that were now in or out of the real curriculum.

The Follow-up

Dr. Brevard did design the format and it required teachers to sketch out in rough terms the content they covered in each area and also asked them to break out that content in the cognitive, affective, and psychomotor domains. The mapping took the year as anticipated. The committee on refining the school's outcomes also took the year, submitting several revisions to the staff along the way as well as involving selected parents and members of the instructional staff at the central office. Drafts were also circulated among the principals of the middle and high school and their staff for comment. That process got those schools thinking about where they picked up their instructional programs in terms of the elementary school. In short, it was a forcing-function for the secondary system to examine its own assumptions about what students had or did not have in the way of skills, knowledges, and attitudes.

How did the school make decisions in the interim? All schools make programmatic/allocational decisions about what should be done, how, and by whom. Without firm data, most of the decisions are based largely on precedent, rules, or traditions. However, the data by Dr. Brevard did result in programmatic adjustments being made by individual teachers. Both content and procedures underwent changes without formal instructions from anyone. Teachers became convinced that in the interim period they could make adjustments in the content, structure, and process to work toward alleviating the problems detailed by Brevard. This cost no money but was a spinoff of the process of involvement.

The weakness of the response was as before; it was sporadic and uneven. Matters of effectiveness could not be determined and were not undertaken. Methods which had proven effective before were used again with no information. Some teachers spent more time than others. The programmatic response was very mixed. If there was a "treatment," it was impossible to really say what it was; but awareness and action did follow.

As the school principal, Dr. Sheila Murphy spent considerable time briefing parents about what was going on and why the staff was so concerned about establishing outcomes. The community response was positive. In a public report to the board, Dr. Murphy commented:

> It's true that we have a lot of data at our disposal in the school system. Most school systems have more data than they really use. We don't use it because first we can't relate it to an overall collective set of outcomes. We tend to respond individually or idiosyncratically. While this is desirable, it is also haphazard. We are trying to learn how to respond collectively. To respond collectively as a school, we have to learn how to think as a faculty and not just as a group of individuals. This takes time and patience. We're learning how. We're working on describing the existing curriculum rather than assuming the curriculum somewhat includes a set of desired outcomes. We're also working on defining where it is we want to go. When we have both, and we expect to at the end of the year, we will proceed to translate those outcomes into program analysis. We will take out tests, those in the central testing program, and those we use at the school, and match them to the desired outcomes. When we have the gaps firmly identified, we will locate them on our curriculum map. After they are located, we will make the necessary adjustments in curriculum coverage, instructional methods, and scheduling to accommodate and close those same gaps.

When Dr. Murphy was asked what the staff was going to do in the interim, she responded:

> We will use our best professional judgment in order to anticipate as best as we can. After all, we have gained some wisdom after being in the business as long as we have. If we've been lucky, 50 percent of what we have been doing should be right anyway. We think we're better than that. From this we expect no revolutions, but we do expect some change. We will come back to the superintendent and the board with a set of recommendations based upon our analysis.

When the superintendent of schools pressed her for more specifics, Dr. Murphy responded:

> What we will do this year is to create a series of skill cards which will follow a student through his or her study at Cedar Creek. On this card the skills of reading, speaking, and listening are identified. The teacher will note the book used and whatever mastery level the student has obtained. This will be passed on to the next teacher who at least will have some idea of the level of exposure if nothing else. We hope that as the actual assessment takes place, the level of specificity will be vastly improved on these cards. This is really a primitive monitoring system so that information about the student does not "slip through the cracks" of the collective memory of our staff. So much time is spent finding out where students are that we think this crude system will greatly help us. Also, we want to stress health in a new and different way than before to form concepts about the body earlier, both to combat drug abuse and to gain new awareness of human sexuality and growth. This will occur, of course, at the upper elementary grades. About positive self-concept we have engaged a consultant from the school of education, Dr. Peter Graff, the noted specialist on children's thinking. We believe that after several workshops we can develop some practical methods to improve and assess this element. It would perhaps be nice to stop school and wait until we know that all of this will be on target when the gap analysis is completed. However, school goes on and we will make the most intelligent guesses we can. We have faith in the process that incorrect responses will be weeded out anyway as we recycle to come closer to our expected outcomes.

At this point Margaret Thatcher, a long time teacher at Cedar Creek, observed to the board:

> You know, I've been at Cedar Creek for over seven years. I was there when old Harold Bowling started it. I helped design the building. Today I think perhaps we are on the road to really understanding in a concrete way what we thought might be possible but couldn't really pull off. We didn't know how to make it work. We didn't know that if you want to make improvements you have to have some idea of what eventually the thing is supposed to do. We were just focused wrong. I think this process will finally put us on the right track but it won't be easy. There aren't any quick and easy answers. We've got to create the

indices to assess and we have to be able to locate them in our curriculum. I'm optimistic that we can do it and that things will be better as a result.

Several other teachers also felt the same way and the board thanked Dr. Murphy for her presentation.

Cedar Creek Today

Today the Cedar Creek Elementary School is still largely self-contained. A curriculum map has been constructed on which the skills, knowledges, and attitudes for each grade level have been distributed for each teacher. Parents also have copies of the map. The map has been revised in keeping with the delineation of outcomes adopted by the school. There are approximately 50 outcomes in the basic curricular subject areas. The recordkeeping system mentioned by Dr. Murphy has been updated and follows the map. The cards are open to parents at any time.

A basic skills learning center has been constructed in which children with special difficulties can be referred for special help during the school day. It is staffed by two resource teachers and some teacher aides.

There were substantive changes in the science, math, and health curricula. The middle school has begun to more closely correlate its curriculum with that of Cedar Creek. Once the outcomes were more precisely specified, curriculum coordination became much easier for the middle school staff. They know now what skills, knowledges, and attitudes the students actually possess. They understand the general sequence which produced the outcomes. They have seen the relationship between what children learn at the elementary school and what they can do to adequately prepare them for the high school.

A special reading project on peer teaching has been instituted for children with poor self-concepts, and the staff regularly assesses growth in this dimension. As a result of developing a precision-oriented picture of pupil growth, the staff has made a quicker adjustment to adapting its program to the learning disabled child and the gifted as well. The differentiation of the program began with a precise description of what was required to obtain the outcomes.

Dr. Sheila Murphy summarized the progress of Cedar Creek this way:

> Today we know where students are and where they are expected to be. We have begun to build a service support system to assist students who are not learning and who have already learned. We are beginning to see that we can only go so far in the traditional structure. We are bumping into limitations in terms of the actual skill differences within the teaching staff and the way the structure prohibits us from really using staff very effectively. Whether we take the next step or not remains to be seen.
>
> However, we have developed a new esprit de corps. We are together as never before. We have acquired greater insights about our own skills as professionals and our limitations. We have learned that defining *minimum* outcomes can become the ceiling of our expectations if we are not careful. We had to learn that the outcomes are really survival skills and that once survival is more or less assured, there is much more to be learned to make life rich and meaningful. We think that the outcomes applicable to all students should account for no more than 40-60 percent of the entire curriculum anyway. But we had to learn that as we went. You can't allow the initial benchmarks to become pre-emptive of your entire program. I believe after two or three more years of making program adjustments toward the outcomes desired we will see how much power our existing program and assumptions really have. It wouldn't surprise me if we have to begin again, but that's a bridge we cross then. For now, we are moving rationally and progressively in a way we have not experienced before and it is rewarding.*

Another School System Beta Assessment

A new Assistant Superintendent for Planning position was created in the Haugan City Schools and filled by Dr. James Feron. His first task was to undertake a needs assessment. A conversation with the superintendent and the Board president convinced him that an Alpha assessment was unfeasible. The system was not interested in examining key organizational or political assump-

---

*Some material in this section was taken from "Hillside Elementary School in the Future: A Document to Initiate Staff Dialogue," Hastings Public Schools, Hastings-on-Hudson, New York (March, 1976). For the most part the account is hypothetical.

tions. Therefore, he asked his secretary to obtain a copy of Board policies in which the goals or objectives of the system were stated. After two days, the secretary returned with the following statement.

> *Philosophy of Education of the Haugan City Schools*
>
> We, the Board of Education, do set forth these statements as a comprehensive philosophy of education by which the city schools are to be administered. We believe they are the guiding principles of this Board and the people of Haugan.
>
> (1) The schools are for the purpose of creating universal brotherhood and good will toward men.
> (2) The schools are places in which every child has a right to feel secure, to be valued in his or her own right, and to find worthiness.
> (3) Children are not adults; they must find enrichment and nurturing sources from empathetic teachers.
> (4) The purpose of teaching is to stimulate the student to become a better person, to seek wisdom where it may be found, and to draw forth from the student the best of which he or she may be capable.
> (5) The function of curriculum is to present to the child in some logical and accepted order the truths of the universe as people have come to know them.
> (6) The purpose of obtaining an education is to become a functional citizen within a democracy and to treasure and perpetuate a democracy.

Dr. Feron was dismayed. The goals were really a mixup of means and ends in which the schools were treated as ends and what they should be doing as the purposes of education. The philosophy was so broad as to provide no real direction for the system. Dr. Feron brought up the philosophy of education at the superintendent's administrative cabinet. It was met with amusement by some. Others did not know of its existence. Said one senior administrator, "Everyone knows that they were purposely stated rather broadly because it enables us to do anything we think should be done."

When Dr. Feron asked if that was its purpose, he was told by the superintendent that the "philosophy" was passed by the previous board who could not agree on much of anything and that it took them two years to put anything to paper. Furthermore, he was reluctant to regenerate this kind of discussion because the board had more pressing matters before it and they would say that the old board already did that.

However, Dr. Feron did obtain permission from the superintendent to conduct a limited field study of the effectiveness of the "philosophy." First, he put together a brief questionnaire. Basically, it asked about 400 teachers to indicate how the philosophy of the board of education influenced their teaching in the schools. He asked 35 principals the same question. The overwhelming response was that most had never seen it; those that had felt it didn't do much for them. Some indicated that they were guided by it.

Jim Feron took the responses which indicated the philosophy was utilized and spent some time interviewing. His first interview was with a department chairperson of math at the junior high school level. He interviewed him during his "prep period."

"Mr. Pearson, you indicated in your response that you found the board's philosophy of education useful in the conduct of your department."

"That's right Dr. Fearon."

"I have a copy of it here. Could you look it over and tell me how you use it."

"Ok, let's see. I take the first principle, you know, the brotherhood one. I don't allow any of my teachers to create permanent instructional groups, you know, tracking. I really don't believe that tracking leads to the creation of universal brotherhood and good will."

"Oh, you interpret the first principle as that which would prohibit any differentiation between learners?"

"Not really, any differentiation which led to feelings that we weren't really brothers."

"I saw the grades posted for the quarterly Algebra exams on the office door, Mr. Pearson. Wouldn't that tend to create some ill will?"

"No, on the contrary, we feel that that meets the board's second goal, making the child feel secure."

"But what about the students who received D's and F's? Their names are right up there for everyone to see."

"We believe that security comes from knowing your limitations."

"Don't some of the students feel badly about that?"

"Well, you know, they have to learn how to deal with that. That's part of learning how to become a functional citizen." James Feron left and interviewed an elementary teacher who believed that part of creating a "universal brotherhood" was conducting daily "Glasser groups" and values clarification. The teacher also felt that any kind of grading of students was a violation of Board policy on making students feel "valued." Still another teacher gave weekly quizzes because that was part of "stimulating a student to become a better person."

This conglomerate of responses was collated into a descriptive narrative for the superintendent. A Board report followed with a request to allow the new planning administrator to "refine" the existing board policy. The board gladly relinquished the chore and Dr. Feron began the task of re-drafting the "Board's policy into student outcome statements. Each phrase was redrafted into a student outcome statement and some new ones were added to incorporate state legislation. The board reviewed and approved the new student-oriented statements. Dr. Feron then developed the statements into a survey that citizens, students, and staff could rank. These were ranked and a public report given to the Board which received wide publicity in the press. The following excerpt is repeated here from the press article.

New Board Goals Show Basics Ranked First
A revised set of Board of Education goals for the Haugan City Schools was adopted last night by a unanimous vote of the Board. Dr. James Feron, new Assistant Superintendent for Planning, presented the Board with the goals after they had been ranked by over one thousand students, three thousand parents, and the teaching staff. Dr. Feron noted that "We found that old Board policies were simply not adequate as guides for system action. They were so broad as to enable any reasonable interpretation to stand as official Board policy. The more specific statements, ranked by the three groups, should provide far more detailed benchmarks for the staff to fulfill the Board's actual intent."

When asked by a member of the audience why the new goals were necessary, Feron responded by saying:

> If you don't know where you're going, any road will take you there. The purpose of specific future-oriented goals is to serve as an effective set of criteria by which the professional staff can operate. Furthermore, when we actually assess the performance of the school system, we will require such criteria as indicators of effectiveness. Without them we will not be able to make much of any kind of test data.

The Board thanked Dr. Feron for his efforts and asked the superintendent when the next report would be forthcoming about system effectiveness. The superintendent responded by saying an assessment plan would be presented in the Spring.

Planning and Politics

Beta designs are clearly the most common with school district or school-based assessments. Their major function is to help focus a district's or individual school's efforts to create a rational plan for change and a sound approach to configuring its resources to attain learner growth. To do so, the outcomes must be phrased in terms of desired learner performance. We hypothesize that one of the reasons goals or philosophies of education have been ineffective in shaping individual or group behavior is the lack of specificity in their phrasing. There are also many obstacles to overcome in the process. Perhaps the major barrier is a political rather than a technical one. Wide disparity within groups in a community can make it extremely difficult to find a consensus. The traditional approach to this dilemma has been to create vague and generic goals to which everyone can subscribe. Because that represents a temporary consensus, there is often reluctance to translate them into more behavior-guiding principles.

We believe that such an approach is mistaken. First, global goals cannot be a substitute for real consensus. Hiding the lack of agreement will not create agreement. Real consensus is made by pursuing specifics and seeking agreement on them. Furthermore, disagreement itself can be the forcing function to seek consensus by continuing to pursue what is acceptable and thereby stimulate the interests and agendas of the other parties.

Too often the fear of specifics is a "cop out" for a lack of expertise or time to complete the process. Nothing is served by "faking consensus" by retreating to ambiguity. Most of all, vague political agreements enable contrary interpretations to be used by the system in carrying out policy and are not effective criteria for making decisions. While they may present, at best, a temporary solution at one level, they create many more problems at other levels.

These kinds of political problems are often more acute for Beta-type assessments because an Alpha assessment starts with no assumptions about system viability. Therefore, Alpha assessments tend to flush out ambiguity more quickly and bring agreement or the lack of agreement much more quickly into focus. Nonetheless, Beta designs and assessments will probably continue to be widely used in educational systems.

(Since the KEY POINTS of this chapter have been stated directly above, there is no KEY POINTS section here, as is found in the other chapters.)

Chapter 11

CONSENSUAL DETERMINING TECHNIQUES IN NEEDS ASSESSMENT

Following the rioting and marching, the bullet-riddled buses and dynamited school buildings which occurred in the West Virginia "textbook rebellion," the assistant superintendent of the Kanawha County Schools observed (Young, 1974):

> We must demand some accountability from the public. We must request that the public delineate explicit goals and objectives for national, state, and local educational programs, and we must assist in the cooperative, participatory process by which goals are developed. Without these explicit goals and objectives in this complex and pluralistic society, education is doomed to a future of chaos, confusion, mistrust, wasted resources, and frustrated parents, students, and educators.

The eruption in Kanawha County has occurred on a much smaller and less violent scale around the country as parents have come to discover that where once their school boards controlled education, they now have apparently lost control to powerful teacher unions and state and federal bureaucracies (Ziegler, *et al.*, 1977). A national institute has been formed to reassert parental control over education and to propose ways that laypersons can become involved to re-establish educational standards (Wolf, 1975).

The needs assessment* process actively involves citizens, educators, and students in three phases of application. The first is the

*Unless otherwise modified, "needs assessment" here means the external or Alpha-mode.

establishment of outcome standards. The second is on-going feedback and reaction to the implementation of means or programs to reach the standards or outcomes. The third takes the form of "downstream" or follow-up evaluation.

The Process of Involvement

In most places in the nation, citizens no longer control the fate of the schools as once they did in town-hall type meetings. Overt control of the schools is manifested in the legal functions of the board of education. The only exception may be sections of the northeast, where some states still mandate annual citizen approval of school budgets or tax levies of various types. However, the content or substantive aspect of curricular control is carefully circumscribed even in these locations. There are a few exceptions where local power groups control the schools by the selection of school board members either through appointment or selection of the candidates who will stand for election.

Short of public referendum on each function of the school, the most obvious form of citizen involvement is the practice of *polling* or *sampling* a given constituency to determine its feelings about significant educational issues (Urban Observatory, 1976). These opinions are then made public, and presumably elected or even appointed officials have some obligation to be responsive to the expression of the sample. The degree to which such bodies are actually responsive are technical and political problems. The more representative a poll is of a diverse constituency, the more the results can withstand criticism from various minorities who may have vested interest in subverting the will of the majority. In Kanawha County, the expression of the will of the majority was not sought; and so the officials of the system were without visible support in battling the Ku Klux Klan, the John Birch Society, self-appointed religious leaders, and others in maintaining a public institution aimed at providing for the majority (Underwood, 1975).

In such crises, the difference between publics is blurred and it is almost impossible to distinguish between them. Boards and administrators have a fear of being persuaded by a minority only to find that the silent majority has been offended. Fear of being manipulated by a vociferous minority is a perennial problem for school system officials, and the needs assessment process provides a method for determining the majority and consensual viewpoint. It should be undertaken in times when a rational discourse and discussion about what it will provide the system can be understood by all parties concerned. Waiting until after a political explosion occurs which has inflamed public passions is not the gateway to a calm, rational assessment of the functions or purposes of schooling.

Polling is not new to the nation, to schools, or to education (Sudman, 1976). Various types of polls have become commonplace. The Purdue Opinion Poll, for example, has been administered to senior high school students for over thirty years (Elam, 1974). The Gallup Polls of Education have been well reported in the public and professional press (Phi Delta Kappa, 1973). A special Gallup Poll conducted in 1974 for the National School Boards Association revealed that "fully 63% of the people were unable to name one thing their school board had done in the preceding year, and barely half the parents of public school children could do so" (NSBA, 1975).

The New York State United Teachers employed pollster Louis Harris to sample their membership to determine whether the AFT or the NEA did a more effective job for teachers (NYSUT, 1976). The *Boston Herald-American* commissioned a study by the Becker Research Corporation on the public's perception of the violence in that city regarding school integration. It revealed that while 78% sought peace and order, a "small hardcore, including one-fourth white parents, prefer to continue resistance even if violence comes" (Becker, 1975).

Taxpayer groups have sampled the general public regarding their attitudes towards the schools. One such group reported that the results of their survey indicated that the public did not feel that the real property tax was a fair way to finance public education, that administrators and teachers were overpaid, and that teachers should not have the right to strike (CPES, 1975).

Professional educational associations such as Phi Delta Kappa have polled their memberships on occasions to determine priorities within their constituency on various issues (Spears, 1973). Some school boards have taken to sampling citizens and parents about the quality of their educational systems. In Brevard County, Florida, for example, the board of education asked a random sample of citizens to "grade" their schools on the traditional A-F scale (Brevard County, 1976). The recent Supreme Court ruling on obscenity mandated that such issues be defined by "community standards." This led the city of Cleveland to send out 280,000 questionnaires to try and define such standards in that city (Stuart, 1977).

The needs assessment process here advocated builds upon a determination of the degree of consensus which exists regarding the functions or outcomes of education. The constituency has been divided into three parts: professional staff, citizens, and learners. Educational outputs* have been treated for some time as the exclusive domain of the professional. Phi Delta Kappa reported the results of a pool of 1020 Kappans on 18 educational outputs as follows in rank order of importance:

1. Develop skills in reading, writing, speaking, and listening.
2. Develop pride in work and feelings of self-worth.
3. Develop good character and self-respect.
4. Develop a desire for learning, now and in the future.
5. Learn to respect and get along with people with whom we work and live.
6. Learn how to examine and use information.
7. Gain a general education.
8. Learn how to be a good citizen.
9. Learn about and try to understand the changes that take place in the world.
10. Understand and practice democratic ideas and ideals.
11. Learn how to respect and get along with people who think, dress, and act differently.
12. Understand and practice the skills of family living.

*These, using a taxonomy of results (outcomes) (Kaufman, 1972), are really "goals," since they are measurable only on nominal or ordinal scales of measurement. To become "objectives" they would have to be measurable on an interval or ratio scale.

13. Gain information needed to make job selections.
14. Learn how to be a good manager of money, property, and resources.
15. Practice and understand the ideas of health and safety.
16. Develop skills to enter a specific field of work.
17. Learn how to use leisure time.
18. Appreciate culture and beauty in the world (Phi Delta Kappa, 1973).

There is some empirical evidence that the public and students would place a different order of priority on the same goals. A ranking of goals in Sarasota, Florida, showed that students placed as their number two goal a concern for ecology or "the preservation of natural resources." In the same survey, this was ranked sixteenth by adults, i.e., teachers and citizens (Chamberlin, 1973). In Hastings-on-Hudson, New York, students ranked as their number one goal, "how to get a job and/or to go on to complete college." The community ranked this goal second, and the professional staff ranked it sixth (English, 1976).

A detailed study in mathematics was undertaken by Baker in which she analyzed the responses of parents, teachers, and students as data sources in the selection of mathematics outcomes at the junior high school level (Baker, 1972). The data showed some revealing differences. Teachers favored practical and basic concepts in arithmetic, while parents rated objectives in operations highest. Parents also included skill with word problems. Students, however, favored esoteric skills such as scientific notation. Professional opinion does not include other data sources, i.e., it does not necessarily rest upon evident universalisms in the selection of outcomes, either for the school system or within subject areas.

Citizen involvement is essential to public enterprises, particularly where the public can influence budgetary appropriations via elected officials. Waning public support of school appropriations measures has forced at least one state to re-examine methods for public involvement. A special publication by the New York State Commissioner of Education on public involvement in school affairs cited the following reasons for increasing citizen participation:

(1) expansion of the opportunity for parents and others to express their expectations for the schools;

(2) a method for increasing the base of information for those responsible for decision making, i.e., board members and top administrators;

(3) a way to increase parental support of the schools;

(4) an opportunity to make better use of community resources; and

(5) a way to create a climate for a reasonable and rational dialogue among and between the various sub-publics in the school district (Nyquist, 1977).

David Tyack (1974) has shown that as boards of education became less dominated by ward selection and moved toward a so-called "non-partisan" and "at large" basis, they came to be dominated by professionals and managerial males. Tyack reports a study in 1916 which showed that three fifths of the members of urban boards of education were merchants, manufacturers, bankers, doctors, or lawyers. That women as one minority were excluded from boards has carried into the present day with only twenty percent representation on state boards of education and less than one percent occupying the role of superintendent of schools on the national level (Fishel and Pottker, 1974).

The influential Committee for Economic Development, which released policy statements on directors for the American school and statements concerning the outcomes of instruction, included no women in its membership. The sixteen-member subcommittee on efficiency and innovation in education included only one female, Katherine Graham, publisher of the *Washington Post* (CED, 1968).

A 1969 study by the Universities of Michigan and Oregon of the characteristics of school board members indicated that 90% were male, 96% were white, 68% were in the age range 40-59, 85% were Protestant, and 44% were Republican (PSBA, 1976). The hegemony of business interests and backgrounds on American school boards at all levels and the exclusion of women and other minorities, not to mention those whose occupations are not professional or business related, causes considerable questions as to whether any one group should develop the outcomes of education as an exclusive prerogative.

If the schools are to be used by all of the children of all of the people, the people should have a more direct and representative voice in determining their outcomes. We hypothesize that techniques which are more representative and directly involve all of the people in such determinations will result not only in more universal outcomes being developed and perhaps different ones than the prevailing genre, but also in the populace financially supporting the functions of the schools at more sustained levels and with less reluctance than current data now suggests (Costello, 1972). This is an admittedly optimistic premise. While the thrust for total community control of the schools has ebbed in recent times, there is continued emphasis on a variety of means for more active school-related citizen involvement. It has been suggested that educators cannot simply stand by and watch the community trying to become involved, or encourage it. Rather, the school system should assign someone on the inside of the system with the responsibility of school community agent or director to insure that there is a steady level of involvement (Deshler and Erlich, 1972).

Student involvement has changed, too, from the blatant and often violent means utilized during the Vietnam War years to the more persuasive forms of actual representation on boards of education, serving as tutors of other students, peer counselors, and various types of community "out reach" efforts (NYSED, 1976-77). Recent information on communities suggests that such notions as a permanent "power elite" which controls the schools are false. Real influence by citizens in school affairs and other community matters is far more "issue specific" than at first realized (Pellegrin, 1965).

For both practical and historical reasons, we feel it is important to widen the area of influence regarding the determination of the outcomes of schooling. The Alpha needs assessment model involves in a formal and planned manner the considered requirements and perceptions of students, citizens (including parents), and professional staff. Formal assessment techniques will be described in which a consensual determination indicates the appropriate outcomes of schooling. Surveys or interviews usually provide various sub-classifications within the basic constituency to be polled or sampled. The most common are cited in Figure 11.1.

*Figure 11.1. A Breakdown of the Most Common
Sampling Sub-Classifications in Needs Assessment.*

	Sub-Classification	Basic Constituencies		
		Citizen	*Student*	*Professional*
1.	Sex	x	x	x
2.	Age	x	x	x
3.	Race (ethnic background)	x	x	x
4.	Education	x	x(level)	x(degrees)
5.	Occupation	x		
6.	Annual income	x		x(salary)
7.	Resident	x		x
8.	Length of residency	x	x	x
9.	Geographical area (precinct)	x	x	x
10.	Number of school age children	x	x(siblings)	
11.	Religious affiliation	x		
12.	Political affiliation	x		
13.	Property ownership status	x		
14.	Grade point average		x	
15.	College/occupation bound		x	
16.	Years in school system		x	x(seniority)
17.	Current assignment		x(grade)	x
18.	Family status (parent status)	x	x	
19.	Occupation of head of house	x	x	

The actual data requested will vary according to the situational decision-making requirements. This means that the educational planners involved with the needs assessment will have to anticipate the kind of data analysis which will be necessary in order for decision-making groups to convert the data to information.

The planners must anticipate not only the decisions themselves regarding outcome priorities, such as answering the question about the importance of certain results in reading versus the performing arts, but also the acceptance by the various sub-publics of the decisions made with their input. Boards of education are required to make decisions often without the advantage of much information or time. Therefore, some boards may not be bothered by what they may feel to be the "technical" aspects of data gathering. For the various sub-publics to have confidence in the ultimate decisions made, the degree to which the polling or sampling is representative of the actual populations involved will be critical.

The solicitation of information about who is being polled or interviewed is important to answer the possible questions of representation. These may follow local requirements to some extent. If, for example, a particular school unit is divided by historical, geographical, or other sub-divisions that are politically viable, it will be important that these are represented in the survey in order to show that the data took them into account. If the school system has minority populations, or large senior citizen or private school constituencies, these delineations may be represented as well.

In approaching the gathering of data about the respondents, the credibility of the survey must be paramount. However, the practitioner is often torn between the requirements of good survey techniques and form advocated by statisticians, and the practical requirements of decision-making demanded by boards or politicians. The statistician wants rigorous pre-testing, conceptually clear terms, and unambiguous phrases with high reliability. Many educational decision-makers, such as boards, do not use anything more complicated or precise than percentage bar graphs. T-scores, means, standard deviations, Chi Squares, point biserials, analysis of variances, and linear regressions do not help in the decision required if the "consumer" does not understand or use the results or the processes which yield the results. When boards are pressed to the wall, they want concrete data; and any clarification of or qualifiers to the data appear to be cases of administrative weaseling rather than methodological statistical rigor.

The languages of the statistician-researcher and the board of education member are usually different, and the parameters place different kinds of demands upon the practitioner trying to satisfy both. Figure 11.2 indicates the problem. Citizen respondents often want survey instruments which are issue specific, whereas educational decision-makers require data which are situation generic. If the practitioner approaches the citizen respondents from the decision-making context of generic data, questions are of a broad,

Figure 11.2. Parameters of Instrument Construction.

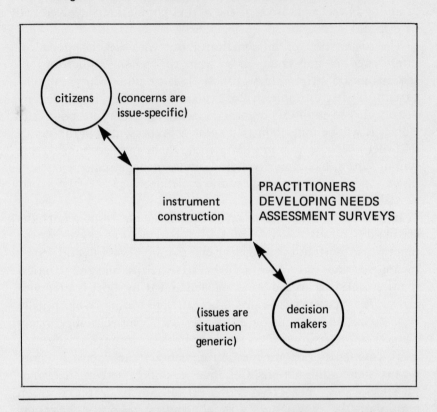

sweeping kind and citizens often react as if the inquiries were unrealistic. On the other hand, should the practitioner approach the decision-makers with issue-specific data, they may dismiss it as being the exception to the rule and not applicable to some other situation.

Practitioners must consider both demands on instrument preparation (i.e., the demands of the decision-makers, board members, and administrators) and the manner in which citizen respondents perceive their most useful input. In most practical situations, tradeoffs will have to be made between both groups and the resulting data collection vehicles and statistical procedures. The problems with developing an instrument which satisfies both groups are exemplified in the dialogue in Scenario 1.

Scenario 1
Problems of Instrument Construction in the Westfalls Schools

*Cast of Characters**

Mr. Leopold Sarasotan, Superintendent

Dr. Arnold Pike, Director of
Instruction

Mr. Reginald Rodson, Vice-
Chairperson, Parents for
Better Schools

Dr. Virginia Koler, Board of
Education, President

Mrs. Alice Clackers, Chairperson, Parents for Better
Schools

Mrs. Clackers: I've asked for Mr. Rodson and I to meet with the Superintendent to discuss what might be in the survey of parents that the board has asked the administration to prepare and administer.

Mr. Sarasotan: Yes, you told me on the telephone that your group had some concerns about the impending survey.

Mrs. Clackers: Yes, that's right. You see, you weren't here four years ago when the previous superintendent did a community survey. Well, that little stunt cost the board a lot of credibility here because there was the feeling in the community that the thing was stacked in favor of the superintendent's biases and it didn't prove anything. The superintendent thought it supported his moves toward open schools and a lot of other kinds of changes and it didn't at all. The community didn't really support any of them.

Dr. Koler: It wasn't quite that way, Alice. I tend to think that only the pro-school people answered it and they tended to think the same way Mr. Maggery did.

Mrs. Clackers: Whatever, there's a feeling of distrust about these sorts of things. We're here to prevent that same thing from happening again. We have here a list of items we feel should be in the survey.

Dr. Pike: Oh, good. We're now in the process of constructing our survey instrument and your input would be very helpful. Let's hear them.

*These, like all other names in scenarios in this work, are fictitious.

Mrs. Clackers: Well, the first thing is a question about patriotism. We think something to the effect, "Should the schools teach patriotism?" The second might be, "Should the amount of taxes we pay be used to support certain educational frills?" The third is, "Should a greater concentration on the basics be made in the earlier grades?"

Dr. Pike: That's not what we had in mind as possible questions, Mrs. Clackers. Those are board decisions anyway. What we want to ask the community is which types of outcomes of schooling do you think are most important? We'll then use a Likert scale to record the degree of importance.

Mr. Rodson: I think you're already on the wrong track. It's too complicated. I don't think most of the citizens know what a Likert scale is anyway. Why does it always have to be filled with a lot of mumbo-jumbo and jargon? Why can't it be simple and to the point?

Mrs. Clackers: You have to ask the people the things that are on their minds. They're concerned about taxes, discipline, patriotism, frills, bureaucrats, and basics. Those are the things they're worried about.

Dr. Koler: Let's see what your format would be like, Dr. Pike.

Dr. Pike: Here's a copy of our preliminary instrument.

Mrs. Clackers: Even the word 'instrument' sounds bureaucratic and cold. Why is it an instrument? It's merely a poll about what the people want in their schools. Why make it fancy?

Dr. Pike: Our first question deals with a list of possible educational goals for the community to approve or disapprove on the five-point Likert scale. Here are some examples:

    (1) students should be able to secure gainful employment upon graduation and not be on welfare;

    (2) students should be able to enjoy the arts and literature which provoke reflection;

    (3) students should be able to know and practice good health habits; and

    (4) students should have a positive self-concept about themselves.

Mrs. Clackers: What on earth could a list like that possibly tell you? Why, I think they're all important. The schools better do all of those things. I'm not going to chose between them. That's like asking me to tell you whether my heart or my liver is more important. God knows, I want both of them.

Mr. Rodson: I don't know what a "postive self-concept" means. That's another example of the excessive use of jargon. You people have to learn to communicate with the common person. You have to deal with what's on people's minds. They know all this stuff. They believe in these goals. Why ask them? What we want to get going here is the poor way tax money is being managed in the school district. We would like more concentration on the basics in earlier grades. We want stricter discipline and we want to get back to sound, basic education.

Dr. Koler: But your kind of survey is what got the previous superintendent into trouble. His survey, if I can remember it, asked a lot of questions about what we call means or methods to reach the goals. That's a board of education responsibility vested in law. We can't give it away. We're elected by the people to make those kinds of decisions. Furthermore, questions about means are not merely citizen plebiscites. They involve the knowledge of the professional. The staff isn't always right; but since it's they who must implement our decisions, their opinions must be solicited and weighed very heavily.

Mr. Sarasotan: The board of education and the administration must make decisions about priorities all the time. "The heart/liver" problem is one we're struggling with every time we approve a budget. We can't run away from it. Many of our educational objectives or outputs can be reached through a variety of approaches. We'd like to know what the community deems most important as outcomes of schooling. That can really help us make better programmatic decisions.

Mrs. Clackers: I don't know a thing about 'programmatic decisions.' That's not my job. I agree it's the board's job. It seems to me that once again the educators will win out. If you want to know what we think, why don't you just ask us in plain English without Likert scales and programmatic decisions?

Dr. Pike: I wish it were that simple, Mrs. Clackers. For the board to have any confidence in the data returned from a survey, they have to be assured that it does in fact represent the people's opinion and not just that of a vocal minority. The board must represent all of the people, even the ones who don't care.

Dr. Koler: I'm sure it must sometimes appear to you that the board just doesn't change its mind when various vocal individuals speak at public meetings. It isn't that the board has made up its mind; it's because the board must be attentive to the opinion of those who don't necessarily come to meetings, but who call us or write us. You've heard of the phrase the 'silent majority.' Well, it's a sad fact but true that most people don't come to board meetings if they feel things are going along ok. They come when they're highly agitated about something and then they want action.

Mr. Sarasotan: What the board requires is a data base that will help them through the budget period so they can reassess priorities and allocate limited funds in the most effective manner possible. They really want to know what kinds of educational outputs the community feels are most important.

Mr. Rodson: That's a good example of jargon right there. I don't know what an output is and I don't think most people in the community would know either.

Mrs. Clackers: I don't know how many times I can say it to you people; if you want to converse with the people, you must speak their language. You've got to come down from your perches and mingle.

Dr. Koler: I think you've made a good point, Alice, but what if you discover that decisions, at least good decisions, those that are far-reaching for the district, don't demand that kind of data or opinion. Suppose that you could decide or had to decide on a matter which would have to stand not only for one thing but a lot of things. The kind of opinion you are advocating gathering would only be marginally helpful.

Mrs. Clackers: I don't think I understand what you're saying, Virginia.

Dr. Koler: Well, let's suppose the community told us they thought we should reduce educational frills. Suppose that 96% of the community agreed with that statement. Now let's suppose that the board interpreted that to mean releasing from employment all the guidance counselors in the schools.

Mr. Rodson: That's not too bad a start I would say.

Dr. Koler: Now suppose that in the middle of the year a group of angry parents stormed the board meeting and demanded that the counselors be returned because no one was making out their children's transcripts and helping them in college placement, no one was helping students select careers or enter into vocational training, and no one was available to refer troubled students to other community social agencies. Suppose the people said at that time they didn't mean fire the counselors when they said "reduce frills," they meant fire the teacher aides, or administrators, or custodians. The board thought it knew what they meant but now they're sorry and they don't know what to do. Counselors are means to a certain range of services and those services in turn produce student outputs or changes in behavior. It's the board's responsibility to know what services produce what outputs. But we've got to establish concrete outputs and that's what we want the community to help us do.

Mrs. Clackers: That may be true and I can see your problem, but people don't get too excited about goals. They get excited about things they can identify with, things they can remember from their own schooling experience. They don't remember goals. They think it ought to be possible to adjust the budget so that some of the excess baggage is eliminated, and the schools could accomplish all of those goals.

Dr. Koler: They may be right on that point, but it's only through establishing objectives that we can test it.

Mr. Rodson: We feel strongly about these issues we brought to you and I thought we might be able to make some breakthroughs but I think I was wrong.

Dr. Koler: I would encourage you to press your opinions. That's your right and responsibility. But I think you too will find it easier to present your case when you know what the schools should be accomplishing. Any advocate is in a hazardous position without concrete goals and we want to have the people involved in setting them, ranking them, and in evaluating whether we have reached them or not.

Dr. Pike: After we've finished constructing the survey, I would appreciate your analyzing it from your point of view. Help us eliminate the excess jargon. If the words we've selected don't communicate properly, we should know it now, and make the necessary changes so we do communicate.

Mrs. Clackers: We want to help if we can.

Mr. Sarasotan: You know, most citizens approach the schools like I approach a computer. I mean, I don't know how to program a computer. I can perhaps make the computer go faster or slower, I can kick it, curse at it, or unplug it, but I can't make any changes in the actual operation of the computer until I learn its language. When I learn Fortran I can change the program. Citizens will not change the schools until they learn the language or at least enough of the language to give different kinds of instructions to the board or to the educators. We all know that computers use a special language. The use of English is confusing. Often we think we're communicating and we really aren't. Your group has to give a little too. For real participation in the decision-making process, you must give some attention to learning the program, the one that makes the school system tick.

Mr. Rodson: That makes some sense. I guess we feel that the use of jargon is a put-down to citizens.

Mr. Sarasotan: Sometimes it is. Professionals can get defensive too. Language can reveal or conceal. We have to be kept honest too.

Dr. Pike: I'll get this new survey draft to both of you within about two weeks.

The second scenario involves a board of education and administration that made too many statistical tradeoffs in administering a survey to a community. Too many corners were cut on costs and for the sake of time. As the scenario will show, the effort had to be repeated.

Scenario 2
Survey Data Is Challenged as Biased in Partridge Creek Schools

Cast of Characters

Dr. Jack Bond, Superinten-   Mr. Winston Miles, President
dent of Schools   of the Board
Mrs. Mary Moncare, Trustee   Mr. Hardy Wilson, Trustee

Mr. Parker Ridgely, Trustee   Mrs. Lena Dewey, Trustee
Mr. Hackamore Waverly, Presi-
   dent, Athletic Boosters

Mr. Waverly: Dr. Bond, Mr. Miles, members of the board, and audience. I've come this evening to raise certain inquiries about the recent community survey conducted by the superintendent's staff and the degree to which it seems to the Athletic Boosters that conclusions from this survey are erroneous and not reflective of the actual feelings of this community.

Mr. Miles: Please be brief, Mr. Waverly.

Mr. Waverly: We're extremely concerned about the board's decision to cut out all junior varsity athletic teams and form a junior symphonic orchestra. I have a petition here signed by over 1800 parents indicating that they want junior varsity sports put back into the budget.

Mrs. Dewey: I thought you were going to point out the erroneous conclusions.

Mr. Waverly: First, the data was not gathered correctly. According to census data, our community has a total population of about 10,000 persons. About 3,000 of them are registered voters. It was to these 3,000 persons that the surveys were sent. According to the board's data, there was an 11% response from the 3,000 mailing. 89% of the community sampled did not return the survey. 70% of the people were not even included in the survey. Even if all 3,000 had returned their surveys, that would have been only 30% of the actual community. We believe the board biased the response right from the beginning by choosing this approach.

Mr. Miles: The board considered a variety of plans, Mr. Waverly, and I didn't see you at any of the meetings we had about it, either. We also operate within a budget, you know. We considered going to a sample of homes but that would have meant training or hiring people to do interviews and we didn't have the time.

Dr. Bond: That's right, Mr. Waverly. We thought we'd get more than the 11% but we didn't. We were very disappointed. But our timelines demand that we go with what we've got.

Mr. Waverly: The biases of the board are well-known, Dr. Bond.

Mrs. Moncare is in the symphonic boosters, and Mrs. Dewey the Urban Art League. Mr. Wilson is a trustee in the civic light opera association. The language of the survey itself seemed to us to discriminate against those who didn't have much education. Does the board know who answered the survey and who didn't?

Dr. Bond: The surveys were anonymous to increase the honesty of the response. We have no way of knowing who responded and who didn't.

Mr. Waverly: What we propose is that the board rescind its motion to cancel junior varsity athletics until a new survey which is representative can be constructed, or we suggest that the board conduct a town-wide referendum in the matter.

Mr. Ridgely: This is ridiculous, Mr. Waverly. You and your supporters had the opportunity to turn in your surveys and be counted.

Mr. Waverly: I beg your pardon, Mr. Ridgely, over half of my group didn't even remember receiving the surveys in the mail. I think if the board were really serious about involving the community, much greater care would have been taken in securing a better cross-section of this town. We're here to tell you that the survey doesn't represent us and we don't think that 11% of 3,000 people of 10,000 people is anywhere near the true feeling of this community! Now is the board responsive to the will of the community or is it not?

Dr. Bond: Mr. Waverly, none of us here were happy with the low response. We wanted at least 80-90% response to have a representative survey. But we didn't get it and we have no way of knowing if a second or third survey would do any better. The alternatives open to us now are to ask the people again, or make decisions without asking them and assume we obtained a representative sample.

Mr. Waverly: We're here this evening to tell you to ask us again. All of us! We want to tell you how we feel. You can begin by asking the people in this audience to vote tonight on this matter to show you how they feel.

Mr. Miles: This is not a town hall meeting Mr. Waverly.

Mr. Waverly: You mean you're going to ignore the fact that over one hundred people came to this meeting tonight to present to you our petition with over 1800 signatures and you're going to pretend that nothing happened at all?

Mr. Miles: I think the board may well have to reconsider the whole idea in possibly a second survey. It may put us off our timeline but I see no other alternative at this time.

In this second scenario the board was challenged not only on the basis of the way it sampled, i.e., the design, but also on the results. Mr. Waverly made a strong case that 11% on a mailed survey was not representative. Sudman calls this poor sample execution (Sudman, 1976). Had the board developed a well-designed sampling plan and executed it well, 11% may have been adequate assuming an appropriate random sample. The lack of adequate control on the sampling and the procedures utilized in the design rendered the board powerless to reasonably and responsibly answer the critics.

While the criticism of the survey in the second scenario largely centered upon poor design and execution, some of the first scenario did touch upon the actual content or items contained within a survey instrument. The decision to include or exclude items in a survey is a matter of *content validity* (Downie and Heath, 1965). Content validity is a non-statistical type of validity. It is a measure of the adequacy of an instrument to include the appropriate number of kinds of items to assess something, such as a course.

A survey instrument possesses content validity when the items included in it correlate with stated goals and objectives and local board policies or other types of educational statements. A simple match and mis-match check can help to determine if the scope of the items is adequate. It should be noted that even the Gallup Polls have been criticized as being too heavily influenced by professional educators in the types of questions asked (Joyce, 1976).

Content validity, then, refers to the extent to which an instrument adequately covers the total array, or domain, of that which should be sampled. This comprehensiveness should include necessary and required skills, knowledge, and attitudes.

Construct validity is a measure of the extent to which a test or instrument measures what it intends to measure—does what it purports to do. When a test or procedure only appears to measure something important, it is said to have face validity. When it actually measures what it is supposed to measure, it has construct validity.

Another use of the term validity refers to the results of the survey and the adoption of the results by the board of education. Validity in this sense refers to the fact that a given level of consensus appears to exist among the respondent groups so that a goal can be included or excluded on the adoption list and perhaps with an overall higher ranking compared to other types of goals. In answer to the question, "Who says that this should be a goal for this school district?" the board responds, "We determined that at least 60% of each responding group must concur that it be a goal. These goals have all attained at least that level of acceptable consensus." The use of the instrument is a method to determine if consensus exists on the goal and it then becomes the means for determining its validity for the school district.

Reliability refers to the ability of any given procedure to produce similar results under similar sampling or field conditions. Virtually all other kinds of polling or survey procedures can be subjected to questioning as in Scenario 2. Therefore, we urge that careful consideration be given to these critical factors. As a possible overview to more serious and sustained reading, the following is a somewhat general and non-technical discussion regarding the utilization of consensual techniques.

Sampling

A sample represents a predetermined number of potential respondents who are hopefully representative of the population at large. A sample can either be designated *a priori* to include a cross-section of characteristics of respondents (in which case it is *stratified*), or it can be established *after* an entire population has been attempted to be polled or surveyed and the response calculated. *A priori* sampling often forces the practitioner to think through procedures and design considerations in more detail and eliminate possible sources of biases rather than attempting to "doctor" a survey after the fact. For this reason, the *a priori* approach is recommended.

In Scenario 2, the board of education sampled only 3,000 persons in a community of 10,000 people. However, an 11% response rate meant that the actual sample was 330 persons. If a stratified sample were desired in which certain geographical or occupational income respondents were necessary to speak to the issue of the "artsy-craftsy set vs. the athletic boosters," the survey might have indicated such data in the return. The board would have to say to the effect that, "of the 330 respondents in the sample, 13% were of income ranges between $40,000 to $60,000 per year." This could be compared to the latest U.S. Census figures to determine if it represented the overall town mean or constituency breakdown. If it did not, the data should be shown to be not representative of the population as a whole. If no such data were available, significant doubt could be raised about whether the sample was representative of the larger population unit.

The degree to which the sample results vary from the population as a whole is called the *sampling error* (Kish, 1965). Sampling errors introduced bias into the results of our example from two sources. The first source were persons who did not respond (non-response bias), and the second source were those people not included at all (non-coverage bias), i.e., the unregistered voters. In the example, 3,000 surveys were mailed out in a community of 10,000 people. In rough terms, sampling error could occur because 7,000 people were excluded from responding and 2670 who had an opportunity to respond did not. Such errors are different from *measurement errors,* which relate to the instrument utilized *per se* and its assumptions (Cleary *et al.,* 1970; Nunnally, 1967).

The manner in which such questions are answered relates to the concept of *randomness. Randomness* helps to answer questions pertaining to the representation of a response as a valid indicator of the population at large. *Randomness* refers to the concept that a subject or respondent included in a survey had as much chance or opportunity to be included or considered as all of the other possible respondents (Guilford, 1965). Error in the selection of respondents introduces bias. Let us assume that the board of education stood outside of the local supermarket and handed out questionnaires instead of mailing them home. What percentage of the population utilizes the local supermarket on any particular day? Would the respondents who answered the survey be as likely to be included if they had been approached in the public library, the tax assessor's office, or in front of church? Staking out a particular location means that there may be a common and systematic element of bias introduced in the selection of participants, that is, each is related to each other in some non-random way, but not representative of the population at large. Contrast this procedure with drawing names from a hat or other types of lottery-based procedures.

If survey respondents can be said to be selected at random, the results of the survey can be assumed to be "like" those of the population as a whole. No matter what sampling procedure is utilized, however, there is usually some sampling error. This can be estimated and probability of that error specified. The best procedure for making sure that a sample is representative of the larger population is to insure that it is large enough (the size variable) and that the procedure did not introduce some selection bias from the respondents, either included or excluded. To deal with these considerations does not require huge samples. The Gallup Poll of Education, which is considered representative of the nation, does not usually include more than 2,000 people!

The first problem confronting the design of the sample is therefore its size. The general rule of thumb is that the larger the sample size, the more likely it is that the results will be closer to that of the population as a whole (Hays, 1963). However, as the size increases, so do the factors of cost and effort required to obtain the sample. Therefore, it is convenient if some optimum size can be calculated. To know how many responses must be in the sample requires some idea of the degree of accuracy required; that is, the educational planner must know if he or she kept sampling the population in the same way, what the probability of deriving a different response would be with a fixed number of repetitions. To know this the statistician calculates a *confidence interval*. This statistic indicates the degree to which the mean of the sample would be expected to be different from the mean of the larger population, if sampling were to be continued to some finite point (Wonnacott and Wonnacott, 1969).

If the practitioner wanted to be sure that the sample mean was falling into the correct range of the population mean 95 percent of the time and would only be outside of the range of the population mean 5 percent of the time, he or she would construct an estimate for a 95% confidence interval. To this he or she would require only one sampling from the large population. By employing assumptions of a normal distribution and specified statistical procedures, a sample is specified. For a confidence interval of 95%, the actual number in a sample may be as low as 384 respondents (Krejcie and Morgan, 1970). The reader desiring a more thorough explanation (with the necessary mathematical background) may consult Hays (1963) or Guilford (1965).

The most useful approach with needs assessment appears to be a stratified random sample. In such a sample, a systematic effort is made to approximate the major divisions of a community's or population's characteristics, such as making sure there are a representative number of people in the sample on such variables as listed in Figure 11.1.

For example, in conducting the Florida State Educational Opinion Survey, four stages of selection were utilized as follows:

(1) counties as primary sampling units;

(2) U.S. Census Enumeration Districts;

(3) neighborhoods-geographic areas containing approximately 30 households; and

(4) households.

At the last stage of sampling, the person in the household selected for an interview was chosen by procedures developed by Kish (1965).

The first stage of the process was spent in determining how many respondents were necessary to complete 1000 interviews. The study anticipated a 15% refusal rate and a 2% non-coverage rate. Therefore, the sampling process was aimed at completing 1170 contacts. However, given certain population characteristics of Florida, this figure was upped to 1400.

Since the household comprised the basic source of selection, the next step was to secure the total list of households in the state. This was then divided by the required number of contacts and yielded a *sampling interval*. The number of households in each county was then divided by the sampling unit to indicate the number of contacts required. Each county was then divided into five sub-strata as follows:

(1) cities of 50,000 or more;
(2) cities of 10,000 to 49,999;
(3) urban places of 2,500 to 9,999;
(4) other incorporated places and densely populated places of 1,000 to 2,499; and
(5) residual or rural areas.

Within each sub-strata of the county, a sample of the enumerational districts was selected in proportion to the estimated number of housing units. Each district was then divided into neighborhoods of approximately three blocks in size. Individual homes were then selected utilizing the sampling interval and a random start (Florida SED, 1970).

The great care to sample proportionately and randomly within the identified sub-strata means that a relatively small sample can provide very reliable information to decision-makers. If properly conducted and evaluated, such a community survey can answer most of the objections which will be raised regarding its representativeness, its size, or its reliability.

Techniques of Securing Participation

Most school districts utilizing the needs assessment have employed a questionnaire which is mailed or taken at some location, or house conducted personal at-home interviews by telephone or face to face (Witkin, 1975, 1977; Tuckman and Montare, 1977). Each technique has special problems which should be mentioned.

Mailed Surveys

The cheapest form of survey or questionnaire is the bulk-mailed survey, which is sent to registered voters or heads of households. One kind of sampling error, i.e., non-coverage, can be easily controlled with the mailed survey. However, the chief liability of the mailed survey has been non-response bias. Non-respondents typically have very different attitudes than do respondents.

Non-response bias can be estimated by identifying some of the non-respondents and interviewing them to ascertain if they possess significantly different attitudes regarding the survey item. Another method is to compare the two groups (respondents and non-respondents) on data which is known for all participants. A third is to make comparisons between early and late respondents. This latter method is based on the concept that a non-respondent is simply a very late respondent (Bridge, 1974). Unless the response rate is at least 80% on mailed surveys, the problems of dealing with non-response bias cannot be easily controlled (Kish, 1965).

Telephone Surveys

Both telephone surveys and interviews raise the possibility of interviewer bias. Also, the question of how to deal with the "not at homes" is raised. In utilizing a telephone poll, it is important to know the percentage of homes by geographical area which have telephones. This data can be secured from the telephone company. A telephone poll in Sarasota, Florida, regarding the year-round school began with no area having less than 70% actual phone coverage. Then a staff of minimally-trained volunteers was given the responsibility of calling every twentieth name in the telephone directory.* Each person was to "call back" the "not at homes" at least twice. Of 2459 calls, 1140 were completed, 756 were not at home (busy signal, out of order, etc.), and 563 refused to participate. Interviewer bias was reduced by providing the pollsters with "scripts" so that a uniform approach was utilized in soliciting citizen opinion (School Board of Sarasota County, 1973).

Despite utilizing the "call back" approach to reduce the non-response, only 46% of the calls made resulted in an opinion being rendered. Twenty-three percent of those contacted refused to provide an opinion. No further contact with this group was made, so it was not known the extent to which their opinions may have differed from those in the respondent group. The disadvantages of the telephone polling technique are that it is more complex to administer, more time consuming, and (without volunteers) more expensive. The element of possible interviewer

*This is an example of attempting to sample randomly within a biased sample—people who own telephones!

bias is always present. Despite attempts to standardize the responses, the degree to which the telephone interviewers "help" the respondents is unknown. In areas with a low percentage of telephones installed, certain groups may be underrepresented in the sample. The advantages are that the work can be "farmed" out and does not take a physical tramping down blocks of houses to complete. "Call backs" are considerably easier with a telephone; however, a telephone interview should not be too lengthy and the questions should not be too complex. Respondents are without non-verbal cues to understand a question. Poor listeners or those with hearing problems are at a distinct disadvantage with this method of polling.

Personal Interviews

Despite costs and time involved with personal interviews, this technique is probably the "blue-ribbon" approach. Begun with a random sample design on a stratified basis, which is a simple random sample within each sub-strata (Hill and Kerber, 1967), the representativeness of the survey can be quickly ascertained. The problem with "not at homes" can be covered by using a weighting procedure which reduces the under-representation of those who were difficult to reach (Politz and Simmons, 1949). The utilization of personal interviews is the most time consuming and costly approach, perhaps even with the utilization of semi-trained volunteers. Even a modest 10% sampling of a community can present an enormous investment of personal time and effort (Frase, 1975). This method is found to be useful even in a very large urban setting with multiple strata (Morgan and Feldman, 1977).

Reporting the Data

Decisions about weighting the data and how it is reported should have been made prior to the design of the survey or questionnaire. Often, practitioners will begin by deciding upon the ways the data will be reported and what the tables and graphs will look like. This is useful in order to design the survey to yield the data required. Since the data is intended to supply information for decision-making, the content of the data collection vehicles should be derived from and be directly relatable to the questions to be answered by the resulting information.

Weighting the data presents both practical and political problems. The Kaufman rationale (1972) has been to treat all of the major sub-groups, i.e., students, staff, and citizens, as equal; greater weighting is not attached to any group of respondents in order to provide them with more influence. It should be remembered that at this stage only outcomes (desired results) are being ranked, not procedures or methods utilized to obtain the outcomes. We believe it is important that the outcomes be decided in partnership and that the partners receive an equal influence at this stage. At later stages, such as the selection of media and methods, the influence of professionals may be heavier. However, all of these points should be decided in advance and the weighting system discussed prior to implementation and reporting (Ohio SED, 1976).

Whatever approach is utilized, the reported data should include the percentage of each group by question or goal. The sampling design should be described along with mean scores, standard deviations, and the standard error of measurement. Whatever information is necessary to understand the sample design should be included, from both the decision-maker's perspective and that of the statistician.

The purpose of reporting the data by categories or major groups is to provide a clear picture of the level of consensus present and which groups it includes or excludes. This is an important procedure to minimize disruption which may flow from the utilization of the data at a later time (Hyman, 1972). Opinions gathered from the public may be transient. An opinion is "a belief that one holds to be without emotional commitment or desire, and to be open to reevaluation since the evidence is not affirmed to be convincing" (English and English, 1958). Opinions are to be differentiated from attitudes, which are more stable. Attitudes are predispositions to respond behaviorally (Shaw and Wright, 1967). If the school system has gathered opinions, then it must take steps to periodically update those opinions.

Even if all the methodological and statistical requirements are ably met in the design of a sample, a more pervasive problem is present. This problem is that ranked goals from the groups are usually prioritized essentially from the experiences of the respondents in the past and present. Yet the function of the goals is to provide for *future* direction of the school system and the individual school building program. This dilemma has been one reason various authorities have stayed away from such procedures. They are suspicious of validating the status quo with its obvious inequities (MacDonald, 1971). Nonetheless, there appear to be few alternatives to utilizing shared techniques of ranking future goals through the perceptions of the present. One possible check on this problem may be the application of the Delphi technique.

The Delphi Technique

The Delphi Technique is an approach developed by Olaf Helmer of the Rand Corporation (1967) to forecast the probability of future events occurring. These probabilities can then become targets for planning, either to avoid or to insure that they are realized. Helmer's approach is based upon the realization that "informed intuitive judgment" of experts can constitute an effective resource in forecasting future events or event probabilities.

Helmer's approach differs dramatically from previous uses of so-called experts. In the past, experts had been brought together in committees or panels to consider various probabilities. This proved to be somewhat unsatisfactory due to intergroup dynamics in which some divergence may have been traded off to conform with majority opinion. The cultivation of considered divergence is a strength of the Delphi method, which is a linear and sequential pattern of questions and responses by the expert group. The procedure does not depend upon group interaction, but does depend upon each expert seeing the responses of the group to various probabilities. He or she is then provided an opportunity to revise a prediction based upon the group's total reaction.

The Delphi technique is therefore not a logical series of extrapolations from models of current reality. Rather, by utilizing informed intuition, such forecasts have been called "quantum leaps" by Weaver (1971) and their rationality can be defended only by explanation. Amara and Salancik (1972) reviewed some of the earlier Delphis utilized in 1964 to predict future events in space exploration. They noted that of 22 major scientific and technological developments expected to occur by 1972, 15 of them were judged to have happened, 5 did not, and 2 were uncertain.

The Delphi technique has been applied to educational studies for a variety of forecasts. Farrell (1969) utilized experts in four fields (educational psychology, secondary curriculum, educational media, and English) to project the responsibilities of English teachers between 1970 and the year 2000. Handley (1970) utilized the same procedure with 236 superintendents, administrators, teachers, state education department personnel, and school board members to react to 53 possible educational events occurring in the next 20 years in Utah. Handley's study also underscored differences between groups on the 53 events. He found that of the five groups responding, the state education department displayed the greatest amount of consensus on the importance of the items and the school board members possessed the least degree of consensus on the same items. School board members had rated the items less important and likely to occur at the latest date possible than other groups.

Both the Farrell and Handley studies indicate differences in approach. The Farrell study generated the items from the experts. The respondents in the Handley study were provided with a pre-developed list from which to react. The advantage of not developing such a list would be that the combined creativity of the groups of experts is stimulated earlier in the initial rounds; and, therefore, the potentiality of the study having a greater scope (leaving out unanticipated events) may increase. The disadvantage of not structuring the likely events is that when generated from the respondents, additional rounds may be necessary simply to clarify and expand the items suggested. A pre-developed list of items is quicker and can be generated and checked from the literature. Comprehensiveness is thus generated from the outset. The expert reaction then serves to validate the comprehensiveness initially selected.

One of the interesting off-shoots of the Delphi has been called the "Focus Delphi" (Sandow, 1972). This variation of the Delphi does not depend upon a panel of experts, but recognizes that many publics must be involved in determining a consensus from which public policy can be generated. The Sandow study consisted of four rounds involving two basic groups, producers and consumers (students). Producers were classified as high school counselors, college faculty, etc.

Description of the Generic Focus Delphi Procedures

As paraphrased from the Sandow study, the general procedures of the Focus Delphi appear to be as follows:

Round 1

1. Identify the groups and individuals to be involved.
2. Ask each person to provide a list of events he or she considers as likely occurrences in the future.
3. Respondents mail in the lists of events in the proper format.

Round 2

1. Planners collate responses by group and develop criteria for selection of responses (included or excluded) and categories.
2. Respondents are asked to indicate earliest possible date for the event occurring and the date by which the event will probably have already occurred—time interval restrictions are specified (20 years, 15 years, etc.).
3. Respondents mail in list of events and times the events may occur.

Round 3

1. Planners collate responses by group.
2. Planners develop four interquartile ranges—one per group per event with the median date shown for the entire group.
3. Respondents are asked to check data and if they thought their original response was still accurate.
4. If respondent's date indication is "outside" of interquartile range, he or she is asked for an explanation.
5. Respondents given options of changing estimation of dates.
6. Respondents may be asked to indicate how important

the item might be to them on a scale of value or for society or the educational institution/field of study.

7. Respondents mail in estimates.

Round 4

1. Planners collate responses by group.
2. Information again is returned to respondents to indicate degree of consensus by group on interquartile ranges.
3. In the Sandow study respondents were asked to indicate which group had the power to enhance or inhibit the event occurrence and which strategy would enhance or inhibit event occurrence.

Utilizing the Results of a Delphi

Delphic procedures can be utilized to rank goals which are presented to groups of parents, students, and professional staff, or those same groups can be used to generate and rank goals as possible educational outcomes. Another variation might be to ask the respondents to read over a list of events considered highly likely to occur by the year 2000 and ask them to rank a list of educational goals in light of these occurrences (McNamara, 1976). Educational goals are then responses to the future. This latter procedure may help reduce a problem of infusing values upon likely future occurrences. An example would be that "by the year 2000 it will be possible to create human life outside of the human body and alter some of its characteristics in the process of development." Rather than argue about the possibility of this event occurring on a time line, the respondent is asked to indicate, if it is possible, what relationship it has for a list of educational goals. Based upon the probability, he or she may elevate an educational goal concerning "moral and spiritual values" to a greater place than some others. This procedure also helps obviate the criticism of consensual educational approaches within needs assessment that rank educational outcomes on priorities solely derived from perceptions of current conditions. The Delphi technique can be used, therefore, as a forcing function to re-examine educational goals in light of future responsibilities. While it may be impossible to totally separate the present from the future, the impact of its consideration is at least included in the consensual determining techniques of the needs assessment process.

The California Association of Secondary School Administrators generated a list of probable events from a variety of sources (CASSA, 1968). A few are listed below to indicate how a list of future conditions may assist respondents within the framework of a Delphi to rank or re-order possible educational goals.

By the year 2000:

1. There will be direct control of the weather and climate.
2. Reanimation will be frequent; death will be appreciably delayed.
3. There will be extensive use of "cyborgs" or artificial human organs.
4. There will be practical use of direct communication with the brain.
5. Average personal income will have doubled and the work week will be 28-30 hours.
6. The end of bureaucracy will have occurred.
7. A large number of urban areas will fall completely under the jurisdiction of the federal government.
8. There will have been a re-thinking and re-evaluation of "work." The values of nonwork will be extended and expanded.
9. The world will have experienced a major war in Africa requiring massive outside intervention.
10. American power will be in a state of deterioration while Mexico and Brazil will be world powers.

Given the probability that any of these ten items will materialize, how would American educational goals be changed? Surely, the decline of the concept of "work" and increased leisure time activities would elevate the "arts" to a higher scale than almost all surveys of educational goals have indicated. It is believed that the use of such procedures as the Delphi is an important contributor to goals which are futuristically accurate for the school's planning purposes.

Other Areas for Consensual Determination

We have spent the major portion of this chapter describing ways in which consensual techniques can be utilized in the needs assessment process to establish outcomes or goals for educational institutions. Two other areas may involve such determinations. After the plans have been made and implemented by educational institutions toward the goals derived by consensus, some sort of feedback is required by which the administration or board of education trustees can decide if adjustments are necessary. Feedback consists of a whole series of activities, some of which are listed below:

a. reports on the results of intra-system competency or minimum essential testing;
b. polls of parents and students regarding their perceptions of the degree to which the plans implemented are reaching the desired objectives;
c. various types of anecdotal studies such as vandalism, utilization of the school buildings by outside groups, and support for taxes or bond issues;
d. teacher judgments about courses or changes in the curriculum;
e. pupil attitudes about school-related changes;
f. studies on pupil grades/placement;
g. various types of budget analyses such as percentage spent on auxiliary services, etc.;
h. accreditation reports of various types;
i. reports on state testing which indicate comparisons with other systems or schools;
j. subjective/descriptive "consultant" evaluations from the state education department in various subject areas; and
k. others.

These types of interim assessments have all been used in the same capacity prior to the implementation of a needs assessment. However, with the establishment and validation of outcome standards, their use becomes more specific and visible. Each group which helped establish the outcomes can be sampled in a variety of ways and with a variety of procedures.

Some of the same procedures can be used to assess outputs *per se.* However, outputs themselves will probably be assessed with various types of objective and subjective tests. Educational results expressed on a nominal or ordinal scale will probably use attitude surveys or various records of judgment by observers. Ratio and/or interval outputs can take the form of a variety of paper and pencil achievement tests. Also, it will be important to undertake some graduate follow-up studies. Many of the most desired educational outputs and related outcomes will not be possible to directly assess until perhaps one/two decades after high school graduation. How many times did a former pupil vote, utilize a public library, attend a symphony concert, run for public office, help improve his or her community, or expand upon personal experiences found valuable in the school? This kind of "downstream" assessment is vital for an educational institution to come to a more definitive judgment about its educational program and how well a given set of solutions worked. One way "downstream" assessment can be reported is shown below.

A Hypothetical Twenty-Year Follow-up Assessment of the
Class of 1958 on the Ten Priority Objectives of 1958
(85% response)

Objective	Percentage Indicating Completion Since Graduation	Ranked Importance in 1957
1. Registered voter and voted in at least three elections, national, state, local.	43%	3
2. Never arrested for misdemeanor or felony.	86%	9
3. Regularly reads newspaper editorial page/writes letters to editor at least once every twelve months.	35%	1
4. Uses public library at least once a month.	37%	6
5. Understands current world conflict situations.	56%	4

6. Is not now unemployed or has not been unemployed in the past ten years for more than six months.   75%   2

7. Found information in school regarding drugs and alcohol abuse helpful.   69%   5

8. Has experienced no serious mental illness or prolonged period of depression.   71%   10

9. Engages in some form of physical exercise at least once or twice a week.   48%   7

10. Has attended a play or art exhibit once in the last year.   17%   8

The hypothetical follow-up study indicates that 35% of the class regularly reads the newspaper editorial page. This was a performance objective for goal one, which was probably related to the basic skills. Perhaps other performance objectives received a higher level of reading, such as the perusal of various technical journals in subject or occupational fields if they were developed for the Class of 1958.

In order to make sense of such data, it is not only necessary to be able to relate the objectives to the stated and ranked educational goals of that period, but it is also necessary to retain socioeconomic* data about the class as well as the school and community. As many of the situational variables as possible should be part of the records. These could include census data; newspaper articles about school activities, names of faculty

---

*Recent years have brought about some dramatic shifts in recompense for various occupational groups (such as streetcleaners, mail carriers, etc.) so that economic data alone can be misleading in an era where plumbers may make more money than professors. Social class (as indicated by such indicators as education level, occupation, etc.) seems to be a promising indicator when used by itself.

members, and their backgrounds. Records regarding the options considered but rejected within the situational variables should also be kept. Twenty years later, it is often difficult to recall why a school staff selected a curricular option over some other type of option. What appears to be the most probable solution to a problem twenty years later is simply the accumulation of data and breakthroughs in curriculum, materials, learning theory, and research since that time.

Unless a series of decisions can be traced from the initial descriptions of the problem and the variables, and unless it can be understood why the educators at a school or district office selected an option over all others possible, the quality of decisions, in so far as they rest upon the capability of the system to improve its diagnosis and intervention strategies, is extremely difficult to determine. Therefore, it is not enough to be able to make comparisons between gaps or needs twenty years downstream. It is necessary to recall the situation which was present as well.

As identified in Chapters 2, 3, 4, and 5, one technique which is useful in obtaining consensus and mutual understanding is the referent of all goals and outcomes to the individual being able to survive and contribute upon legal exit. Asking all partners to consider their goals in terms of enabling the learners to survive and contribute tends to be a reifying experience. Opinions and biases tend to be reduced when the external referent is used (see Figure 11.3).

It has been said by some critics of the consensual determining techniques of the needs assessment that "there is no special wisdom in the masses." If this is an excuse for not involving students as consumers and parents and citizens as taxpayers in the establishment of educational outcomes, we would disagree. We don't believe that merely polling any constituency and finding a consensus necessarily establishes a special kind of wisdom or verification of eternal or latent "truths." On the contrary, we see the needs assessment process as an imperfect tool which is perfected with successive applications. Since the state of perception and wisdom is a constantly evolving process, each successive approximation of reality retains at least a parallel vision of that same reality. The opinions of the clients and taxpayers of the

Figure 11.3

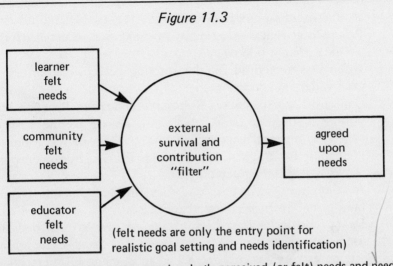

A needs assessment process requires both perceived (or felt) needs and needs substantiated and justified by external reality.

schools are an important part of establishing a hold upon reality, and we believe it is an invaluable parallel process to supplement the practice of the professionals who heretofore have made such decisions in isolation.

No system which extensively involves students, citizens, and educators is going to stray too far from contemporary social values, either directly applied or projected through the Delphi procedure. The alternative is either to find a procedure or approach which does not rest so heavily upon existing social realities and values, or to return the operation of school systems to the authority of a new elite, a danger we would oppose. Besides, the future is not some objective point waiting for us "out there," but an extension of the present and within our contemporary grasp. The future is now.

KEY POINTS

1. Involvement of the educational partners (community mem-

bers, educators, and learners) is essential to successful accomplishment and change.

2. Representativeness is essential to make sure that all of the partners are considered.

3. Polling, as a method for determining perceptions, has been used widely in education.

4. Consensus (agreement) is essential to educational change, and polling is a method for determining consensus and perceptions. Agreement between the partner groups on what is important for the schools to accomplish is determined by a process of gathering perceptions.

5. A community is diverse, and just randomly sampling community members is liable to have biases.

6. Strata exist—characteristics of people and groups may be used to gather people together on the basis of common attributes (such as sex, age, social class, income) and to make sure that a sample includes all of the important variables (strata) to be considered.

7. "Cleanliness" of statistical sampling and instrument design often suffers at the hands of lay people. When politics and rigorous methodology clash, rigor often is asked to suffer.

8. Some "trade-offs" are often required, but at no time should the validity and reliability of the data be bargained away. It is better to have no assessment at all.

9. Validity is the extent to which something does what it says it will do, and reliability is the extent to which it does it consistently. Both are important in surveys and polls.

10. Sample definition and selection is a complex business. Make sure it is done correctly. It is not a business for amateurs.

11. By correctly designing a sample and instruments, many allegations of bias and prejudice may be met. "Plan in advance" is good advice.

12. There are a number of ways to collect data and determine consensus—fit the tools and techniques to the application, not the other way around.

REFERENCES

Amara, R.C., and Salancik, G.R. Forecasting: From conjectural art toward science. *The Futurist,* June 1972, 112-116.

Baker, E. Parents, teachers, and students as data sources for the selection of instructional goals. *American Educational Research Journal,* Summer 1972, *9*(3), 403-411.

Becker, J.F. A sweeping demand for peace, order. *Boston Herald American,* August 16, 1975.

Brevard County Schools. Public rates schools better than last year in comprehensive opinion survey. *Insight,* February 18, 1976. The survey was conducted by Hubbell and Associates of Port Huron, Michigan.

Bridge, G.R. *Nonresponse bias in mail surveys: The case of the Department of Defense post-service survey.* A Report for Defense Advanced Research Projects Agency. Rand Corporation, R-1501-ARPA, July 1974. 25 pp.

California Association of Secondary School Administrators. *Education now for tomorrow's world.* Report of the Curriculum Committee, Sub-Committee on Curriculum Objectives, 1970-2000, May 1968. 80 pp.

Chamberlin, J. Adult-student gap illustrated by survey. *Sarasota Herald-Tribune,* August 1, 1973, Section B.

Cleary, A.T., Linn, R.L., and Walster, G.W. Effect of reliability and validity on power of statistical tests. In E.F. Borgatta and G.W. Bohrnstedt (Eds.), *Sociological methodology.* San Francisco: Jossey-Bass, 1970, pp. 130-138.

Committee for Economic Development. *Innovation in education: New directions for the American school.* A Statement by the Research and Policy Committee, New York, 1968. 74 pp.

Costello, T. Implications for community participation. In T.V. McKelvey (Ed.), *Metropolitan school organization,* Volume 2. Berkeley, Calif.: McCutchan Publishing Corporation, 1972, 105-122.

CPES. CPES education questionnaire enjoys good response. In *CPES taxpayer* of New York State, Albany, New York, March 1975. 2 pp.

Deshler, B., and Erlich, J.L. Citizen involvement: Evolution in the revolution. *Phi Delta Kappan,* November 1972, pp. 173-175.

Downie, N.M., and Heath, R.W. *Basic statistical methods.* New York: Harper and Row, 1965.

Elam, S. Is belief in the open society wavering? *Phi Delta Kappan,* December 1974, p. 233.

English, F.W. Preliminary analysis of the results of the educational goal ranking survey. Hastings Public Schools, April 2, 1976, Hastings-on-Hudson, New York. 25 pp.

English, H.B., and English, A.C. *A comprehensive dictionary of psychological and psychoanalytic terms: A guide to usage.* New York: David McKay, 1958.

Farrell, E.J. *A forecast of responsibilities of secondary teachers of English, 1970-2000, A.D. with implications for teacher education.* Unpublished doctoral dissertation, University of California, Berkeley, 1969. 504 pp.

Fishel, A., and Pottker, J. Women in educational governance: A statistical portrait. *Educational Researcher,* July-August 1974, p. 5; and National Education Association, 26th Biennial Salary and Staff Survey of Public School Professional Personnel, 1972-73. Washington, D.C., the Association, p. 9; as reported in *Sex equality in educational administration,* AASA Executive Handbook Series #7, Arlington, Virginia, 1975, p. 2.

Florida Department of Education. *Florida educational opinion survey.* Tallahassee, Florida, 1970. 225 pp.

Frase, L. et al. *Goal prioritization and needs assessment in the Flowing Wells Public Schools.* Flowing Wells Public Schools, Tucson, Arizona, 1975. 36 pp.

Guilford, J.P. *Fundamental statistics in psychology and education.* New York: McGraw-Hill, 1965.

Handley, D.T. *A forecast and analysis of educational events identified by Utah educators.* Unpublished doctoral dissertation, Utah State University, 1970. 118 pp.

Hays, W.L. *Statistics.* New York: Holt, Rinehart, and Winston, 1963.

Helmer, O. *Analysis of the future: The Delphi method.* Rand Corporation: Santa Monica, Calif., March 1967, P-3558. 11 pp.

Hill, J.E., and Kerber, A. Chapter seventeen, Numerical aspects of sampling. In *Models, methods, and analytical procedures in education research.* Detroit: Wayne State University, 1967, 203-239.

Hyman, H.H. *Secondary analysis of sample surveys: Principles, procedures, and potentialities.* New York: John Wiley, 1972.

Joyce, C. Who counts for what? *Network,* November 1976, *2*(3), pp. 1 and 7.

Kaufman, R.A. *Educational system planning.* Englewood Cliffs, N.J.: Prentice-Hall, 1972.

Kish, L. Biases and nonsampling errors. Chapter Thirteen in *Survey sampling.* New York: John Wiley, 1965, 509-573.

Krejcie, R., and Morgan, D. Determining sample size for research activities. *Educational and psychological measurement,* 1970, *30,* 607-610.

MacDonald, J.B. Curriculum theory. *Journal of Educational Research,* January 1971, *64*(5), 196-200.

McNamara, J.F. Trend impact analysis and scenario writing: Strategies for the specifications of decision alternatives in educational planning. *The Journal of Educational Administration,* October 1976, *14*(2), 143-161.

Morgan, L., and Feldman, D. Needs assessment in higher education: The Mott Foundation community college model. *Educational Technology,* November 1977, *17*(11), 48-53.

National School Boards Association. *The people look at their school boards.* NSBA Report Number 1975-1, Evanston, Illinois. 47 pp.

New York State Education Department. *Recycling resources: Models for shared learning.* A Report of the 1976-77 Commissioner's Student Advisory Committee. State Education Department, Albany, New York. 15 pp.

New York State United Teachers. Part IV Harris poll, preliminary report: Does the AFT or the NEA do a more effective job for teachers? *New York Teacher Magazine,* March 7, 1976, 17-20.

Nunnally, J.C. *Psychometric theory.* New York: McGraw-Hill, 1967.

Nyquist, E.W. An occasional paper from Commissioner of Education Ewald B. Nyquist. State Education Department, Albany, New York, January 1977. 15 pp.

Ohio Department of Education, Division of Planning and Evaluation. *Needs assessment guidelines.* Columbus, Ohio, 1976. 31 pp.

Pellegrin, R.J. *Community power structure and educational decision-making in the local community.* Eugene, Oregon: Center for the Advanced Study of Educational Administration, 1965. 12 pp.

Pennsylvania School Boards Association. *Bulletin,* September-October 1976, *40*(5).

Phi Delta Kappa. Kappans rank three R's first. *News, Notes, and Quotes,* September 1973, p. 5.

Politz, A., and Simmons, W. An attempt to get the 'not at homes' into the sample without callbacks. *Journal of the American Statistical Association,* March 1949, *44,* as cited in NSBA, *The people look at their school boards.*

Sandow, S. *Educational policy formulation: Planning with the focus Delphi and the cross-purpose matrix.* U.S. Office of Education Policy Research Center, February 1972. 72 pp.

School Board of Sarasota County. *A feasibility study of the year 'round utilization of school buildings in Sarasota County,* October 2, 1973.

Shaw, M.E., and Wright, J.M. *Scales for the measurement of attitudes.* New York: McGraw-Hill, 1967.

Spears, H. Kappans ponder school finance questions. *Phi Delta Kappan,* March 1973, 486-489.

Stuart, R. Cleveland tabulates first returns of survey to determine obscenity. *New York Times,* July 14, 1977.

Sudman, S. *Applied sampling.* New York: Academic Press, 1976.

Tuckman, B.W., and Montare, A.P.S. The many uses of PDK's goal attainment tests. *Phi Delta Kappan,* April 1977, *58*(8), 610-613.

Tyack, D. *The one best system.* Cambridge, Mass.: Harvard University Press, 1974.

Underwood, K.E. Educational crisis in Kanawha county. *The School Administrator,* AASA, January 1975, 4-5.

Urban Observatory of Metropolitan Nashville-University Centers. *Community survey of public education in metropolitan Nashville,* August 1976.

Weaver, W.T. *An exploration into the relationship between conceptual level and forecasting future events.* Unpublished doctoral dissertation, Syracuse University, 1969. 359 pp.

Weaver, W.T. The Delphi forecasting method. *Phi Delta Kappan,* January 1971, *52*(5), 267-272.

Witkin, B.R. *An analysis of needs assessment techniques for educational planning at state, intermediate, and district levels.* Alameda County School Department, Alameda, California, May 1975.

Witkin, B.R. Needs assessment kits, models, and tools. *Educational Technology,* November 1977, *17*(11), 5-18.

Wolf, R. Citizen juries evaluate schools. *Citizen Action in Education,* Winter 1975, *2*(2), p. 4.

Wonnacott, T.H., and Wonnacott, R.J. *Introductory statistics.* New York: John Wiley, 1969.

Young, K.M. School storm centers: Charleston. *Phi Delta Kappan,* December 1974, p. 267.

Ziegler, L.H., Tucker, H., and Wilson, L.A. How school control was wrested from the people. *Phi Delta Kappan,* March 1977, 534-539.

Chapter 12

PROJECT, PROGRAM
AND STAFF DEVELOPMENT

A recent and now common application of needs assessment has been as a requirement of federal projects and programs. Various federal and state regulations now demand some sort of needs assessment as part of project development or as a lead-up activity to staff development. However, since the quality and understanding of the writers of such guidelines vary rather substantially from state to state, and from agency to agency, what is meant by needs assessment is often confusing (see Chapters 2 and 3). This is apparent in examining the guidelines. Some merely desire a polling of the public, goals ranked in various ways, a review of the literature to spot "the needs," or needs determined by the writer's subjective opinion. An increasing number, though, are demanding a rigorous output- and outcome-oriented assessment.

The procedures specified most often utilize the "gap concept" of a needs assessment, that is, the difference between a fully functional program and a not so healthy one. A needs assessment in this context does not challenge the validity of the solution itself, something done with an Alpha or external needs assessment of outcomes. If the practitioner has utilized a system approach to develop the program *per se,* then the most appropriate solution has probably been identified.

A project or program is, therefore, a solution to some larger problem or gap; and the most difficult aspect of project development is that educators bypass the identification of an adequate problem statement prior to developing programs or projects as solutions. The following dialogue, which occurred in the superintendent's conference room of a hypothetical medium-size school district, will serve to illustrate the context in which this often happens.

What Is the Problem? A Dialogue in the East Willow Public School District

Cast of Characters

Bertrum Jones, Ed.D., Superintendent

Malcolm Mavix, Director of
Projects

Alice Higgins, Ph.D., Associate
Superintendent

Clarence Terry, Elementary
Principal

Fornice Albumum, Ed.D., Coordinator, Special Educa-
tion

Dr. Jones: When I talked with Alice yesterday, she indicated that Mal and Clarence had already developed some preliminary ideas for our federal project application; and, as she spoke, I began to get concerned about where we are going with this thing. So I got you all together this morning to review where we are.

Dr. Higgins: That's right. I have to admire Mal's and Clarence's energy at this thing, but I have some doubts about the ultimate outcome, so I mentioned to Bert that we should talk.

Mr. Mavix: Well, I don't really understand. Clarence and I thought that the concept of the dial-access system was well understood and we were proceeding on that basis. I mean, after all, we've spent I don't know how many meetings on this thing, met with consultants at the state university in the AV department, and we've been spending a lot of time on it.

Mr. Terry: I have most of the staff really going on this thing. We've seen the film from the Ball Foundation developed by Avis Blanchard when he put dial-access into Grape School in Akron, and I've sent teachers to Grape to investigate it. Besides, the guidelines indicate that technical methods to improve instruction will be given priority ranking. What have we got to lose? I'm with Mal, I don't really know why we're here.

Dr. Jones: I'm not sure that even if we get funded, a dial-access system is what we want or require. I want to retrace the development of the idea of this thing. Would you do that Fornice?

Dr. Albumum: Ok, Dr. Jones. I went to our national conference in Chicago and saw a film, the one that Mal mentioned, developed by the Ball Foundation and Grape School. I thought that it had some potential so I mentioned it to Clarence. He said that he had just finished reading about it in the elementary principal's magazine and got all excited. He called up this guy who is the assistant director and got him to send us the film, which he showed to his staff. I'm not sure all the staff is as excited as Clarence thinks they are, and I've heard some rumblings that the executive board of the teachers association is troubled by some of the implications of the system. It wasn't peaches and cream in Akron either. The teachers union really objected to it.

Dr. Jones: Ok, Fornice, let's leave the staff out of this for the moment, but I think that's an important factor too. Right now I want to concentrate on why we picked a dial-access system. I still don't know how we ended up with it.

Mr. Mavix: Well, it seems simple to me. For years we've had to march kids to the AV room to show films. We've had squabbles among teachers over times and films. Sometimes the films arrive late and sometimes they're not in the best shape to boot. We waste so much time just getting in to see the film and going back and forth that it's a waste of time, period.

Dr. Higgins: The problem is that we're wasting time in showing films?

Mr. Mavix: That's right. A dial-access system means that a teacher can just look into the catalog at any particular time during the day when a film is desired. No scheduling is necessary, no extensive delays, no hassle. If the children are discussing the Great Depression and don't know what the Dust Bowl was, the teacher can reach into the catalog, dial the right number, and presto, a short film comes on the screen about the Dust Bowl. Instant reinforcement of the concept. The teacher has the kids when they're ready. Think of the increased motivation and spontaneity in the classroom.

Dr. Higgins: I think some teachers will resent competing with TV. Heavens know, they do it enough now and lose. Some are afraid that it won't supplement their educational programs, but supplant them.

Mr. Mavix: Any teacher who can be replaced by TV *should be!*

Dr. Higgins: Some teachers just feel the idea is pure luxury. The amount of planning for them to effectively use it will be enormous. The Association will ask for more planning time in the next negotiations. That's all we have to have when the board is complaining about the lack of teacher productivity now.

Dr. Jones: Interesting as all this discussion is and certainly important, it still misses the point I'm driving at.

Mr. Mavix: What's that?

Dr. Jones: What problem will the dial-access system solve? I mean *what is the problem?* I don't buy the idea that the problem is wasting time showing films in the schools. Why do we show films? We aren't competing with the movies. I don't feel compelled to transform the school system into the immediacy of sitting in front of a TV set or a Saturday morning watching cartoon shows. I'm not interested in saving time just to save time. That smacks of the old work ethic. Pleasure is bad, leisure is bad, and only work is good. Saving time becomes a goal in itself. Time is valuable; so, therefore, when we save it, we are good. Baloney. I'm more interested in what we do with the time we've got. What do we require for the time we want? To what ends will the time be spent?

Mr. Terry: The dial-access system is a solution to the perennial problem of motivation.

Dr. Jones: What you're saying is that children aren't properly motivated in your school?

Mr. Terry: No, I think they're motivated. It's just that I think a higher level of motivation could be present in every class with a dial-access system.

Dr. Higgins: You keep forgetting the human element, Clarence. You can put dial-access anywhere if you want; but if teachers aren't convinced it's better, they won't use it so you'll have spent a lot of money on hardware that won't ever be applied.

Dr. Jones: As I said before, I think teacher acceptance is important, but it's not the crucial problem now. The crucial problem is that we don't know what the problem is. We've got a fixation on a dial-access system and we're goaded by the fact that some federal dollars will support it, or we think they will. My question is—and I think it's the only question that makes a difference—will children learn any better or any more than if we had picked a series of ten inspirational lectures for them to attend with their teachers? Why a dial-access system over inspirational lectures, sensitivity training, individualized tutoring, aides in the schools, or even merit pay?

Mr. Mavix: I don't think there's any question that children won't learn better with this system.

Dr. Jones: Well, with the concerns Alice has mentioned about teacher perception, I'm not sure. But leaving that aside for the moment, let's assume that children will learn better or more, how much more and what will they learn? Did you consider inspirational lectures, that is, charismatic talkers?

Mr. Mavix: Come on now, Bert, inspirational lectures, really!

Dr. Jones: No, I'm serious. I want to know on what basis did you consider and eliminate alternatives, other possible solutions?

Dr. Albumum: He didn't. He was sold on dial-access from the beginning.

Mr. Mavix: I did consider some other possibilities; but based on my experience, I didn't think they had the impact possibilities of the dial-access system.

Dr. Jones: Your own experience was the criterion then for selecting or rejecting alternatives?

Mr. Mavix: I guess that's about it.

Dr. Albumum: How can you be so sure your experience is the only one that counts?

Mr. Mavix: That's the essence of educational leadership, isn't it? I mean, an administrator has to act on what's good for kids. He has to be a child advocate. What else can you go on besides faith in your own abilities and experiences?

Dr. Jones: There are times when that is all an administrator has. But there are times, and I think this is one of them, when we have more, or we ought to have more. In fact, I believe that leadership is putting one's views forward to be challenged by the insights of others and by the clients themselves, the students, and ultimately put to the test of use—does it work and does it accomplish something worthwhile?

Mr. Terry: Well, if you left it up to the teachers or some of the parents, *McGuffy's Readers* would do fine! Some of them couldn't thread a sixteen millimeter projector if their lives depended on it!

Dr. Jones: That's not the point, Clarence. We've lost sight of the fact that we don't really know why we got all jazzed up on the dial-access. Do you know what the children at your school aren't learning that they should learn? Do you know what is NOT happening?

Mr. Terry: Well, some of our achievement test scores don't look too hot, but neither do those of some other schools.

Dr. Jones: No, no. What specific skills, knowledges, attitudes aren't being acquired that should be learned at your school?

Mr. Terry: I don't know. I don't think we've ever really identified them that way. I mean we've been following the district's curriculum guidelines all along.

Dr. Higgins: We know that those guidelines are too vague and lack validity anyway. Our curriculum development process hasn't been good. The process has been carried on by an elite few defining what others should learn, and it hasn't helped bridge the gap to how teachers really select content and how they shape their methods!

Mr. Terry: I don't really disagree with that, Alice.

Dr. Jones: Alice's point is, Clarence, that a dial-access system may be the right solution, *after* we've done our work on problem definition. Right now the only criterion we have for validating the selection is your experience. You might be a world traveller, have extensive experience in all grades, worked in all kinds of teacher environments, and with all kinds of kids . . .

Mr. Terry: I grew up in this Town, Bert, I've never worked anywhere else.

Dr. Higgins: I think what Bert is saying, Clarence, is that we must have a broader base upon which to make solution decisions. If all of East Willow's graduates stayed in East Willow, then maybe experience only in this town would be adequate. But as I recall from our last follow-up study on our high school graduates, less than 23% of them stayed. Most of them went to Megapole City, other states, and some to foreign countries. Local experience is important, and it's the base for decision-making in our board, but it simply isn't the sole base for decision-making. It can't be. We'd be doing our students a real disservice.

Mr. Terry: What should we do? We've invested so much time in this project.

Dr. Jones: I don't want to take any proposal to the Board of Education that doesn't really lay out the problem, the gaps, the things that aren't happening in terms of what kids now learn and what it is they must learn. That's the essence of problem identification. If, after we've learned what that is in specific terms, we look at all the possible solutions available and decide that a dial-access system best fits the requirements, then I would wholeheartedly ask the board to submit the project.

Mr. Mavix: Then you're not saying that dial-access is out?

Dr. Jones: I'm not saying that anything is out or in. I'm saying we haven't done our homework. Frankly, I don't blame a lot of the staff, or the teachers in general, for being somewhat cynical about innovation and federal projects. Some of the stuff that's been funded is pure garbage and some of it represented good ideas which are now failing for the wrong reasons—they didn't go with the real problems. If they did anything at all, it was a miracle. Maybe they'll buy that stuff at the state education department, but the time has long passed when this district will submit anything that hasn't been well thought out and after we've gone through a sound needs assessment.

Dr. Higgins: They don't do it at the state education department anymore, either. The new crew that's in now is asking some tough questions about proposal planning.

Dr. Jones: Yes, and while I know that technological developments are a priority because of the past influence of NDEA, no technological gimmick is going to fly without a sound rationale and assessment procedure accompanying it.

Mr. Terry: Well, what do we do now?

Dr. Jones: If you've built in momentum, I don't want to stall it. The momentum will have to be altered to include an adequate needs assessment somewhere. That's Mal's job. Also, I think from what Alice has said there is some suspicion, how much I don't know, about the dial-access system among the staff. I don't think any innovation will go very far that depends on a denigration of teachers and their efforts as its rationale. We might be cynical ourselves at the negotiating table when we're quibbling over nickles and dimes, but I don't think we'll go very far if that attitude carries over into project development. We're not negotiating now. We should be engaged in problem-solving, and that really requires teachers' help, not their antagonism. There are enough teacher complaints about this system to supply you with momentum to go 'most anywhere. If we can't devise a system that will help teachers and be perceived as help by them, we will have already failed to exert positive leadership. I think we have to maintain the momentum we have, recoup, and regroup. I'd like to have a new developmental timeline presented to the administration as soon as possible, Mal. Also, I would hope each faculty council has a chance to critique it as well.

Mr. Mavix: That will lengthen the timeline some, but I guess there are not many alternative courses open. We either have a sound proposal or no proposal.

Dr. Higgins: If we do come up with a dial-access system as the solution, then, we ought to be able to count on staff support. Furthermore, we can have greater confidence that it will really help children learn.

Mr. Terry: Well, this has really been a lesson for me. I won't go off half-cocked again, that's for sure.

Dr. Jones: Don't be apologetic, Clarence. You may be right. Sometimes our intuition is right. Intuitive leaps are responsible for much human progress—but much error as well. Our planning process should be able to encourage intuition as the wellspring of insight, but supplement it with the kind of hard analysis that can hone it into something a lot more powerful. Planning is not a substitute for wisdom. However, wisdom alone can't deliver the results of an applied system of human resources to vast enterprises. That takes planning. I think the needs assessment process required by project guidelines is a nice blend of intuition and public validation that will provide a fairly solid base for problem identification and solution. We should re-examine it closely. Let's get to work.

The East Willow dialogue has occurred many times in many places. As educators, we are prone to jump to conclusions, confuse problems and solutions, and to state a problem as the lack of our particular desired solution. If we are convinced that there is not enough individualized instruction in the schools, it is the lack of individualized instruction that becomes the problem. This lack, discrepancy, gap is not a problem but the absence of *our* solution. The solution ends up, unfortunately, to fill the gap with our "pet answer." If the problem is the lack of individualized instruction, then the solution has to be to increase the degree of individualized instruction. In this case, individualized instruction is both a means and an end (Weber, 1977).

The outcome of an enterprise is the end desired, and possible solutions are the possible means to achieve the desired end. Solutions may be programs and/or projects, unless a project is aimed at helping define the ends *per se,* as in financing a needs assessment process. The following are solutions or means to attain improved pupil learning in the schools.

A Partial List of Solutions or Means in the Schools

career education	flexible scheduling
bilingual education	sex education
differentiated staffing	individualized instruction
dial-access systems	physical education
Chemistry II	social studies
community education	mini-courses
student store	the basics
ecology	Title I
student government	instructional television
art	drama
computerized instruction	audio-visual equipment
vocational education	interscholastic athletics

Curricular subjects are also means. They are simply a convenient wrapping or organizational center for facts, knowledges, and skills being grouped one way as opposed to some other. Certain mathematical techniques or concepts could as easily be grouped under philosophy, where mathematics originated, or in vocational education, home economics, religion, music, business education, or science. An argument over subjects *per se* is an argument about solutions. Most arguments in education are arguments about solutions, especially the lack of a particularly sought after solution by proponents. The "Back to Basics" movement is a good example. However basics are defined, and typically they have not been defined well at all, it is the lack of basics that is the problem, not the lack of a specified range of pupil learning. The presence or absence of the "basics" appears to be the solution to poor school discipline, falling test scores, loss of parental control, lack of taxpayer support, and "watered-down standards" (Peterson, 1977). One prominent newspaper viewed the restoration of *Beowulf* in the high school English curriculum as a healthy response to sagging test scores (*Post*, 1977). The argument leaves aside what students should know after they have studied *Beowulf*, i.e., what does a study of *Beowulf* deliver to students as opposed to one viewing of *Star Wars*? Of *Gone with the Wind? Happy Days?*

Perpetual arguments over solutions mean that education is continually subjected to fads—first liberal fads then conservative ones. Both liberals and conservatives play the same game and both are guilty of perpetuating educational fads. With the expansion of knowledge, what students could study in school is almost limitless. What they *must* study is the question that needs assessment attempts to answer. It does this not by arguing over programs or subjects, but by defining the outcomes outside of programs and subjects, because programs and subjects are means and not ends. The interplay, juxtaposition, and shaping of means are almost endless. We do not view the current scene as a battleground for the inclusion of one to the exclusion of something else. Rather, we view the right question as the appropriate shaping, interplay, and juxtaposition of what exists with new facts, knowledges, and attitudes.

A needs assessment of the most basic variety (Alpha or external type) is the base for determining what means are accomplishing important ends. If the correct ends or results are not being attained, then all the means currently being used to attain them must be re-examined. The assumption is made for the purposes of *this* chapter that the most appropriate, valid, and useful ends or outcomes desired have been defined, and that now the school system is ready to apply a gap analysis of its programs or means used to attain the desired ends.

The Precedent of Accreditation

The accreditation process is a good example of a means-type (or internal variety) of needs assessment. A gap analysis is performed by a visiting committee who look at a school compared to accreditation standards and local standards. They are basically trying to assess whether or not the school is meeting a given set of criteria.

Typical accreditation reports do not deal with how well students are learning or not learning, or how useful that learning will be when they enter society. Rather, accreditation teams compare the present situation to some set of standards. For example, if the standards indicate the expected level or scope of courses to be found in a particular subject area are such-and-such, accreditation seeks to determine if all the courses fulfilling that scope are included. The difference is a gap or discrepancy in the level of courses. The gap would be met by developing the required number of courses.

If the ratio of guidance counselors "should be" 1/250 students and the school has a ratio of 1/350, then there is the "lack" of a certain number of required counselors. This goes on to involve square footage for locker rooms, presence or absence of necessary lab equipment, presence or absence of a school philosophy, adequate administration, pupil/teacher ratios, building cleanliness, etc. This is a needs assessment of sorts, that is, the status quo is being compared to a desired future condition. However, it should be remembered that it is the *means* of the status quo being compared to the *means* of some future desired condition.

A Program Needs Assessment

Other kinds of internal needs assessments engage in a perceptual analysis of respondents and develop gap or discrepancy statements on the basis of these perceptions. A sample is shown in Figure 12.1. The results of this hypothetical survey are shown below in Figure 12.2.

Once the returns were collated, the administrative staff at the school compiled two lists. The first list consisted of programs or areas that were ranked of greater importance by parents than the current emphasis indicated they were receiving, that is, a mismatch

Figure 12.1. Parental Review and Ranking of Programs at Roosevelt Junior High School.

Directions: Dear Parent, we are anxious to find out how you feel about our educational programs at Roosevelt. Down the left side of this survey find the names of our major educational programs. In the middle find a five-point scale which indicates the degree to which you feel that program may be important. If you think it is *very important*, circle the number five, etc. On the next scale indicate the degree to which you think the program is now emphasized at Roosevelt. Please feel free to add your comments on the reverse side about any aspect of the survey or our programs here at Roosevelt.

Clyde Barstow, Principal

Existing Program at Roosevelt	The Degree to Which You Think This Program Is Important					The Degree to Which You Think The Program Is Now Emphasized				
	Very Important	Important	Somewhat Important	Not Very	Don't Know	Strongly Emphasized	Receives Some Emphasis	Does Not Receive Enough	Should Not Be Emphasized	Don't Know
	5	4	3	2	1	5	4	3	2	1
1. Physical education and physical fitness	5	4	3	2	1	5	4	3	2	1
2. English/lang. arts	5	4	3	2	1	5	4	3	2	1
3. Reading	5	4	3	2	1	5	4	3	2	1
4. Mathematics	5	4	3	2	1	5	4	3	2	1
5. History/geography	5	4	3	2	1	5	4	3	2	1
6. Home economics	5	4	3	2	1	5	4	3	2	1
7. Industrial arts	5	4	3	2	1	5	4	3	2	1
8. Art	5	4	3	2	1	5	4	3	2	1
9. Music	5	4	3	2	1	5	4	3	2	1
10. Study skills	5	4	3	2	1	5	4	3	2	1
11. Career education	5	4	3	2	1	5	4	3	2	1
12. Extra-curricular activities	5	4	3	2	1	5	4	3	2	1
13. Health education	5	4	3	2	1	5	4	3	2	1
14. Sports/team activities	5	4	3	2	1	5	4	3	2	1
15. Guidance/counseling	5	4	3	2	1	5	4	3	2	1
16. Testing	5	4	3	2	1	5	4	3	2	1
17. Homework	5	4	3	2	1	5	4	3	2	1
18. Self-responsibility	5	4	3	2	1	5	4	3	2	1
19. Library/library skills	5	4	3	2	1					
20. Special education programs	5	4	3	2	1	5	4	3	2	1

Figure 12.2. Hypothetical Parental Ranking of Programs at Roosevelt Junior High School (83% response).

	Existing Program	Degree of Perceived Importance	Degree to Which Program Emphasized
1.	Physical education and physical fitness	2.88	3.02
2.	English and language arts	4.87	3.16
3.	Reading	4.89	2.67
4.	Mathematics and computation	4.37	4.23
5.	History and geography	3.66	3.50
6.	Home economics	3.01	2.75
7.	Industrial arts	2.53	2.74
8.	Art	2.14	2.51
9.	Music	2.85	2.90
10.	Study skills	4.25	2.80
11.	Career education	3.15	2.15
12.	Extra-curricular activities	3.32	3.01
13.	Health education	3.92	3.86
14.	Sports and team activities	2.47	3.58
15.	Guidance and counseling	3.89	3.24
16.	Testing	4.54	3.48
17.	Homework	4.67	3.12
18.	Self-responsibility	4.52	3.41
19.	Library and library skills	3.33	2.59
20.	Special education programs	2.65	3.45

between importance and emphasis. This list is indicated in Figure 12.3.

The second list (Figure 12.4) shows programs that parents thought were receiving more emphasis than their perceived importance required. The data generated by the survey proved to be interesting, but hard to utilize. This is one of the major difficulties in actually applying this type of survey data.

Figure 12.3. Programs/Areas Ranked More Important
by Parents than Current Program

Program	Perceived Importance	Amount Emphasized	Difference
1. Reading	4.89	2.67	- 2.22
2. English/language arts	4.87	3.16	- 1.71
3. Homework	4.67	3.12	- 1.55
4. Study skills	4.25	2.80	- 1.45
5. Self-responsibility	4.52	3.41	- 1.11
6. Testing	4.54	3.48	- 1.06
7. Career education	3.15	2.15	- 1.00
8. Library/library skills	3.33	2.59	- .74
9. Guidance/counseling	3.89	3.24	- .65
10. Extra-curricular	3.32	3.01	- .31
11. Home economics	3.01	2.75	- .26
12. History/geography	3.66	3.50	- .16
13. Math/computation	4.37	4.23	- .14
14. Health education	3.92	3.86	- .06

Figure 12.4. Programs/Areas Ranked Less Important
by Parents than Current Program

Program	Perceived Importance	Amount Emphasized	Difference
1. Sports and team activities	2.47	3.58	+ 1.11
2. Special education programs	2.65	3.45	+ .80
3. Art	2.14	2.51	+ .37
4. Industrial arts	2.53	2.74	+ .21
5. Physical education	2.88	3.02	+ .14
6. Music	2.85	2.90	+ .05

For example, the major negative gap between what parents thought was important and the program of the school which was perceived to be the weakest occurred in reading. What would school officials do to improve the reading program? Suppose the reading scores for the school were above average. The actual data base for determining a gap must still be obtained because school officials cannot simply accept parental perceptions of programs as *prima facie* evidence that the reading program is weak. School officials may decide that a public relations campaign is required to inform parents that reading scores are above average, that the school reading laboratory ranks among the best in the region, and that speed reading is available for students to take as an elective.

Suppose, however, that there is no test data to show that pupil reading scores are above or below any comparative population. What then does the school do with this perceived discrepancy? It still must seek factual data about pupil reading ability as the base for administrative decisions. Perceptual data may be based on fancy or fact. While perceived gaps may indicate the actual perception level of parents, they are not adequate alone as a base for decision-making.

The second perceived gap was in English and language arts. Here parents indicated that the school's programs were not strong enough. What does the administration and staff do to strengthen the program? Do they require one composition per week and also satisfy parental perceptions that not enough homework is being assigned? Do they require more book reports, handwriting lessons, upgraded textbooks, fewer films, more memorization of famous speeches or poems such as *Beowulf?* The range of options is so great as to befuddle most administrators. A choice of one or more possible solutions may not improve the program or convince parents the program is in fact strong. On what basis do parents decide a program is weak or strong?

The third and fourth gaps from parents present similar problems to the school but add some new dimensions as well. To improve the perceived strength of the school, is every teacher required to give homework? How much more homework? To improve study skills, what does the school do? It could require each student to take a four-week unit in "study skills." It could require a test to be passed in which the student demonstrated knowledge of how to study or where to find certain information. Should every teacher and every subject teach study skills? To what extent are they being taught now? What are the actual study skills that should be taught?

Homework and study skills cut across the school curriculum. They affect everyone. Choices about where such gaps are specifically located or how they may be closed are vague. Again, numerous choices open to the administration and staff may not be the ones that form the data base upon which parental perception rests. Furthermore, there may be no real gaps once the actual study skills *per se* are located and defined in the curriculum.

On the other side of the question, the school discovered that parents felt it emphasized sports and team activities too much as well as special educational opportunities for the gifted. The administration is sure to face the wrath of the team booster clubs if it tries to de-emphasize sports, and it will endanger federal or state requirements in special education if it de-emphasizes its special education program. The latter is being mandated by state and federal laws and regulations, and the school has considerably less latitude in changing the emphasis upon these programs.

There is strong suspicion that the level of information which is available to parents about the school program influences percep- tions of program strength. If certain areas of the curriculum are regularly described in the community press and others are not, the public's perception may be that the number of column inches devoted to school activities is a rough gauge of their importance to school officials and the amount of emphasis received at the school itself. What the public doesn't know and the school cannot control are the biases of the newspaper editors and reporters. Team sports and new federal laws for the gifted and learning disabled child are news. Homework and study skills are not news. The intervening variables of the press and the amount of information are difficult for the school to control.

Perceptual surveys are popular and usually the public responds to them fairly well. They are good public relations in that the image of the concerned school staff trying to be responsive to public perception is undoubtedly presented. However, the results of such surveys are extremely difficult to utilize in actual decision-making beyond serving as the basis for various PR efforts, or as a rationale for the members of the staff or administration to develop their "pet projects" as possible solutions to fill the apparent gaps.

When the data from perceptual surveys are tabulated, the apparent gaps may not be based on actual educational gaps at all, but on the biases of the local community press, TV, or radio stations. While this is important information in terms of community perceptions, it is not the hard kind of information upon which curricular and instructional priorities can or should be established. Such priorities should be based upon the importance of skills, knowledge, and attitudes for students and the degree to which students do not possess the desired levels of competency. Gaps should be the actual differences between such specifically identified skills, knowledges, and attitudes and the degree to which they have been acquired by a given student population (Drumheller, 1971).

Programs or areas are, again, *means to ends.* Altering the means may have little or nothing to do with actual learning, but may simply be a different way to package the same practices that have always been utilized in the schools. Perceptual surveys are too prone to be influenced by extraneous factors, such as the most recent press coverage or the results of the latest Gallup Poll.

Some Application Considerations

James McNamara (1977) has examined the differences between operational or field research and academic research. He found several significant differences. The first is that academic research begins with the identification of an estimate of the parameters of a study based upon a sample of cases. The result is a statistic upon which certain inferences can be made about the larger population. Operational research, such as the kind of perceptual survey just reviewed, is not based upon statistics but upon including all of the population in a survey. The population forms the parameters of the study. Conclusions from such a study are not a matter of estimating confidence intervals as required in more academic research, but of determining the general integrity and accuracy of information obtained. Thus, in our survey, confidence intervals could be developed; but the issues raised about the utility of the data and how perceptions are formed generate serious questions regarding data integrity. While "academic" research frequently spends time defining samples, in school-based surveys, such as that reported, the sample and universe are already defined. Operational research in the context reported is really social policy research, and its most valuable function is to form a reliable and valid information base for decision-making. While such research and responses may be reliable, the validity is sufficiently in question so as to be risky to accept at face value. Policy-making would be extremely dangerous on the basis of the data generated if the data were supposed to be "representative."

The necessity to involve the public in evaluation efforts and the requirements for sound policy-level decisions have not yet been adequately explored in the literature. Most efforts underscore the importance of citizen involvement, but fail to show how such involvement actually helps decision-makers influence what students may or may not learn. Sweeping policy-type decisions pertaining to program development or emphasis are extremely difficult to translate into the things that teachers teach or do not teach, or into what students learn or do not learn. Furthermore, they are extremely difficult to isolate in terms of the school's influence in assisting students in acquiring them.

In order to be most useful to decision-makers, the actual skills, knowledges, and attitudes that should be acquired or learned must be identified and decision-makers must be more specific about what it is that the schools should do. Debate about the "basics" will not appreciably improve the ability of the schools to respond to the public demand for anything, until the basics are operationally defined and until the existing school curricula can be made sufficiently explicit to be able to isolate and locate the points in the system where it is supposed to teach the identified skills, knowledges, and/or attitudes. Without such precise location, the ability of the schools to actually respond to criticism is limited to exhortation of agreement with the "basics," but without the ability to deliver the desired outcomes. For any human organization to respond to criticism and to change or alter organizational relationships or the flow of resources to a different and possibly more effective configuration, objectives must be sufficiently clear so as to be able to discern if they have been reached to a greater or lesser degree than some other alternative configuration employed. If outcomes or desired goal statements are so vague that almost any configuration would be acceptable, then the organization has no ability to make determinations regarding effectiveness.

Schools' goals have traditionally been so nebulous as to include almost any function desired by society and to tolerate almost any strategy or decision which influenced resource configuration as appropriate. As long as the public does not more explicitly define the outcomes and/or school leaders refuse to assist the public to be more precise about its desires, the schools will be convenient social scapegoats for all kinds of societal failures. At the same time, they will still be unable to respond to the cries for accountability and to the success or the lack thereof for minority learning.

To a large extent the social effectiveness of the schools lies in the definition of their role. Such definitions must answer, or at least come close to approximating a response to, such questions as "schooling for what?," "schooling to enable students to learn what?," or "schooling to enable a society to achieve what goals?"

The functions of American schools have traditionally been so inclusive that they cannot exclude by definition paradoxes, contradictions, or conflicts. Schools have become for some students the gateway to the good life, for others vast cells of containment, and for still others a mechanism for co-opting their ambitions to alter the society in fundamental ways. Fuzzy mission statements allow schools to continue favoritism, acts of overt or covert discrimination, and practices which reinforce negativism and human frustration by continued operational failure experiences for some students, whether by default or by purposive action.

Various social forces are demanding a more accountable management of the schools for results. On the other hand, the same social forces appear to require such vague goals that the management cannot fix upon a mission statement which will enable them to be more responsive. It may well be that to provide the schools with a firmer operational set of objectives would be to expose the society itself to its prejudices and to strip away the verbiage which allows the schools to prepetuate social inequities. Exposing the schools to sound management practices would be to reveal the extent of injustice fostered in them and supported by the existing power arrangements of the larger society. Society, therefore, may simultaneously demand and resist having the schools become more accountable.

Strategies for Project Development

The most concrete manifestation of the educator's response to such paradoxes is to find appropriate means to define and channel social response and expectations for the schools. At the same time, we believe it is the educator's responsibility to point out these contradictions and paradoxes as they arise, returning them to various socially elected or appointed bodies either for temporary or long lasting resolution.

While we don't believe that every possible contradiction can be resolved, we do believe that forcing such agencies, groups, and boards to confront the contradictions and paradoxes is essential to sound educational leadership. We are very aware that on issues which have support in wide constituencies of varying opinion, the grounds for consensus are usually more tenuous than on those with narrower support. We believe that, with the process of public involvement available to practitioners, these bands of consensus or agreement are possible to operationalize and will provide educators with a firmer base upon which to install better management systems than have existed in the past (Gonder, 1977).

Furthermore, we believe the first prerequisite to the creation of such a system is the derivation of a more specific, valid, and reliable set of objectives for students. We also recognize that the basis for such consensus is more or less stable and that continuing efforts must be made to define the validity and utility of the objectives as well as the basis of consensus, particularly one which does not favor the automatic extension of the status quo. Definition cannot be allowed to result in "freezing" any kind of force field for the educator. Such a field is the result of dynamic tension which is in a period of ebb and flow and which must be consistently appraised, re-appraised, and mapped. The educator is not a silent participant, a mere objective observer. On the contrary, the educator is a dynamic participant in this process and can help shape the forces which may be present on the field at any one time.

Perhaps the most concrete course of action for the educator is to use project development as a base for changing the existing management system.

Project Development and Needs Assessment

Regardless of the specific guidelines, a project developed around the following basic questions will not be too far off target when applied. A good project will answer specifically the following questions:

(1) Why this problem versus all other problems?

(2) Why the selected solution over all the other available alternatives?

(3) How will one know when the problem is solved?

Why This Problem Versus All Other Problems?

A problem is a need selected for closure. A project must operate from the needs and then define the problem not in terms of a pet solution and the absence of that solution as a gap or need, but as a lack of appropriate, valid, and desired responses in a specified situation, and the results which come from a successful intervention. Therefore, the problem cannot be "the lack of individualized instruction," the "lack of educational TV," or the "lack of adequate curricula." These represent *solution* statements. The problem must be stated and might well flow from such indicators or systems as follows:

- Forty percent of the twelfth grade could not read the editorial page of *The New York Times* with at least 80% comprehension as measured by teacher certification on a performance test.
- Sixty-two percent of the ninth grade could not recognize the basic art forms of the Romantic period.
- When asked to describe themselves by looking in a mirror, 68 percent of the fifth graders used more negative descriptors than positive descriptors.
- Eighteen percent of the eighth grade could not list the basic functions of the three branches of the U.S. government.
- Only 21 percent of the tenth grade could engage in

creative problem solving to find three ways to resolve a described human relations crises in a simulated family environment.

If the project is aimed at improving a means to pupil learning because of funding requirements or guidelines, then the problem can deal with the difference between a desired response and the actual response. For example:

I. A responsive school is deemed to have the following characteristics:

(a)   responsiveness as determined by a creative and useful response to an innovative or novel challenge;

(b)   high level of productivity or output as evidenced by an ability to increase outputs without substantially increasing costs;

(c)   high-level ability to utilize conflict situations to define and attain new levels of interpersonal and intergroup consensus as exhibited by peak periods of conflict followed by higher levels of productivity;

(d)   high morale due to participative structure as exhibited by sustained increases in productivity, responsiveness, and ability to utilize conflict positively;

(e)   increased social utility as judged by satisfaction levels of clients and the board of trustees or governing agency with a decrease in complaints regarding services to clients.

II. The current school does not possess the following characteristics as determined by:

(a)   extensive delays (4-5 months) in meeting novel or innovative situations. Breakdowns in communication, backlogged problems, and crises management are the major modes and characteristics of the school;

(b)   productivity by any measure has not increased, or has remained stable. By almost all measures (dollars per man hours, pupil achievement, dollars per pupil expended, etc.), the school is less productive than before;

(c)   conflict leads to paralysis and not to higher levels of consensus. The school avoids conflict. It is rarely allowed to surface and much energy is consumed trying to escape it;

(d)   morale is low and getting lower. Structure is becoming more elite, more bureaucratic, more clogged with rules and regulations, and less open to input from a variety of levels;

(e) the satisfaction levels of clients is decreasing. Funding agencies are restive and calling for drastic re-appraisals of current methods of financing and of allocating responsibilities. Some are calling for the abandonment of the current school by creating competing structures which are more responsive than the existing one.

While it can be shown that the school is defined and supported to help students learn better, its lack of appropriate and responsive characteristics impedes its ability to assist learners in an organizational (collective) sense. These are examples of gap statements, problem symptoms, or problem statements delineated in terms of defined needs. This needs assessment is of a Delta mode, since it is looking at gaps between the effectiveness of a current solution (the school as it exists) and a required solution (the school as it should exist when it is responsive).

When there is a listing of gaps, one should determine why one or more of the gaps (potential problems) should be selected for elimination or reduction versus all of the gaps which could have been chosen. Thus, one asks the question and intends to answer it of "why this problem (or need) versus all other problems (or needs)?" This is basically a needs assessment question—of all the needs which were or could have been identified and selected, what is the rationale for selecting the need (or problem) which was selected?

In this above example, a number of gaps were identified. If one or more were to be selected for resolution, why were they selected? One criterion suggested earlier was to select among the needs by asking two simultaneous questions:

- what does it "cost" to meet the need, and
- what does it "cost" to ignore the need?

A more crass phraseology would be:

- what do you give and what do you get?

Returning to the East Willow scenario, why did Mavix and Terry select the dial-access system versus all other solutions? If they had asked why this problem versus all other problems, and if they had understood the differences between means (the dial-access system) and ends (still unspecified in terms of criteria external to the East Willow School), then they might not have had the interaction we witnessed. By asking why a given problem has been selected instead of all the others which could have been selected, there is a "forcing" of thought back to basics and back to what *matters* in education—learners' survival and contribution external to the schools, upon their point of legal exit.

In our examples in this chapter, much of the activity is related to goals and objectives internal to the schools. If one were to adopt the frame of reference of an external (or Alpha-type) needs assessment, then these questions might emerge:

East Willow

- How well or how poorly are the graduates of our high schools doing in getting into college, finding jobs, or otherwise being productive in our society?

- When we examine the graduates or "pushouts" who are not at the survival/contribution point, what specific characteristics do they display, and which of the characteristics would have been positively altered by one or more school experiences?

- What is the relationship between the current curriculum and the successes and failures of our learners after they legally exit from East Willow? Is there any "value added" from what our schools contribute versus no schooling?

A Responsive School

- What are the relationships between the managerial/administrative procedures and characteristics, and the performance of learners?

- What are the relationships between teacher performance and characteristics, and learner performance and characteristics?

- What are the relationships between what our school does and how it does it, and the survival and contribution of our learners after they legally exit?

When we ask the question, "Why this problem versus all other problems?" we are pushing ourselves and our educational partners toward the tough but critical issue of picking problems on the basis of what must be accomplished with learners in order for them to survive and contribute once they leave the school system. It also prevents us from picking solutions before the *problems* have been identified and validated.

What Are All of the Possible Solutions to the Problem? Too often the criteria for selecting a desired solution are not listed or mentioned. Rather, they are implied. Too often there are conspicuous blanks in projects in this regard. Some project guidelines are now mandating that all alternative solutions be listed. To return to one of the examples previously cited:

- Forty percent of the twelfth grade could not read the editorial page of *The New York Times* with at least 80% comprehension as measured by teacher certification on a performance test.

Possible solutions to the problem (if it were one to be selected and the "what should be" identified on the basis of empirical evidence) are listed below:

1. Do nothing. Continue as is and see what percentage of the students cannot read the editorial page next year. Perhaps it will get better, or the newspaper will become easier to read.

2. Change newspapers. Make it the editorial page of the local newspaper with a lower level of reading comprehension required.

3. Drop the standard. Newspapers aren't important anyway.

4. Develop a new standardized test and administer it prior to the twelfth grade to see why students cannot read.

5. Develop a new approach to teaching reading at the secondary level.

6. Change the elementary textbook series in reading.

7. Write a federal project to improve the reading by some novel approach.

8. Re-test with a parallel instrument that measures the same thing.

9. Send elementary teachers to inservice training sessions on teaching reading.

10. Increase the percentage of time at the elementary and secondary levels in which reading is taught as a separate skill.

11. Bring in specialists from the university for further diagnosis.

12. Organize a curriculum task force to upgrade the reading curriculum.

13. Formulate a requirement at the tenth grade level and do not allow any student to graduate who cannot pass prior to the twelfth grade.

14. Force students who cannot pass a preparatory exam to go to summer school.

15. Change the structure of the school library and ask the librarian to supervise a study hall for poor readers.

16. Organize a student tutoring program in which good readers tutor poor ones.

17. Develop several alternatives to the traditional reading program, such as reading from comic books, mechanical manuals, "hot rod" magazines, and gossip columns.

18. Send the poor readers to a commercially operated reading center.

19. Devise a reading test for teachers to see if they know how to teach reading.

20. Organize a tutoring class for parents to help their children at home on special assignments.

21. Develop a resource room for students with special reading problems.

22. Develop a parent volunteer program to tape record all lessons requiring reading so that students can listen to someone reading their textbooks and learn in spite of their handicaps.

The solutions could perhaps be expanded to include 50 to one hundred or more alternatives. In developing the alternatives, it is important to include "do nothing" as an appropriate response and to ask: what is the cost of ignoring the problem? Too often solutions are discarded because they will cost something to implement. What is forgotten is that doing nothing usually carries a cost as well. Deciding to do nothing *is* a decision (Greenwald, 1973).

Sometimes the cost is in prolonged failure and longitudinal impact, that is, it will accrue in the next several years, not immediately. Thus, doing nothing about poor reading scores at the elementary level may not have any cost there; but later, at the secondary level, it may lead to special classes with reduced enrollment, extra effort in developing a less strenuous curriculum, special teachers, counselors, and other personnel to cope with negative students, and extensive vandalism in the school building.

Why This Solution Versus All Other Solutions?

The project developers have an obligation to indicate the full extent to which alternative solutions were considered and then have a useful rationale to support the criteria by which some were included as possibilities and some were not. Some of the most common criteria by which solutions are selected are as follows:

(1) *Cost*

Expensive solutions are difficult to fund, particularly if they are risky or demand an innovative response.

(2) *Expertise*

Some solutions clearly fall out of the range of capability of the personnel who must implement them. This can be partially overcome (in some cases) with inservice training (staff development).

(3) *Time*

Some solutions are too cumbersome and time consuming to be within the limits of a project funded on a year-to-year basis.

(4) *Complexity*

Some solutions are so complex as to be impractical.

(5) *Acceptability*

Some solutions are not acceptable because they would change the group influence structure.

(6) *A priori decisions*

Some funding guidelines already lean toward a solution. Solutions which do not lean the same way are considered inappropriate.

(7) *Demonstration of competence*

The project proposal in some way does not conform to guidelines or fails to adequately explain how the proposed solution will work.

(8) *Conventional wisdom*

Every field is dominated by conventional wisdom. This wisdom or orthodoxy spills over into acceptability in terms of the range of responses and those who would have to implement the changes. Proposals which fall outside the ranges of conventional wisdom are very risky from the perspective of the funding agency. Such wisdom may be dignified by a (biased) literature search or from a selective review of existing research.

The above eight criteria can be stated any number of ways. Many times they may not be stated at all but are implied. However, in more specific form they comprise the criteria for selection or rejection of solutions which are proposed to be funded and possibly implemented. In simple terms a project proposes a solution that is not too costly, is supported by the literature and/or current research tracks, doesn't take too long to implement, is acceptable to those funding and those who must implement the changes, is not too complex, is within the guidelines as a possibility, and is within the range of existing competencies of the personnel submitting the proposal. With these in mind, it is not too difficult to see how truly innovative solutions to problems are rarely funded and why human progress is very slow in terms of results—no matter what may be the field of endeavor.

The most revolutionary breakthroughs in human history often represent simply the shedding of conventional wisdom. Some examples are cited below:

- the heliocentric versus the geocentric theory of our planet's place in the solar system;
- understanding of human blood circulation;
- how human diseases are spread and how they may be eradicated;
- notions in physics of motion and rest (absolute vs. relative).

How Will One Know When the Problem Is Solved?

If an organization can state the conditions by which it will know if the problem is solved, then evaluation is considerably less of a problem. If, however, the problem has been stated as the lack of a "pet" solution, then the problem is solved when that solution is implemented. If, for example, the problem has been stated as the lack of individualized instruction, as we have previously discussed, it can only be responded to by *more* and not by an alternative at all. If the problem is not defined as an actual gap in student achievement, the means/ends problem will continue to plague administrators and boards.

Examples of Project Schematics. Figure 12.5 shows the sequence of major project activities, beginning with a needs assessment and ending with the development of a change model for a school district. Figure 12.6 indicates how each component is related to a project objective and the cost per month on the basis of project activities.

Programs developed on this systematic basis, in which the four basic questions have been answered, are much more direct and to the point in constructing and stand a far better chance not only of being funded but of actually making a *difference* after funding has been secured (Krathwohl, 1977). No amount of technical diagrams or jargon can take the place of a well thought out and constructed proposal based upon the paradigm presented. The key appears to be differentiating between means and ends and then logically selecting a solution which describes the conditions by which one will know if it has been effective (Law and Bronson, 1977).

Staff Development

Staff development is the term which describes attempts by school systems to attain one or more of the following aims:

(1) assess the individual skills of various staff members (teachers, supervisors, assistant principals, etc.) or levels (middle management, top management, etc.) in relation to existing problem priorities;

(2) focus certain system skills upon designated problems, i.e., to re-arrange them or to prioritize them. This relates to the question of "time on task," a critical finding in the research on learning; and/or

(3) to add to or to upgrade the existing array of skills, knowledges, or attitudes of levels of staff to increase repertoires to solve previously unsolved problems or emerging problems.

Needs assessment is utilized in staff development as a basic diagnostic tool to ascertain various skill levels and to help focus and change such skills so that the school system can effectively engage in better instruction (English, 1976).

While the linkages between teaching skills and learners are plain and straightforward, the research specifically tying them together is bound up in some rather complex problems (Berliner, 1976).

Figure 12.5. Analysis/Sequence of Major Project Activities.

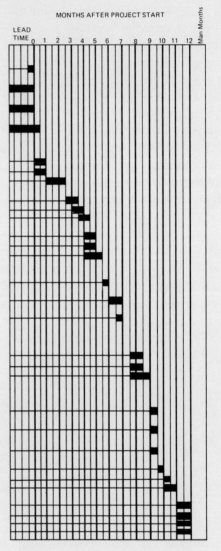

Figure 12.6. Determination of Monthly Cash Flow for Project.

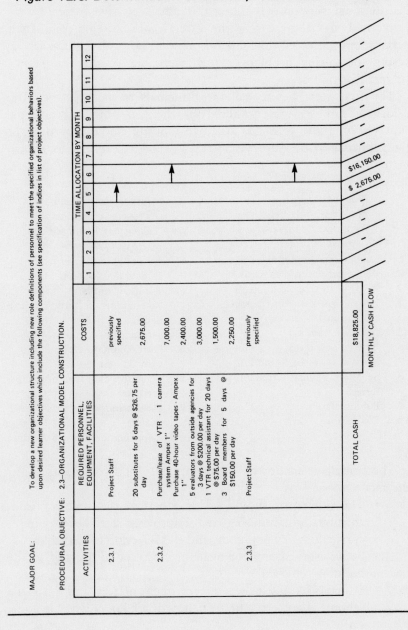

MAJOR GOAL: To develop a new organizational structure including new role definitions of personnel to meet the specified organizational behaviors based upon desired learner objectives which include the following components (see specification of indices in list of project objectives).

PROCEDURAL OBJECTIVE: 2.3—ORGANIZATIONAL MODEL CONSTRUCTION.

ACTIVITIES	REQUIRED PERSONNEL, EQUIPMENT, FACILITIES	COSTS	TIME ALLOCATION BY MONTH											
			1	2	3	4	5	6	7	8	9	10	11	12
2.3.1	Project Staff	previously specified												
	20 substitutes for 5 days @ $26.75 per day	2,675.00												
2.3.2	Purchase/lease of VTR - 1 camera system Ampex 1''	7,000.00												
	Purchase 40-hour video tapes - Ampex 1''	2,400.00												
	5 evaluators from outside agencies for 3 days @ $200.00 per day	3,000.00												
	1 VTR technical assistant for 20 days @ $75.00 per day	1,500.00												
	3 Board members for 5 days @ $150.00 per day	2,250.00												
2.3.3	Project Staff	previously specified												
TOTAL CASH		$18,825.00												

MONTHLY CASH FLOW

$16,150.00

$ 2,675.00

One example of how a middle-sized system went about an internal staff development effort pertained to the role of the instructional supervisor. The major administrative officers were concerned about increasing the effectiveness of this role. Their perceptions indicated that supervisors were not assisting the school system in solving problems which were out of their respective subject disciplines.

The first step was to ask the principals to indicate the "top priorities" of services rendered to them by the instructional supervisors. They were also asked to indicate where they thought the priorities of the supervisors really were. The results are shown below.

Principals' Views of Top Services Which Should be Rendered by Supervisors	*Principals' Views of Priority of Services Currently Rendered by Supervisors*
1. Curriculum development	1. Resource to the Supt.
2. Coordination of curriculum	2. Budget development
3. Help in textbook adoptions	3. Public relations
4. Help principal in teacher evaluation	4. Evaluation of building program
5. Inservice training	5. Working of federal projects
6. Provide new ideas	6. Curriculum development
7. Serve as resource to Supt.	7. Provide new ideas
8. Selection of instructional materials	8. Selection of instructional materials
9. Public relations	9. Help principal in teacher evaluation
10. Evaluation of school program	10. Coordination of curriculum

The principals made the following anecdotal comments about the supervisors:

• The supervisor should become part of the building team, continually evaluating and improving staff development, curriculum development, and the selection of materials.

• Supervisors should be available to respond quickly to the building program.

• Supervisors must get out of their offices and into the schools; they can't help if they don't know what is going on.

- Public relations is fine, but teachers and principals require help and that is more important.
- Supervisors are afraid to take a stand on a controversial book, they won't help the principal out of this kind of jam.

A simple discrepancy analysis can be made from the comparison just indicated. First, treat the principals' views of how the services should be ordered as the "correct" list of priorities. Then compare the present perceptions of the principals to the "correct" list. The results would be as follows:

Gap Severity

1. Help in textbook adoptions (total gap)
2. Inservice training (total gap)
3. Coordination of curriculum (8)
4. Resource to the Supt. (6)
5. Public relations (6)
6. Evaluation of school program (6)
7. Help to principal in teacher evaluation (5)
8. Curriculum development (5)
9. Providing new ideas (1)
10. Selection of instructional materials (0) (no gap)

The above data could be used to re-structure the services of supervisors to more nearly coincide with the perceptions of principals *if* principals were the only client group requiring service and *if* supervisors possessed the necessary skills to accommodate the new focus level. However, the first assumption is incorrect. Another client group served by instructional supervisors are teachers. A survey of the teachers indicated the following:

Teachers' Views of Top Services Which Should be Rendered by Supervisors	*Teachers' Views of Priority of Services Currenty Rendered by Supervisors*
1. Resource/consultant to teachers	1. Working on federal projects
2. Inservice training	2. Budget development
3. Communicating to parents	3. Initiating new ideas
4. Employing teachers	4. Communicating to parents
	5. Evaluation of building program

5. Working with special students
6. Resource to faculty meetings
7. Assist in pupil diagnosis
8. Initiating new ideas
9. Resource to principal
10. Teacher observation

6. Employing teachers
7. Assist in pupil diagnosis
8. Resource to principal
9. Inservice training
10. Resource/consultant to teachers

Sample teacher comments about the services rendered by instructional supervisors were as follows:

- Too much time is spent in bringing in new programs via federal dollars. The "feds" aren't always right. We should concentrate on sound, basic instruction.
- The supervisors can function better only if they are aware of actual classroom situations. Often they are too far removed from the classroom, the teachers, and the students. Their plans and suggestions are impractical and ineffective. They must be sure that they really understand what is happening in the schools. Only then can they be of real service to teachers and exert a positive influence.
- Workshops could be provided to teach skills development for children above or below grade levels in content areas.
- Work individually with some special students who require the special expertise.

A similar kind of simple comparison could also be made with the teachers' perceptions. Now examine the last group of clients served by the instructional supervisor, the central office staff.

Central Office Administrators' Views of the Top Services Which Should be Rendered by Supervisors

1. Coordination of curriculum
2. School building program evaluation
3. Budget development
4. Teacher observation
5. Initiating new ideas
6. Selection of materials
7. Employing teachers
8. Resource to principals

Central Office Administrators' Views of Services Currently Rendered by Supervisors

1. Selection of materials
2. Resource to principals
3. Inservice training
4. Working on federal projects
5. Coordination of curriculum
6. Employing teachers
7. Teacher observation
8. School building program evaluation

9. Working on federal projects
10. Inservice training

9. Budget development
10. Initiating new ideas

A perusal of the three perceptions indicates that the supervisors come closest to satisfying their bosses' ideas of priorities. They are most responsive to central office requirements. Each client group views its own priorities and problems as the most demanding and those to which the supervisors should be most responsive.

The data also indicates the problems affiliated with doing an assessment of one group's effectiveness in the eyes of others. Imagine a similar survey performed for the classroom teacher with groups consisting of parents, students, colleagues, and the principal. Role conflict is common in many situations in school districts.

Perhaps the greatest asset of such data collection is that it can reveal whether or not consensus is possible for a given level or role. Activities in staff development are important foci upon which to design a training group. If only the board of education or top management defines the skills required for a group, other client groups may suffer. The interdependencies involved in assessing gaps in skills or knowledges of the professional staff should take into consideration the level above and the level below each layer of staff to be trained. In some cases, more than just those.

What should be remembered is that the final criterion of the effectiveness of staff development must be an improvement in pupil learning. Individual happiness, group morale, increased skills, and employee productivity are meaningful only if students are more effectively served and they learn more and with increased efficiency. Too often, staff development efforts assume that once certain skills are acquired or once certain problems are resolved on an intergroup or interpersonal level, the results will be shared with learners and the school will become more effective. There is no reason to assume that this will in fact occur unless and until staff development efforts deliberately create measurable bridges between staff and students and improved student learning, and an additional bridge is built between learning outputs and societal outcomes. From this perspective, staff development, like program and project development, is a means to an end.

KEY CONCEPTS

1. The gap concept of comparing desired and actual status or conditions can be applied to means or ends. One example of the gap process applied to means is accreditation. Another is a program assessment where a collection of resources is compared to certain standards.
2. Perceptual surveys ask the respondents to share their feelings or opinions based upon their current perception of either the status quo or a future desired condition.
3. Operational research differs from academic research on the basis of purpose and the manner in which sampling occurs. Academic research attempts to draw inferences to a larger population based upon findings or conclusions. Operational research is interested in one population, usually a school or school system group, and is interested in data for decision-making for that population group.
4. Operationally defined means that general statements or intentions are translated into specific actions required to create an entity, or supply criteria by which the existence or non-existence of something may be determined, so that it is possible to see what they mean in terms of "doing" or "results."
5. Bands of consensus refer to the parameters in which agreement is expected or desired to be obtained.
6. Successful proposals for activity generally ask and answer these questions:
   * Why this problem versus all other problems which could be considered?
   * Why is this solution selected versus all other solutions which could be considered?
   * How will we know when we have been successful?
   * How much will it cost?
   * How will it be managed to assure success?
7. The above questions relate to the concept and application of a system approach.

REFERENCES AND BIBLIOGRAPHY

Berliner, D.C. Impediments to the study of teacher effectiveness. *Journal of Teacher Education,* Spring 1976, *27*(1), 5-13.

Drumheller, S.J. *Handbook of curriculum design for individualized instruction.* Englewood Cliffs, N.J.: Educational Technology Publications, 1971.

English, F. Staff development: The nine lives of inservice training. *Inservice,* October 1976, *10,* 2-3.

Greenwald, H. *Direct decision therapy.* San Diego: EDITS, 1973.

Gonder, P.O. *Linking schools and the community.* Arlington, Va.: National School Public Relations Association, 1977.

Kaufman, R. *Educational system planning.* Englewood Cliffs, N.J.: Prentice-Hall, 1972.

Krathwohl, D.R. *How to prepare a research proposal.* Syracuse, N.Y.: Syracuse University Bookstore, 1966. Second edition, 1977.

Law, A.I., and Bronson, W.H. *Program evaluator's guide.* Princeton, N.J.: Educational Testing Service, 1977.

Lewin, K. *Principles of topological psychology.* (F. Heider and G. Heider, translators). New York: McGraw-Hill, 1936. Reprinted by Johnson Reprint Company, 1969.

McNamara, J.F. *Practical significance in administrative research.* Unpublished paper prepared by the UCEA-University of Rochester Career Development Seminar on "Research in Educational Administration," May 16, 1977.

Peterson, B. SAT scores, 14-year slump laid to TV, schools, blacks, women, a decade of distraction. *Washington Post,* August 24, 1977.

The Washington Post (editorial). The test scores. August 25, 1977, p. A-26.

Weber, G. The cult of individualized instruction. *Educational Leadership,* February 1977, 326-329.

Chapter 13

NEEDS ASSESSMENT IN
NON-EDUCATIONAL CONTEXTS

In all cases, a needs assessment is an outcome gap analysis. There are a series of processes which lead to outputs, and these outputs will lead to outcomes. In each application the extent to which the anticipated outcome is related to survival and contribution in our society, the more relevant and practical will be the needs assessment and the resulting planning.

Assumptions concerning the utility of the required results can be no better than the reality of those assumptions. In business, industry, and the military, there is frequently little or no systematic attention paid to the utility and validity of the criteria used in planning. Most frequently, the usefulness of the planning referent is assumed usually by someone very high up in the organization. Rank may or may not be correlated with the ability to know the requirements for human survival and contribution in our society—now and in the future.

Industrial and Business Applications of Needs Assessment
The Carron Corporation has been located in Upper Lowe, New York for thirty-nine years. The years during World War II were good to them, and they manufactured slide rules for engineers, drafting, and applied sciences. The boom held up after the war, and the company experimented with lightweight metal, and ultimately shifted to aluminum after much research. Engineers missed the familiar wood; but aluminum caught on, and sales spiralled. Carron Corporation's earnings rose, and the company executives settled in for a long and profitable life.

Soon they gave employees profit sharing, and Upper Lowe grew to love and respect the corporation. The unionization movement failed for the last twelve years; but it looks as if the employees might elect a bargaining unit this year, now that the profit sharing portion has been removed and the company says it cannot pay cost-of-living raises anymore. The slide rule business is almost a curiosity now; the cheap and much more flexible hand calculator has captured 94% of the market, and things look grim for all—management and labor.

The President has called in a consulting firm to conduct a needs assessment—a term he heard at a Management Association of the Northeast meeting. He wanted to know who "needed" slide rules and the consulting firm went forth. They plotted sales figures in different parts of the U.S. and foreign countries and suggested that the "need" could be increased by appealing to conservatives and traditionalists with a "good-old-days" campaign and by noting that one should have a slide rule for when the batteries burn out in the electronic calculators.

The Carron Corporation is about ready to move ahead with the suggested "last-ditch" strategy.

With many business and industrial concerns there has been a classical confusion between marketing and needs assessment. They have assumed that their product is viable and useful and the only thing required is to find out how to sell it and to whom. As in educational applications, there is a confusion between means and ends. There has been an assumption that the only problem is to sell what is on hand—the basic assumptions about the product line remain unchallenged.

Marketing is generally concerned with selling (or finding out to whom to sell and where) and will not consider an Alpha-type assessment in which the gaps between current outcomes and desired outcomes are defined external to the corporation and its product line.

Most industrial and business organizations have a product or a product "dream" and build both the item and the market. Those who have a viable product "make it," and those who do not fail. There is a product-orientation and a product-centering in business. Anyone questioning the viability and utility of the company product line is usually purged.

The classical problem with corporations is their failure to appropriately define their product line. Most company personnel tend to think they are in the business to sell a product, not to make money. Confusions arise, and many companies go out of business. Times change and so do the demands for goods and services.

Why then should a company continue to ask questions only about how to market a given product? Should not profit-oriented organizations ask more basic questions relating to what the current and future requirements of citizens are so that they can identify and fill possible gaps? "Find a need and fill it" was once sage advice. Many companies do not follow it, but rather adhere to "see what you've got and tomorrow will take care of itself." It doesn't always happen that way! Unstated assumptions are just as disastrous in business as they can be in education.

In order to be optimally responsive, a company must look at the society at large and determine the survival and contribution levels of the clients. In some cases, new markets and new products will be identified and defined. In others, variations to existing products can be determined and successfully sold. In a few cases, a company might shift to a new business, sell out, or otherwise change its focus.

What would have happened, for instance, if the railroads two decades ago had examined the requirements for their own survival and had looked at the market as being (1) extended over time, (2) changed on the basis of the requirements for people to survive themselves, and (3) predictable to some extent. If this had been done and if there had been a needs assessment in which requirements *outside* of the railroad were examined without the underlying assumption of being in the "railroad business," the railroads might have owned airplanes, busses, and trucks as well as rails and rusting cars. They would have noted a requirement (and a continuing one at that) to move people and material; and there were some places where railcars could do "just right," but other places where it was best done by other vehicles. Additionally, they might have noted the differing requirements for people and material and might have chosen the delivery mode on the basis of requirements generated from reality instead of from history or fantasy. This is not to say that marketing is unnecessary or wrong. It is useful and important—*after* it has been decided what to sell, and not a moment before.

If a company such as our hypothetical slide rule corporation had put aside its current product line and examined requirements of people outside of the corporate island, it might have become a distributor for electronic calculators, or even assembly plants. Facts do not cease to exist simply because one chooses to ignore them! Looking beyond the myopia of organizations and products can result in continuing economic health.

The steps to be taken by our hypothetical corporation would have begun on a continuing basis very early, perhaps ten or fifteen years ago, when the concepts and tools of needs assessment were first known and available. A corporate planning group might have been set up and charged with "pre-marketing" activities, including noting the needs (as gaps in outcomes, not process) of the society as well as the needs of workers, management, and stockholders.

With the slide rule safely tucked away so as not to contaminate their planning requirements, they could have noted the goals and objectives of the stockholders (who might have been happy with a given return on their investment regardless of the product line), the goals and objectives of the workers (probably to have pride in what they do as well as to earn enough for a happy life), the goals and objectives of the management (probably the same as the workers, but with a deep commitment to helping engineers and scientists figure things out simply and well), and finally the goals and objectives of society.

This last item is an important and comprehensive one, and is no mean undertaking. It requires that current and future trends be identified and that one look at a very "big" picture—much bigger than slide rules or widgets. Other gaps could be located and prioritized by looking at future requirements for survival and contribution and by looking at ways in which much of the market is now or could be served with large institutions and products already "in place." For instance, computers were already being made and one company was dominating the market—no room? Electronics promised microcalculators and processors, and the market for slide rules could be seen as evaporating rapidly. Yet people had to add, subtract, multiply, and divide. What could be done to service that group and help them survive and contribute? Many possible methods-means could be conceived including:

- electronic calculators,
- mini, special-purpose calculators for market, school, estimating for small businesses, etc.,
- TV games,
- TV-driven home computers,
- home games for learning,
- school games for learning, etc.

In other words, an Alpha-type needs assessment could have identified that the current product line, no matter how well marketed, would eventually dissolve, and also could have identified requirements for other related products which would use the know-how, interests, talents, and resources of the existing company.

This hypothetical story is not a happy one. The company went bankrupt because the marketing consultant group did not know how to look outside of the product line and did not consider new vistas and horizons which would build upon the current resources and external needs. The plant is now vacant, and the last slide rules have been bought by a New York City marketing firm which is planning to market them as memorabilia for nostalgia buffs. Of course, it did not have to end that way. *Questioning assumptions is not only for educators, but for anyone who wants to help others to survive. If you want to survive, make sure your business is helping others to do the same.*

This example is not a far-fetched one. Most planning, whether it is in education or business and industry, usually starts with assumptions which might be hard to support if one were to look outside of the present company and the existing product line. Yet most books on marketing and planning which are used by business and industry start with, at best, a Beta-type needs assessment. This almost assures that the status quo will be maintained and that the long-term survival of the corporate entity is in jeopardy. Changes characterize our society and thus our markets. We can either adapt or die. Learning how to market better is a short-run solution; external or Alpha-type needs assessment is for the medium and long-run.

Another Example
The Great Disconnect and Northern Phone Company has had a

successful business. In actuality, it "owns" the market. It has high-quality service, makes its own equipment, and does research. It hires top-notch people, trains them well, and promotes from within. The education and training people set the standard in training in the field, and they are "on top" of all the new training methods. They do research, and they report their results at all of the professional society meetings. The company spends a lot of money, and it expects a lot in return.

The Assistant Vice President for Training at a subsidiary has just attended a training session on self-concept and laterality (brain hemisphere dominance) and its effect on performance, and is ready to apply the techniques to an experimental training program for linespeople. He hires a consultant to design an instructional system based upon the research work on hemispherical dominance of the brain, and waits to see the results.

People learn better in this pilot study—mastery is up 13% over a control group, and he is ready to implement it in measured fashion throughout his territory. But then more data comes in—the post-test scores were up 13% but some young hire carried the study further and measured the "value added" to the new training program in terms of operational effectiveness and efficiency on the job (after the completion of training). He found that there was no measurable gain six months later for this test group! The experimental group scored higher, but did not do any better on the job! The new training concept was shelved, and he decided to do some work on locus of control as a variable in improved training. An experimental group was formed . . .

In this example, a "solution" occurred before the problem had been identified and justified. In fact, the company started with a Gamma needs assessment and wanted to determine if this new possible training method would work better than other possible training methods. When compared to the existing program, it was found to be better. But when compared to what had worked in the field before, this new method was no better or no worse. Like so many other methods which frequently fail for the wrong reasons, this one was selected before the actual problem was identified and defined.

An external or Alpha-type needs assessment seemed to be in order. Instead of picking a solution and assuming the importance and viability of the existing training objectives, it was appropriate to determine if the current skills, knowledges, and attitudes of workers were required for doing the job, and further, if the job itself was important for the company.

The Task Analysis Problem. Very frequently, a task analysis (a potentially powerful tool; cf. Branson *et al.,* 1975, and Mager and Pipe, 1976) is the starting place for determining training requirements. Often, a supervisor or employee is asked to list the tasks and operations required to successfully complete a job (such as motor pool supervision). These tasks are listed, analyzed, charted, and serve as the basis for another task analysis—a learning task analysis which identifies and defines learning requirements and pathways. Gagne's (1977) latest edition of *The Conditions of Learning* offers an excellent source for this type of activity—one which is of critical importance if used correctly and at the proper time in the design of purposive learning change subsystems.

Based upon this newest task analysis, methods-means are selected, designed, developed, implemented, evaluated, and frequently revised. The instructional system has thus been designed, developed, and implemented. Objectives are frequently achieved, and the evaluation usually halts. In our hypothetical example, however, there was another step in the evaluation—did the new system add anything to the person's ability to later complete the task? This will only be likely to occur when:

- there is a direct relationship between the task analysis and the job to be actually accomplished;
- there is a direct relationship between the job's importance and the organization's ability to meet consumer demands and requirements; and
- there is a direct relationship between the company's goals and objectives and the requirements of paying consumers.

In most cases, the utility of any task or set of tasks is based upon historical precedent or expert judgment. If one feels lucky, then it will be worth the individual risk. If one feels that the assumptions should be verified, then an Alpha-type needs assessment would be in order.

In the above case, an Alpha-type needs assessment would have indicated the gaps between current services and the communication requirements of the paying subscribers. From these needs, associated performance requirements for the linesperson job could have been developed—ones in which the *actual* job requirements served as the basis for planning and delivery of training.

In this hypothetical case, it might not have been the self-concept training or the laboratory basis which were weak. Rather, perhaps the objectives of the course were either wrong or incomplete, and thus the training strategy (laterality and self-concept) was no more inappropriate than operant conditioning or norm-referenced testing. The solution did not fit the problem, and this was not defined or discovered. The only discovery was that the current group of trainees were found to be no more effective than previous trainees using different techniques. It was not the new methodology which was at fault but the objectives!

Many good ideas never reach true testing due to the fact that the correct problem has never been defined nor justified. In business and industry, it is important that a company not only identifies the correct solutions, but also makes sure that it has the correct mission objectives and performance criteria—for the whole company—which are usable for the definition of subsidiary outputs and methods and means. Without this, outputs might be approved; but if unrelated to external criteria, the outcomes will not be achieved.

This is a bit slippery, but worth dwelling on. The outputs of a corporate entity must be training of personnel, preparation of marketing materials, or development and production of materials for sale. The outcomes should be a product which sells and which brings back a reasonable return on investment. Thus, the outputs are internal to the organization; the outcomes (or results) are external to it. Outputs should be related to and derived from the required outcomes; the activities and internal results of the company must be designed to achieve the required outcomes of the corporation. This is usually done only by assumption.

In order to assure that this will be the case, a formal and systematic needs assessment is required. Without it, the results may be haphazard, costly, and disappointing.

Needs Assessment in the Military

It seems axiomatic to those outside of the military—"there is no problem about what the military does, it fights." There are some who even see the military mission as "readiness" or in times of peace, "training."

Some who are in the military see it the same way. Like civilian agencies, and similar to education, military people see their jobs in terms of processes, not results. Training, fighting, and readiness are all processes. What are the outcomes for the military? Survival? Why not? Contribution over and above survival? Certainly.

Perhaps a possible mission objective for our military would be to identify and overcome any one of several possible threats to the citizenry from external or internal forces which are illegal or against existing treaties and international agreements. This is an outcome, and it is measurable. It relates directly to survival, and survival is a prerequisite to any contribution. Failure to distinguish means and ends in the military can be just as wasteful and devastating as in the civilian, educational, or public sector. Let's see a hypothetical example.

> In a meeting of the board of overseers for a military college, whose job it is to train future command officers, the recommendation was made to individualize instruction and self-pace wherever possible.
>
> Immediately, a competition was held to provide detailed training for the staff, supervisors, and instructors in self-paced, individualized, modularized instruction. A hard competition was fought; and the successful bidder was a developer of instruction who was well-known for work in evaluation and who had developed and validated an extensive individualized training program in evaluation-based training. The work was good, and it resulted in predictable performance change. All of the faculty and staff were trained, passed the training program, and were given diplomas. In turn, each was required to form a team and develop an individualized instructional program for her or his course.
>
> There was much anguish as faculty, staff, and commanders argued the merits of individualized, modularized education. Courses were developed, validated, and implemented, and criteria were set. After much arguing and resistance, the curriculum was individualized and was meeting most of the objectives. The greatest problem came in "soft" courses such as management and leadership, but this too was accomplished at long last. Courses which had high turnover of content were also developed, but there was a special task force assigned to keep them updated and corrected.

After the fourth year of operation (and many, many visitors later), there was one last attempt to dis-establish this approach; but it failed, and the approach was institutionalized.

Then, a visiting team of external evaluators and auditors were invited in by a Congressional fiat, and the outputs of the school were compared to outcomes required of officers in the field. An evaluation was made of the effectiveness of the individualized curriculum, and there were no noticeable benefits. Another team did the same study, and the same results held. The approach was dis-established.

This is not a far-fetched possibility. It could happen in our public schools, and it could happen in our military schools. Good ideas fail here for the wrong reasons as well.

In this example, a Delta-type needs assessment was made. What has to be done to fill the gap between current instructional methods and individualized ones? This question was asked rather than the Alpha-type question which would have asked, what are the discrepancies between our current skills, knowledges, and attitudes for survival and those which are likely to be encountered currently and in the future? Based upon this external referent, the gaps indicated would serve as the basis for distinguishing entry-level officer skills, knowledges, and attitudes and those required. Then curriculum and curriculum content would be determined on the basis of these discrepancies. Then, and only logically and rationally then, could there be some choices relative to methods of delivery, such as individualization, modularization, and self-pacing.

In this hypothetical example, the difference between the process (individualization of instruction) and the required outcomes (ability to survive and contribute in the world of possible conflict) was blurred and obliterated. The outputs were substituted for the outcomes, and a methods-means (process) was substituted for the desired results. Individualization became the end, whereas it should have been a possible means to the desired and required end.

Individualization is a powerful tool when applied correctly and when it is the best choice among alternatives. It is not useful (perhaps even harmful, for that matter) in and of itself. Means are only meaningful in context of the desired ends.

Actually, the hypothetical military school should probably be using much in the way of self-instructional or self-paced instruction; but without knowing WHAT should be taught, changing the delivery methods can hardly be expected to make much of a difference. Useless content, no matter how well or how expertly delivered, is still useless.

Another good idea failed for the wrong reasons, and the school will probably not have the opportunity to use this powerful tool because it will be thought of as a failure for many changes of command and many cycles of memory.

Let us look at another possibility.

> Air Force pilots have to be trained to rigorous standards. They not only command expensive equipment, but the lives of their crews and citizens throughout the world depend upon their skill and judgment.
>
> Educational technology has been recognized early by this branch of the service, and their research and development have contributed to the entire field. In fact, the first large-scale teaching machine was developed under contract for this service.
>
> They are on the cutting edge.
>
> Recenty, one branch of this service decided to use audio-visual devices and self-paced instruction in an attempt to improve proficiency and reduce training time.
>
> The objectives for flight training on a new rotary-wing aircraft were put in such a form, developed, validated, re-written, implemented, and evaluated in the training context. Ninety percent of all trainees reached a score of 90 or better on the criterion-referenced test. It was approved and became operational.
>
> Later, follow-up studies on the relationship between the outputs of this "systems-designed" course and the regular methods used showed that there was lower in-field performance than with the regular method of delivery, although there was a savings in time.
>
> Headquarters decided that the savings in time was not worth the lower performance, and the methods were scrapped. They were not to be used for some time in this branch of the military.

Again, the focus was on the methods, not on the outcomes required. While the systematic design of instruction is powerful and useful, it is not an end in and of itself. In order for any design to be effective, the objectives have to be correct.

In this hypothetical case, the analysis of objectives was taken from existing sources, and instruction was designed to achieve objectives which did not represent what had to be done ultimately in the operational world with the aircraft. The training was effective (it achieved criterion levels on all validation tests), but the objectives were not completely valid and useful.

If an external needs assessment were accomplished (Alpha-type), data would have been generated relative to a number of issues and concerns, including whether or not the aircraft was necessary,* and what were the requirements for in-field operation. These, then, would have served as the measurable objectives against which alternative methods and means (strategies and tools) could be selected. The military is a societal agency charged with specific responsibilities. It is often judged on processes, but its real job is assuring our survival and ability to contribute. If we are conquered or killed, we are incapable of both survival and contribution.

It is of critical importance that the military separate but understand the interrelationship between means and ends. Further, it is important that military personnel are not trapped within the confines of their service or command, but can look at

---

*In many cases, the researcher or developer is apprehensive about delving into the issue of whether or not a command decision was the correct one (such as a new aircraft, a battle order, or the like). If one is responsible for the successful accomplishment of a mission, it is important to determine if the mission is achievable in the first place. If it is not (for instance, if a given aircraft is destined for failure in the planned operational environment), then no amount of subsequent planning (internal-type needs assessment) will be successful.

It is suggested that an Alpha-type needs assessment is imperative for any planning and doing effort. At worst, the data can corroborate the decision already made from higher-up; at best, it can prevent one from continuing an error for which he or she can later be held accountable. It is not easy to question an order, but it is best to do it with data than with raw emotion or, worse, with failure which should not have been one's responsibility.

Needs assessment is a tool for better assuring a person's success and the success of his or her "boss."

requirements of the entire military service as the basis for their activities. It isn't easy, but it means survival—for the citizens and for themselves.

It is almost ironic to present this section for the military—they have been pioneers in instructional system technology and development. Laboratories in the Air Force, Navy, Army, and the Marines have researched and developed instructional improvement concepts and tools which have served as inspiration and examples for business, industry, and education.

Yet, it is this exact expertise which has to be harnessed and managed correctly, by noting that these approaches are possible means to desired and required ends, and not ends in and of themselves.

IT IS IMPORTANT TO NOTE THAT THIS RELATIONSHIP AND DISCUSSION IS IN NO WAY CRITICAL OF OR NEGA-TIVE ABOUT EDUCATIONAL TECHNOLOGY OR TECHNO-LOGICAL APPLICATIONS. IT IS STATING ONLY THAT THEY REPRESENT POWERFUL TOOLS AND TECHNIQUES WHEN PROPERLY APPLIED. IF APPLIED INCORRECTLY OR TO THE WRONG PROBLEM, THEY WILL FAIL. SO WOULD ANYTHING ELSE INCORRECTLY OR INAPPROPRIATELY APPLIED. THEY ARE ALTERNATIVE MEANS WHICH SHOULD BE SELECTED ON THE BASIS OF REQUIRED OUTCOMES. A PROPER AND APPROPRIATE NEEDS ASSESS-MENT CAN PROVIDE THAT REFERENT.

Again, the lessons and techniques suggested for education in this book are appropriate for use in the military. In most instances, there may be a simple substitution for educational-con-text words and phrases. Both are similar in that they represent socially sanctioned institutions charged with changing behavior in order to accomplish a specified set of results. Both work with people and through people. Both require support of the public and monetary and physical facilities. Both are open to public scrutiny, frequently by incorrect and often irresponsible critics using incorrect and irresponsible criteria. Both can be made more successful by applying needs assessment tools and techniques.

Needs Assessment in the Non-Education Public Sector

Education is not the only public sector activity which could benefit from needs assessment concepts and procedures. Planning is quite well established in areas such as housing, transportation, welfare, employment, and other public areas. When needs assessment procedures are used in these areas (yes, the word is in their lexicon now as well as education's), they are usually Delta and occasionally Gamma-type needs assessments. These activities, like all others, have the same common underlying fabric—people. And these people have a tendency to start with internal-type needs assessments.

A hypothetical case study:

Modest City (population of 90,000 in a county of 140,000) was known to be a good place to live. It had several institutions of higher learning, much government, and a long tradition of respect for other human beings. The citizens prided themselves on hospitality and their quality of life. Large, canopied streets abounded in the city limits, and traffic jams happened for just 15 minutes each morning and each evening.

New housing developments sprung up to the north and to the northeast of town, and the poorer sections on the south stayed poor. The upwardly mobile people moved to the northern reaches of the city, and finally to the country north of town. Speculators began buying the northern part of town a number of years ago and, to "everyone's surprise," the freeway came through the town on the northside, not the southside.

The traffic jams got worse, by this small town's standards (now there might be a tie-up for 17 minutes), and talks of widening roads started. The city and county councils were for it, but a few "kooks" in town wanted to preserve the local close-in residential areas and avoid in-town noise and air pollution. The progressives (their label) argued for expansion, growth, and economic well-being. The residents (labeled "little old ladies in tennis shoes" by the opposition) argued that widening roads would exceed air and noise pollution standards, would drive affluent close-to-town people out into the suburbs, would destroy the city tax base, and would ultimately leave the inner-city a low-cost housing ghetto. They brought law suits, and the battle was on.

The state transportation people studied the problem, and made their report. Widen the roads, they said, and allow traffic to flow easily in and out of the city. Allow the employees in to work and spend money, and let them go back home at night. Land was purchased, and tempers flared. Lawsuits continued, and the in-town homeowners met in furtive bands to "cut off the machine."

Some streets were widened, and the traffic increased, not decreased. It was then found out what larger cities had known for some time—widening roads that go someplace increases traffic, since it becomes a more attractive route for motorists. More widening was planned to accommodate the new traffic influx, and the arguing continued. But the "master plan" by the Department of Transportation was not to be denied . . . "science" was invoked by the councils to show that they were correct, and indeed, they argued, scientific planning and needs assessment had shown the way!

The story has a predictable ending—the streets were widened; traffic increased, dumping more and more cars in town, creating strains on other streets; and people started moving out to the suburbs—that is, those who could afford to leave a house and sell for less due to the air pollution and noise increases. Poor people moved into the once-desirable homes, and their budgets did not allow them to keep up the houses as they had been kept previously. Crime rose in town, and suburban shopping centers started getting more and more business because shoppers did not want to go into town at night and risk mugging or assault. The city was small within the city limits, larger and larger in the county, and the city tax system considered defaulting on their municipal bonds for a hospital and streets since the tax base had moved out of town. The county supervisors dragged their feet on plans for "unification," since it was not to their advantage to pick up the "downtown blight and burden."

The city council is now trying to get a previously built but inadequate circle route around town expanded to four lanes, with limited access so that traffic can move in and out thereby relieving the in-town congestion. They now realize that this might have been better than "blasting" through streets without looking at the desired traffic loads and patterns as the goals.

This hypothetical example is what can happen if people start with a Delta-type needs assessment and plan the solutions without verifying the problems. Much of public-sector planning is, unfortunately, of this variety.

It should be noted that public agencies (and many private ones) are organized in terms of solutions to be delivered rather than by possible problem areas. Examples of this might be seen in the labels or titles of agencies: transportation, housing, welfare—all *solutions* (or potential solutions) to problems. Within this nomenclature there is little or no way for new problems to be identified and justified, or new solutions to be designed or implemented. For example, if one is working for a department of transportation, then the solution to all problems would likely be seen as "transportation." Thus, the solutions are frequently pre-determined by the labels and assigned functions; and this is usually the invitation for Delta-type planning and needs assessment to take place.

Additionally, we reward workers for solutions delivered, not new problems and unique solutions designed and offered! We have shifted our emphasis from "find a need and fill it" to "come up with a quick and dirty solution—regardless of the problem."

We have before us a problem of major magnitude in education, military, industry, business, and the public sector—how do we change from old ways and means to new and more productive ways of looking at problems, defining them, and then solving them so that they "stay solved"?

This problem cuts across all areas, and thus we suggest that the methods and techniques presented in this book be considered for application (with appropriate modifications of language and examples) in other-than-education situations.

KEY POINTS

1. Needs assessment is a concept and a tool which can be used in areas other than education.
2. The major points, models, and considerations discussed in previous chapters are immediately usable in non-educational contexts. All that is required is a "re-coding," using the words which are familiar to that non-educational arena.
3. Much planning and needs assessment in non-educational contexts, as well as in education, usually start at the Beta, Gamma,

Delta, Epsilon, or Zeta levels. The effects are the same as in education; good ideas fail for the wrong reasons.
4. There is often a confusion between marketing and needs assessment. Marketing is usually an effort to find buyers for a product or product line already in existence. Needs assessment (Alpha or external type) is designed to find out what a product line should be.
5. Task analysis is frequently used in military and industrial settings to determine requirements. It is a powerful tool but it is often asked to perform a function which it is incapable of performing—determining what should be accomplished—not determining that which is currently being done. Thus, people often substitute task analysis for needs assessment, mission analysis, and function analysis. Also, they frequently fail to distinguish between a task analysis designed to determine current activities and a task analysis which determines learning requirements.
6. As in other areas, it is important to ask the correct questions as well as to use the correct tools. The effort has to come in that order. Confusing means and ends in non-educational contexts can lead to disappointing results.

REFERENCES AND BIBLIOGRAPHY

Branson, R.K., et al. *Interservice procedures for instructional systems development.* Phase I, II, III, IV, V and Executive Summary. Florida State University, Center for Educational Technology, Tallahassee, August 1975.

Gagne, R.M. *The Conditions of Learning.* Third Edition. New York: Holt, Rinehart, and Winston, 1977.

Mager, R.F., and Pipe, P. *Criterion-referenced instruction: Analysis, design and implementation.* Los Altos Hills, Calif.: Mager Associates, Inc., 1976.

GLOSSARY

ACCOUNTABILITY: the process of determining what proposed results have been achieved.

ACCREDITATION: a means or internal type of assessment of a school or a program.

ALLOCATIONAL DECISIONS: the method or manner in which organizational resources are dispersed within the system or school.

CONFIDENCE INTERVAL: a statistic which indicates the probability to which the obtained mean score of the sample is "like" the estimated mean score of the larger population or universe.

CONFIGURATION: the manner in which work is assembled or the resources of the organization put together to accomplish the mission.

CONTEMPORANEITY: a concept of Kurt Lewin's that everything is happening at once.

CONTENT VALIDITY: the degree to which the actual items in a survey reflect the total scope of educational outcomes within state law/guidelines and board policies, and later the extent to which school district goals/objectives have attained a consensus to be included on the district's total list of possible outcomes.

CONVENTIONAL WISDOM: the development of certain orthodox approaches or explanations of problems or data which often preclude more creative or insightful approaches from being formulated.

CURRICULUM: the planned means by which inputs are used and managed to obtain validated ends (outputs and outcomes).

341

CURRICULUMLESS GOALS: output statements of student growth that are not developed as the exclusive domain of any particular curriculum.

DEEP CHANGE: change in an individual or organization which is not superficial or cosmetic, but involves a basic shift or modification of current values, goals, and/or behaviors.

DYSFUNCTION OF BUREAUCRACY: problems created by the organizational form known as bureaucracy.

EDUCATIONAL PARTNERS: learners, implementers (including teachers, administrators, school staff, consultants), and society (including community members and employers).

EDUCATIONAL TECHNOLOGY: the application of a systematic process for identifying and resolving problems in education which are based upon documented and verified needs.

ENDS: the results from using processes, procedures, tools, and how-to-do-its. Ends include products, outputs, and outcomes.

ESSENTIAL TASKS OF MANAGEMENT: the basic functions of management are to define the purpose of the enterprise, to acquire the resources to carry out the mission, and to configure the resources efficiently and effectively to accomplish the mission.

EXTERNAL NEEDS ASSESSMENT: a gap analysis which requires that the underlying basis for planning and accomplishment be the future survival and contribution in the world to which learners will go when they exit educational agencies and enter society. Any needs assessment has to consider both current societal requirements and future ones.

FACE VALIDITY: the extent to which something appears to measure that which it purports to measure, without consideration as to whether it does or not . . . just so long as it appears to do so.

FORMATIVE EVALUATION: evaluation which determines the effectiveness and efficiency of methods, means, and procedures at any point in the system approach model process.

GAP CONCEPT: a discrepancy or difference between two desired states, either means or ends.

GOALS: desired organizational results (e.g., curriculum) measurable on nominal or ordinal scales of measurement.

GOAL-FREE EVALUATION: the determination of results, both positive and negative, which can be observed after-the-fact, without planning any measurement or previously identified evaluation procedures or vehicles. This is designed in such a way that there is no disruption of the intervention which would be attributable to the evaluation itself.

HUMANISM: the process of being responsive to ourselves and to the needs and characteristics of others in a legal and mutually agreed upon useful manner. It is the treatment of human beings on the basis of human characteristics, and the inclusion of each human into the determination of both the means to be used with them and by them, and their inclusion in the decision about ends. It also recognizes that humans change and are changeable, and that any system or procedure which is used with them and by them must be changeable and responsive.

IATROGENIC PROBLEM: a problem created or made worse by the application of an inappropriate solution.

INPUT: the raw materials used by a process to achieve a product or output; e.g., needs, teachers, dollars, buildings.

INPUT RATIOS: the relationship between resources and clients or staff.

INTERACTIVE CURRICULA: the curricula which emerge as the result of intergroup reactions and dynamics.

INTERNAL NEEDS ASSESSMENT: a gap analysis which allows for the investigation and determination of needs to be restricted to the boundaries of the organization sponsoring the assessment. It assumes (knowingly or unknowingly) that the basic assumptions and ground rules of the organization are correct, or implies that they cannot be challenged.

MEANS: the processes, procedures, tools, or how-to-do-its which are used or usable in converting inputs to any end. These ends could include products, outputs, or outcomes. These are not results, but are ways of achieving results.

NEED: the measurable gap, or discrepancy, between current results and desired/required results. It is not a gap in processes, or means, but a gap between ends.

NEEDS ASSESSMENT: the formal harvesting, collection and

listing of needs, placing the needs in priority order, and selecting the needs of highest priority for action. This process includes the partners in planning, which in education are the learners, the implementers, and the society. It requires that there is a consensus of the partners in the prioritization of needs, and it strongly urges that the process include any additional external referent of survival and contribution when determining need priorities.

NEEDS ASSESSMENT TAXONOMY: a relationship and order between various types of needs assessments. In this one, there is a different type of needs assessment to correspond to each of the six functions of a system approach model:

- Alpha-type: assumes few or no "givens" relative to goals, objectives, and requirements (synonymous with "external" needs assessment).
- Beta-type: assumes the goals and objectives of the implementing agency (or the agency under study) are the boundaries of study and change.
- Gamma-type: starts planning on the basis of a gap analysis relating to solutions and methods-means.
- Delta-type: starts with a gap analysis relative to the implementation of the selected methods-means.
- Epsilon-type: examines gaps in results which have derived from the internal planning which started with Beta-type through Delta-type needs assessments.
- Zeta-type: determines gaps at any point in the system approach process model.

NON-COVERAGE BIAS: the degree to which a sample may be skewed because a segment of the population was not included in the sample design.

NON-RESPONSE BIAS: the degree to which a sample is skewed by the lack of an answer from a certain segment of the sample.

OPERATIONAL RESEARCH: an investigation which is based upon the assessment of the entire or actual population rather than estimates or parameters developed from sampling a population. Operational research is therefore based upon the integrity of the information being obtained.

ORGANIC GROWTH: the notion that no constraints on people in

an organization will result in an improvement of learning.

OUTCOME: the results or "ends," as the impact on an individual's ability to survive and contribute in society. (Possibly indicated by their consumption being equal or less than their production.)

OUTPUT: the "end" of an organization, agency, or agent which may or may not positively affect an outcome.

OUTPUT RATIOS: the relationship between costs of achieving output objectives per client or group of clients.

PERCEPTUAL SURVEYS: questionnaires of a client group or constituency based upon their subjective opinions of the area being assessed.

PLANNING (SYSTEM): the purposive determination of goals and objectives based upon needs, the determination of requirements to meet needs, and the identification and recommendation of methods and means for achieving the required results to meet the needs. Also possibly included in planning is the application of the above to the actual achievement of the required results.

PREACTIVE CURRICULA: the curricula which are prepared prior to instruction.

PROCESS: any how-to-do-it of any agency or agent used in achieving a package or output.

PRODUCT: any materials, goods and services, or packages which contribute to an output.

RANDOMNESS: the concept that those respondents included in the survey had no more or no less "chance" of being included than any other respondents. They therefore can be "representative" of the larger population as a whole.

RELIABILITY: the consistency with which something is accomplished.

SAMPLE: a predetermined numerical unit of a larger population or universe which can be considered representative of that population or universe.

SAMPLING ERROR: the degree to which the results obtained from the sample do not reflect the population or universe as a whole due to bias in the sampling strategy or tools.

SOFT TECHNOLOGY: planning, needs assessment, and system planning which are processes. (Synonymous with "educational technology.")

SOLUTION GAP: not the difference between a future desired status and the current status, but the absence of a preferred solution.

STAFF DEVELOPMENT: an effort by a school system to intervene in the life of a system to upgrade or change existing skill levels in order for the system as a whole to become more effective in improving learning.

STRATIFIED SAMPLE: systematic selection of the important variables or strata within the larger population, such as age, income level, religious affiliation, or political preference.

SUCCESSIVE APPROXIMATION: the process of the refinement of target objectives and the appropriate selection of means to reach them by repeated applications of a system approach with subsequent needs assessments.

SUMMATIVE EVALUATION: determination of the results of implementing the selected methods-means in terms of meeting pre-specified objectives and the meeting of identified needs (if needs have been identified).

SYSTEM APPROACH: a formal planning and doing process which intends to identify and meet defined, validated, and justified needs. It includes the identification of problems based upon needs, the determination of solution requirements and the identification of solution alternatives, the selection of solution strategies and tools, determination of performance effectiveness and efficiency, and the revision of any or all of the previous steps and outcomes (at any time in the process) based upon the extent to which the designed system has met the validated needs.

SYSTEMS APPROACH: a process for systematically determining the requirements for solving a problem including all of its complex interactions, selecting from alternatives the best methods and techniques, designing and delivering the methods, evaluating the results, and revising as required. This may be seen as the last four of the six-step system approach process. When needs are identified in a systems approach, they are of the Beta, Gamma, or Delta variety (internal).

TECHNOLOGICAL APPLICATIONS: hardware and things, such as educational television, computers, and the like, which are used to enhance interventions and improve performance of learners.

TRANSFER: the applicability of learning in one situation to another situation—the transfer of skills, knowledges, and attitudes.

ULIDITY: the joint set, or intersection, formed by validity and utility. If something achieves that which it set out to achieve, and it was worth achieving, it is said to have "ulidity."

UTILITY: the value or worth of something, especially an accomplishment or result of the application of a method.

VALIDITY: the extent to which something accomplishes that which it set out to accomplish.

VALUES: predisposition for an individual to act in a given manner in a specific situation.

WEIGHTING THE DATA: the idea that the responses to some respondents should count more heavily in the calculation of the total population responses.

INDEX